PHILOSOPHY

The Fundamental Problems

PHILOSOPHY

The Fundamental Problems

Joel J. Kupperman

St. Martin's Press New York

Library of Congress Catalog Card Number: 76-28136
Copyright © 1978 by St. Martin's Press, Inc.
All Rights Reserved.
Manufactured in the United States of America.
09
fedcb
For information, write: St. Martin's Press, Inc.,
175 Fifth Avenue, New York, N.Y. 10010

cloth ISBN: 0-312-60573-0
paper ISBN: 0-312-60574-9

Preface

In writing this book, my goal has been two-fold: to create a book that is real philosophy (not merely summaries of various people's positions), and one that can be read with profit by intelligent people who have had little or no previous acquaintance with philosophy. In pursuit of the second goal, I have eliminated many technicalities and minimized the use of footnotes, but in no case have I knowingly done this in such a way as to render the argument weak or uncontroversial. No connected philosophical exploration such as this one can expect to be taken as correct on all points. My hope is that students and their teachers will enjoy disagreeing with the book, and that it will stimulate interesting philosophical rebuttals.

There is not sufficient space for me to acknowledge all the help received, over the years, from philosophers in discussions of the topics explored in the following chapters. I do wish to mention a special debt to Jerome Shaffer, my colleague for the last ten years, whose rare combination of professionalism and humanity I have admired and benefited from. I am grateful to the University of Connecticut for two years of leave, 1973-1975, and to the Provost and Fellows of King's College, Cambridge, for their hospitality during that period when the preliminary work that went into this endeavor was done. Thomas McCormack and Thomas Broadbent of St. Martin's Press gave me some very useful advice at the inception of the book, and as it went along, Patricia Klossner and Peter Phelps were voices of reason and good judgment. I benefited greatly from the comments, which seemed to me both generous and acute, of a number of anonymous readers engaged by St. Martin's. Karen Kupperman, my wife, has helped me with both her encouragement and her good sense. Carolyn Eggleston and Edward Cone of St. Martin's have saved me (and the reader) from a number of unnecessary words and awkward constructions.

Somewhat more intricate versions of chapter 5 and the latter part of chapter 6 have appeared in the *American Philosophical Quarterly*, 1975 and 1978; the roots of chapters 3 and 8 are to be found in the *British Journal of Aesthetics* and in *Mind*, both in 1975. I am indebted to these journals and to their editors, Nicholas Rescher, Harold Osborne, and D. W. Hamlyn, for permission to publish in this book material that appeared in the journals.

Joel J. Kupperman

Contents

PHILOSOPHY

The Fundamental Problems

1 What Philosophy Is

It is normal to begin any general account of a subject by explaining what the subject is. Geography books begin with a definition of the science of geography; chemistry books tell what chemistry is. Therefore it is appropriate to begin this book by saying what philosophy is. This turns out to be a far more complicated task, however, than explaining what geography or chemistry is.

One reason for this has to do with part of the answer: what philosophy is. Philosophy centers on debate and controversy. Now, debate and controversy occur in all fields of knowledge, but in almost all they are regarded as way stations on the road to truth. Typically, the aim of a subject is to find some truth, and one of the marks of having found it (or some passable approximation) is the emergence of scholarly consensus in that particular field. In light of this goal, debate and controversy look like temporary disruptions, which are useful only because they enable us to get beyond debate and controversy and to reach some consensus about the truth.

Philosophy is not like this. Philosophers generally agree that philosophy is concerned with truth. But it is unusual for philosophers to agree that some specific philosophical investigation has reached the truth; and when such a consensus has been reached, it has rarely lasted long.

In other words, in philosophy, unlike the great majority of disciplines, debate and controversy are the norm and are not thought of as disruptive episodes on the way to truth. Philosophers besides are supreme individualists. There are "schools" of philosophy, which are distinguished by common assumptions and common method; but there have usually been rival schools, as well as philosophers who could not readily be identified with any school. It sometimes looks as if almost every philosopher has had a different conception of what he or she was doing from every other.

Thus we cannot expect to arrive at any characterization of philosophy on which philosophers generally will agree. Also, no simple characterization of philosophy can be adequate. Whatever simple characterization were attempted, it would be clear that numbers of competent philosophers carry on their work differently. Philosophy is a variety of enterprises, not one narrowly definable kind of enterprise. Therefore what we are looking for is complicated, not simple; and even then it will be controversial.

Where there is so much disagreement in theory, it is best to begin at the level of fact. We can begin with a few commonsense observations about the characteristic practice of philosophical inquiry.

The subject matter of philosophy is various: knowledge, goodness, reality, and causation are favorite topics. There is philosophy of science, philosophy of history, and philosophy of art. In each area of philosophical investigation, philosophers generally direct their attention to the most central or basic concepts—more often to what knowledge is than to what a hunch is, more often to the concept of virtue than to the concept of repentance.

The most salient feature of philosophical inquiry is one already mentioned, the role of argument and controversy. In the sciences argument and controversy are usually treated as means to an end: the attainment of correct answers, on which there will finally be agreement. Skill in argument is valued less highly than skill in arriving at correct answers. In philosophy, on the other hand, argument is often treated as much more than just a means to an end. It is often remarked that "what you see on the way is as important as where you get to." Skill in argument, too, is usually highly prized. Indeed, the value of philosophy in the education of nonphilosophers is often ascribed to its usefulness in promoting skill at argument and analysis. Philosophy, it is often claimed, teaches a student to think clearly and to produce good arguments; and these abilities are valuable in many endeavors, not to mention life as a whole.

The relation of arguments to their conclusions, in philosophy, may seem puzzling to an outsider. On the one hand, arguments get won or lost. The argument is not simply a ritual dance or a display of skill. Conclusions are genuinely accepted or rejected on the basis of argument, and an impartial observer can often recognize that a view has been reasonably established as correct, or has been refuted, by means of argument.

On the other hand, refutation often is not final. The views of a great philosopher, such as Plato or Descartes, may be passed by or refuted, and thus ignored for hundreds of years, only to be revived later by intelligent practitioners of philosophy, perhaps in a slightly new form. The beginning student of philosophy is struck by the relevance of the old great philosophers—that their views are still taken seriously and can be made party to live controversies of some import. This is unparalleled in other branches of knowledge. The physicist who reads Newton, or the chemist Lavoisier, does so only for historical interest. The philosopher reads Plato or Descartes generally for more than historical interest.

This brings us to a nagging question. Is there progress in philosophy? Philosophers disagree sharply in their answers to this question. At one extreme some who take very seriously the history of philosophy answer "No." They offer in evidence the facts just alluded to: the ways in which the old great philosophers loom large in contemporary philosophical work, and are never superseded in that role. At the other extreme many philosophers answer an unqualified "Yes." They point chiefly to the progress of analysis, especially in the twentieth century. Concepts have been understood that had never been satisfactorily explained. Theories of meaning have been exploded; mistakes have been corrected that will never be repeated, except by the incompetent.

An intermediate position is arguable. It is true that there has been great progress during the last fifty years in understanding the ordinary use of the terms that play a part in philosophical inquiry. It is true also that throughout the history of philosophy mistakes have been corrected which are then not repeated, save by the incompetent. One can consider all this as a general advance in philosophical sophistication. On the other hand, when a mistake has been corrected, it is usually possible—and often happens—that sometime later a more sophisticated position, embodying the same general point of view as the original mistake, but not vulnerable to the same objections, is seriously espoused by competent philosophers. When one takes Plato and Descartes seriously, on some questions no modification of their views is required; but on other questions one is taking seriously what might be called "revisionist" versions of Plato and Descartes—Plato and Descartes as they might have been. General points of view survive, even if specific forms of a position do not always do so. In philosophy one can say in general that much more of the old survives, and plays a vital role, than in other branches of knowledge. Progress is less complete.

Functions of Philosophy

On this issue, as on many others, one can contrast two views of philosophy: philosophy-as-logic and philosophy-as-conceptual poetry. From the former point of view, philosophy unveils logical structures and the meanings of terms. Philosophy of science investigates the logical structure of scientific theories and the meanings of the key terms used in the sciences; philosophy of history does the same for history; and ethics performs this task for the language of morality. In this view, philosophers can hope to arrive at objectively correct answers to their questions. When philosophers of the past are read with more than historical interest, it is because they often have important insights into logic and language that are still relevant today.

To think of philosophy as unveiling logical structures and meanings of terms is to think of philosophy as investigating what we are committed to, or are justified in saying, on the basis of certain utterances. For example, a philosopher might investigate what we are committed to, or are justified in saying, if we accept that "X knows Y." This is to investigate the logic of "knowledge." A number of philosophers have argued that "X knows Y" commits us to "X believes Y"—that it is impossible to be said to know something unless one believes it. In this view, knowledge logically implies belief. Some philosophers have claimed that knowledge logically implies the absence of any risk of error, that "X knows Y" commits us to the assertion that there is no possibility of X's being wrong about Y. Other philosophers have insisted, against this claim, that the ordinary use of the word "know" is such that we are willing to ascribe human knowledge even while admitting the theoretical possibility of human error. In ethics, it has been claimed that "X owes money to Y" logically implies that, all relevant considerations being equal, X ought to pay Y: that is, if we accept the first judgment, we have to accept the second. One reply is that whereas "X owes money to Y" justifies the conclusion that, all things being equal, X ought to pay Y, it does not logically imply that conclusion. That is, the grounds may make it reasonable to accept a conclusion without forcing us to accept it. Philosophical analysis can disclose what conclusions are supported by a given assertion, and what conclusions we are forced to accept.

From the point of view of philosophy-as-conceptual poetry, recent advances in logical sophistication might be compared to the advances in understanding of perspective that occurred in Italy between the time of Giotto and the High Renaissance. These advances make the painters of the High Renaissance perhaps more skilled than Giotto, but not necessarily better. In the same way, recent advances in philosophy have not been advances in what is most important.

Of course, philosophy is not literally the same as poetry: great poetry is distinguished by, among other things, the beauty of its language; whereas great philosophy often is not written well, let alone beautifully. Argument typically does not play the role in poetry that it plays in philosophy. The point of speaking of philosophy as conceptual poetry, however, is this. Great poets often provide a distinctive vision: we prize not only the beauty of Shakespeare's and Milton's language, but also Shakespeare's world and Milton's world. Some philosophers also provide a distinctive vision of the world, not by use of the imagery or wit of the poets, but by subtle and strange changes in the role of the central concepts of their philosophies. The world that Spinoza or Berkeley presents to us is not our familiar world. Spinoza identifies the universe with God, and Berkeley claims that all reality is mental. Part of the appeal of such philosophers is the appeal of their world: to enter into an unusual vision of reality is an exciting experience, one which at the least can refresh our ordinary vision of the world.

Thus in this view philosophers, like poets and painters, at their best offer us a distinctive vision of the world. Philosophers do this by their management of concepts, and the vision they present is distinguished by its conceptual structure from the familiar one. Needless to say, no two great philosophers offer us the same vision of reality, any more than two great painters render a landscape in the same way. Accordingly, to judge a great philosopher's vision by the standards of another great philosopher's vision, or by the standards of our own vision of reality, is badly mistaken. To read Spinoza with the question foremost in mind "Is it true?" is to be insensitive to his accomplishment.

As we have already indicated, there seems to be some truth in both of these views of philosophy. Physicists are reduced to saying that light behaves in some respects as if it were waves, and in other respects as if it were particles. One might say that philosophy too behaves in some respects as if it were logic, and in other respects as if it were like conceptual poetry. Perhaps, too, some philosophers function in a way which fits one model better than the other. The philosophy-as-

conceptual poetry view may be more illuminating as a characterization of Spinoza than of recent Oxford philosophy; it is, indeed,
distinctly unilluminating in relation to most twentieth-century British
and American philosophy.

There are other major views of the nature of philosophy besides
the two already mentioned; and it would be hard to argue that any of
them is altogether devoid of truth. A traditional view of philosophy is
as ethical education. In this view, the primary role of philosophy is to
teach us what a good life consists of; and even the abstract and
nonethical tenets of philosophy play their part, insofar as knowledge
and understanding are part of a good life. It is because of this view that
Spinoza entitled a highly abstract metaphysical treatise *Ethics*. The
great philosophers of ancient Greece were not shy about pointing out
the characteristics of the best way of life. Socrates as a philosopher
was a "guru" in the recent colloquial sense of the word. Philosophy-
as-ethical education asserts that the character and personal history of
the philosopher can be exemplary of his philosophy, which may be one
reason why so much of the philosophy of Socrates has been presented
to us in a biographical context. As impressive as this ideal of
philosophy is, it has been less influential in recent centuries than it once
was (for a number of reasons, some of them bad); and it is difficult to
regard most articles in philosophical journals today as having much
role to play in ethical education.

Another major view of the nature of philosophy is this. Proponents of the philosophy-as-logic view often dwell on the role of the
philosopher in examining concepts ordinarily used in daily life, or in
special disciplines. In this view, we do not know what we mean by
"knowledge," "goodness," or "cause" until the philosopher unveils
the logical structure of the ordinary use and spells out the meaning: the
thoroughness of the philosopher's investigation, and the explicit
attention to context and to logical connections, enables the philosopher's analysis of meaning to be of a different order from anything
available in dictionaries.

At this point an alternative view, philosophy-as-conceptual
engineering, makes its departure. Why should we merely *analyze* the
concepts we already have? Why not *improve* upon them and create
either totally new concepts or new forms of familiar concepts? In this
view, the motive for creating new concepts consists of more than sheer
playfulness. The concepts of everyday life, and of special disciplines,
typically reached their present form some time ago, before we knew as
much about the world as we now know. Our concept of freedom
predates modern psychology; our concept of cause predates modern

physics. This lag in our concepts can lead to awkwardness and impede the progress of our investigations; or it can lead simply to a lack of clarity in some of our everyday patterns of thought. The philosopher, in this view, can remedy the defects of our present conceptual systems by adjusting them to present needs and present knowledge.

A fifth major view of the nature of philosophy is that of philosophy-as-discovery of truth about the world. This view is reflected in the practice of Greek philosophy before the time of Socrates. It also may help us to become aware of aspects of the philosophy of Socrates, Plato, and various European philosophers of the seventeenth and eighteenth centuries that often are overlooked. However, this view has not found much favor in recent years, at least in Britain and America. The sciences, it has been held, discover truth about the world; and philosophy is not a science. When we report the nature of the world, philosophy (philosophy-as-logic) tells us the truth about the logical structure of our reports; but the truth about the world itself is in the province of the sciences.

As recently as a few years ago I would have concurred with this dismissal of philosophy-as-discovery of truth about the world. But now it seems to me that this view, like the others, cannot be entirely dismissed: there is some truth to it, also. One of the things philosophy sometimes does is to discover, or attempt to discover, truths about the world that do not fall within the province of the sciences. How this plays a part, or at least could be argued to play a part, in the philosophical quest is a theme of this book.

The Realistic Dimension in Philosophy

Reality enters into the world of philosophy in a number of ways. In the purest case, it can be argued that a philosophical issue turns out to be an issue about reality. That is, after philosophers have analyzed the meanings of the relevant terms, and clarified the sense of the central questions, the issue boils down to "Is such and such the case?" and the answer is to be found in the world, and not in philosophical analysis itself. Philosophers clear the ground, but then one has to look to see what is the case.

A familiar example of a question that arguably has this character is "Does God exist?" This is the central question of chapter 10 of this book. Philosophical analysis helps to clarify what kind of question this is, and what can count toward answering it. But philosophical analysis itself cannot supply the answer; what is needed is some experience after death, or special religious experience now, or faith (of a positive or negative sort). The question counts as philosophical for two reasons. First, philosophical analysis is required before one can provide a reasoned answer. Secondly, however one arrives at an answer, it is unlikely to be in the ordinary scientific way. People normally do not decide whether God exists by looking through a telescope or by performing laboratory experiments. The question of God's existence looks like a philosophical question about reality.

The central question discussed in chapter 5 is an outstanding example of one that also arguably has this character, although here the point is far less obvious and the matter much more disputable. When great philosophers of the past raised the question of whether physical objects exist, they were raising, I shall argue, a question about reality. The ultimate answer lies in brute fact: whether physical objects exist "out there."

Now, this is how the question "Do physical objects exist?" looks at first to beginners in philosophy. The question appears to be a straightforward one as to whether those chairs and tables we keep bumping into, or using, really do exist "out there." They certainly *seem* to exist "out there"; so almost anyone's first impulse is to take the question to be one of fact, and to think that the answer is obviously "Yes."

However, the arguments against thinking that chairs and tables exist "out there" are unsettling. If all we really have to go on is our experience of chairs and tables, and if this experience is in our mind, how can we be sure that there is a nonmental cause of this mental experience? Just because we have some kind of mental image, or visual perception, of a table, or a sensation of bumping into one, what entitles us to be sure that "out there" exists something which causes these experiences? If we stick to what we *know*, we would have to say that we have the visual experience and the feeling of the bump, and that there may or may not be something which has caused these things. Further, if we consider that all we *know*, all we have to go on, is in our experience (i.e., in our minds), we come to realize that we have no clear idea of what the table "out there" would be like if it did exist. A table "outside" our minds would be nonmental and therefore radically different from anything we can think of, which is perforce mental. A philosopher pursuing this line of thought can lead us to wonder whether it even makes any sense to talk about chairs and tables "out there."

Our discussion of these arguments, and of the general issue, can be postponed until chapter 5. Enough has been said at this point to indicate some of the grounds on which a thoughtful person might decide that the question "Do physical objects exist?" is not what it first seems. Many recent philosophers have swung to the view that the issue is not a factual one at all, and that the old great philosophers who asked whether physical objects exist were merely playing games with language.

Against this background, the position of this book is counterrevolutionary. The issue of whether physical objects exist is, indeed, not entirely what it seems; but the argument of chapter 5 is that, nevertheless, it is primarily a factual issue, just as the naïve person would have thought. Something like this will also be argued, or at least raised as a possibility, about a number of other major issues in philosophy, discussed in chapters 6 through 10.

Thus the reader should be aware that this book has an ax to grind. Philosophy is inherently controversial, and that applies to this book as well. A general work on philosophy which never took sides would not be itself a work of philosophy. A general book, such as this one, which does take sides, and argues for its own conclusions, can be argued against. The conclusions can always be rejected. For a student, part of the interest of reading philosophy can consist in formulating arguments against the writer.

The theme of this book is the realistic dimension in philosophy. However, if the book considered only issues of what is real, it would be one-sided. A great deal of philosophical work traditionally has centered on definitions, or the search for explanations of meaning that would do the job of definitions. This, after all, is a central concern of those philosophers who think of philosophy as composed of varieties of logic. Chapters 2 and 3 begin by pursuing problems of this sort. We begin, that is, by asking the meaning of such words as "ethics," "morality," and "art."

However, even here questions of reality enter in. We cannot explain what morality is without considering the real world: the ways in which societies characteristically put pressure on individuals in some parts of their lives, and leave them alone in others. To ask what the word "morality" means is to focus on a meaning and not on reality. Nevertheless, there is a realistic dimension here too, and we must look into it while we answer the question of meaning.

The issue of political obligation, which is taken up in chapter 4, again has something like a realistic dimension. Questions of obligation need philosophical analysis. But in the end, one asks questions like "Is it the case that I am obligated to obey commands of my government?" or "Is it the case that I am obligated to help the poor?" Philosophical analysis itself cannot carry us all the way toward answering these questions. Whether we can consider these questions of "what is the case" as concerned with reality is a moot point, depending on how broadly we are willing to use the word "reality." But they are, in any event, like questions of reality in that, after we finish clarifying the issue, we have to turn away from analysis and decide what is correct. Do we really have certain obligations, or don't we?

Thus there is more than one way in which philosophy can be spoken of as having a realistic dimension. Even if our concern is with the meanings of terms—with becoming clear about them, or with inventing or modifying meanings in a revelatory way—we must consider the function that our terms fulfill in the real world. If we are concerned with what is good or with what our obligations are, we can ask whether something really is good or whether we really do have a certain obligation. And, finally, some philosophical questions turn out to be unequivocally questions about reality. In these cases philosophy is directly a study of reality.

SUGGESTED FURTHER READING

Edwards, Paul, ed. *The Encyclopedia of Philosophy*, in 8 vols. New York: Macmillan, 1967. This has become the standard work for reliable brief accounts of philosophers, schools of philosophy, and philosophical positions and problems.

Copleston, Father Frederick. *A History of Philosophy*, in 8 vols. London: Burns & Oates, 1951-1975. This is widely considered to be the best history of Western philosophy ever written. For a more than brief, but less than book-length, account of, say, Spinoza or Hegel, consult Copleston. This work is recommended much more highly than the better known *History of Western Philosophy*, by Bertrand Russell.

Matson, Wallace. *A History of Philosophy*. New York: American Book Company, 1968. A good one-volume history of philosophy.

Hutchinson, John. *Living Options in Philosophy*. Honolulu: University of Hawaii Press, 1977. This contains perceptive summaries of major philosophical traditions. It has the merit of including Asian as well as Western traditions within its purview.

The following modern classics are themselves philosophy but also propound distinctive views of the nature of philosophy.

Russell, Bertrand. *The Problems of Philosophy*. First published 1912; reprinted Oxford: Oxford University Press, 1959.

Ayer, Alfred. *Language, Truth, and Logic*. First published 1936; reprinted New York: Dover Books, 1946.

2 The Nature of Ethics

What is ethics? This sounds like a request for a definition, or something that does the job of a definition: distinguishing ethics from, say, aesthetics or pharmacy or the study of sewer systems. In due course we shall attempt to provide something like this. But it is desirable to be aware, first, of other questions lurking behind the simple question "What is ethics?" They include the disturbing question "Why do we have ethics?" It is possible to imagine a world in which no one ever makes judgments that certain things are good or bad, right or wrong. Why isn't our world like that, instead of as it is at present? Similarly, when we come to discuss morality, behind the question of what morality is lurks another question: Why do we have morality?[1]

This is to say that even in this philosophical enterprise there is a realistic dimension. Later in the book we shall encounter the realistic dimension in its raw form. We shall ask questions directly about reality. But even here, where we are asking about the meanings of words—words such as "ethics"—we cannot get satisfactory answers without understanding why these words have been needed. And to understand how words are needed is to understand something about the real world.

In what follows, an account of the nature of ethics is provided that does two jobs. One is drawing the external boundary of ethics: distinguishing an ethical judgment from other kinds of judgments, and an ethical problem from other kinds of problems. In relation to this we can ask why there is ethics at all. The second job is drawing internal boundaries: making clear important distinctions between different kinds of problems and judgments within ethics. The chief internal boundary to be drawn is between problems and judgments termed "moral" and problems and judgments generally placed within the purview of ethics but not termed "moral." Here the specific question of the function of morality arises.

We shall begin by drawing the external boundary of ethics and then proceed to examine some of the internal geography.

What Ethics Is

The conception of ethics we will explore is a very broad and traditional one. It is familiar enough to have some claim to being the major traditional conception. Before exploration begins, however, we should mention some alternative conceptions of ethics that are much narrower. Three may have some special immediate appeal.

A particularly narrow conception is implied by use of the word "ethics" for the code appropriate to a profession. "Medical ethics" is violated when, for example, a doctor entertains guests at a party by disclosing confidential details of a patient's case history. Generally speaking, of course, doctors ought to adhere to medical ethics, and lawyers ought to adhere to legal ethics. However, we recognize that doctors and lawyers have obligations also as husbands, fathers, wives, mothers, citizens, or simply human beings, and that in some cases these obligations may supersede what would normally be the demands of medical or legal ethics. Ethics is concerned with all of these obligations, not just with professional obligations.

A related narrow conception is implied by a very common use of the word "unethical." It is unethical for a man selling his house to use the services of two agents if he tells neither that he has engaged the other. It is unethical for an author to submit his manuscript to more than one publisher at once, unless he discloses this to all concerned. It is unethical for a man to take money in advance for services that he knows he will be unable to perform.

This sense of "unethical" has at least some relation to written or unwritten codes governing what we have a right to expect as fair treatment from others. To call a man unethical in this sense is to suggest that he has violated such a code. It also suggests that he has not dealt fairly. To murder someone, however, is not "unethical" in this sense; we certainly would use some different word of condemnation. Neither is wasting one's life in idleness "unethical." Ethics is usually conceived of as concerned with deeds such as murder, and with how in general one spends one's life, not merely with what is "unethical."

A third narrow conception is especially tempting to anyone concerned with social control of people's actions. When one thinks of ethics, one may think of right and wrong; and when one thinks of right and wrong, one may think of a list of "Thou shalt not"s, of the actions forbidden by the great old codes of morality, such as murder, adultery, theft, and false promises.

These classic "Thou shalt not"s all lie in the area of ethics known as morality. Ethics has traditionally, however, been concerned with more than morality. When Aristotle, in the *Nicomachean Ethics*, praises the contemplative life, a life centered on intellectual activity, he does not suggest that to pursue the contemplative life is morally right and to pursue any other kind of life is morally wrong. Yet he was writing ethics. Similarly, when G. E. Moore, in the final chapter of *Principia Ethica*, claims that those states of mind are most valuable which involve love of a worthy object or admiring contemplation of the beautiful, he too would not claim that it is morally wrong never to have such states of mind, or even to eschew such states of mind. Yet he too was writing ethics. Ethics thus comprises more than morality. One of the tasks of this chapter is to delimit and discuss the part of ethics that lies outside of morality.

It might be tempting to define ethics in terms of judgments, or problems, about what is right and wrong, or good and bad. Broadly speaking, of course, ethics does concern itself with right and wrong, good and bad. But it is not alone in this territory. We speak of actions as right and wrong in cases in which both problem and judgment fall within etiquette rather than ethics. Deciding the right way to introduce new acquaintances to one another, or to eat cherries in a restaurant, is not an ethical matter. Aesthetics deals in judgments of good and bad. It may be that there are logical relations between, on the one hand, the judgment that a play or a novel is good, and, on the other hand, judgments of value that fall within ethics; but judging a play or novel good is not itself an ethical judgment. We even speak of certain knives as good, implying that they perform their function well. This, again, is not an ethical judgment.

Judgments of right and wrong, or good and bad, are commonly termed "evaluative judgments." Ethical judgments, then, are just one species of evaluative judgments. Aesthetic judgments form another species; so do judgments of etiquette or social propriety; and judgments of the goodness of knives, baseball players, carpenters, show dogs, and ant poisons also count as evaluative. Our first problem, then, is to analyze the distinction between ethical judgments and other kinds of evaluative judgments. It will not do simply to say that ethical judgments are prescriptive, meaning that they give us guidance in deciding what to do; aesthetic judgments and judgments of etiquette also give us guidance, as do judgments of what knife to use, which baseball player to have on our team, and so on.

Here are six general features of ethical judgments. The first three features are shared with other evaluative judgments; the second three describe features of ethical judgments not shared with all other forms of evaluative judgment. This characterizes ethical judgment, but judgment and problem are correlative: the solution to an ethical problem is a correct ethical judgment, and an ethical judgment is one which solves, or attempts to solve, an ethical problem. Thus the six features add up to a distinguishing characterization of ethics.

1. Ethical discourse commits us to differential grading: that is, to speak in ethical terms is one way of rating some things as better or worse than others. Aesthetic judgments also involve this: we rate some works of art as more beautiful, or better, than others. Ordinary practical judgments also have this feature. We speak of one knife as better for some purposes than others, and we speak of the right way and wrong ways to assemble an engine. Even judgments merely of taste, as when we judge one brand of vanilla ice cream to be nicer than another, have this feature. This feature, in short, is shared by evaluative judgments generally. Ethical judgments characteristically are formulated in words such as "good," "bad," "right," and "wrong," but other kinds of evaluative judgments also may be put in these terms.

2. Ethical judgments, again like other evaluative judgments, cannot be arbitrary. Something cannot be right, wrong, good, or bad for no reason at all. It is even impossible for one brand of vanilla ice cream to be nicer than another for no reason: if none of the qualities in which they differ makes any difference, then it is contradictory to say that one brand is nicer than the other; if some quality or combination of qualities makes a difference, then that they are as they are is a reason why one brand is nicer than the other.

To say that any evaluative judgment must have a reason is not to say that anyone who makes an evaluative judgment must be able to provide a reason. A person looking at a painting may come to the conviction that it is a good painting, but after much time and struggle find it impossible to articulate any of what it is that makes the painting good. Similarly, an act may seem morally wrong to one who finds it difficult or impossible to give reasons to support this judgment. However, it is nonsense to say "The painting is good for no reason at all" or "The act is morally wrong for no reason at all." There must be reasons, even if one cannot find them.

3. It is also true that any particular ethical judgment commits one to a universal judgment. If X is good (bad, right, or wrong), it is good (bad, right, or wrong) because of some of its qualities or characteristics. Then anything else which has these features will also be good (bad, right, or wrong). This leads to the universal judgment that anything that is in relevant respects like X is good (bad, right, or wrong). This is the thesis of universalizability argued by the contemporary Oxford philosopher R. M. Hare in *Freedom and Reason.* The thesis holds not only for ethical judgments but for all evaluative judgments. If X is a good knife, then a knife which is in relevant respects like X must be a good knife. If Y is nice, then something which is in relevant respects like Y must be nice.

4. Ethical judgments are distinguished from other evaluative judgments in having what might be called a "conclusive" relation to conduct. It is always true that what is ethically right is what one should permit oneself to do; what is ethically wrong is what one should not do; what is ethically best is what one should pursue; and what is ethically bad is what one should avoid. On the other hand, the best knife is not the one to use if, under duress, one is cutting what ought not to be cut. The best play is not the one to attend if attending a poor play will help to prevent the suicide of its playwright. The nicest ice cream is not the one to eat if buying it encourages a dairy in its cruelty to animals.

In other words, if we are deciding what to do, the full range of correct ethical judgments that can be made about our situation tells us what we ought to do, what is permissible, and what we ought to avoid. Some ethical judgments, taken by themselves, are conclusive. For example, if something is ethically wrong, it simply ought not to be done. Other ethical judgments may give us only a part of the picture. To know that something is good may encourage us to aim at it, but only when we have a clear view of the other assets and liabilities of possible courses of action can we decide what to do. However, the ethical judgment that something we might achieve is good needs to be supplemented here, not by some other kind of judgment, but merely by other ethical judgments. Thus the ethical judgments that we can bring to bear are in aggregate conclusive.

As many writers on ethics have pointed out, ordinary practical judgments do not have this conclusive character. The aggregate of practical judgments that we make of a course of action may tell us that the course of action works, and perhaps even that it may achieve something we very much want; but the course of action is wrong if the goal is evil. There may also be reasons why something that is beautiful should be destroyed, or why something that is very nice should be avoided.

The difference between ethical and other evaluative judgments can be seen if we qualify ethical judgments to bring them closer to other kinds of evaluative judgments. One might by qualification of ethical judgments arrive at a class of *pro tanto* judgments: judgments of what is good or right *insofar as* certain factors are considered. Thus the ethical judgment "X is the right thing to do" can be qualified to provide the judgment "Insofar as there are certain purposes or functions for which X is best suited, X is *pro tanto* the right thing to do." The *pro tanto* judgment now has the force of an ordinary practical judgment. Or the ethical judgment "The experience of X involves states of mind of the highest value" can be scaled down to the judgment "To the extent that one considers aesthetic features in the experience of X, the experience *pro tanto* is of great value." This has much the same force as a favorable aesthetic judgment of X.[2]

The way words look often makes it difficult to distinguish the *ethical* use of such terms as "good" from other evaluative uses. Thus it has been possible for many philosophers to regard the way we speak of something as a "good knife" or an "extra-fancy apple" as having important implications for ethics.[3] However, to bear in mind the distinction just made is to remove such confusion. The word "good" when used in connection with certain nouns of classification (e.g., "knife," "show Pekingese," "poison") implies standards which have the effect of restricting judgment to certain features of what is judged. Thus, in normal contexts, when we judge whether it would be good to use a certain knife, we restrict our attention to whether the knife cuts and handles well. It is only when other features of the situation are extraordinary (we are not cutting vegetables but using the knife to commit murder) that they are attended to and our judgment becomes ethical. In most contexts, on the other hand, when we speak of a "good experience," or of something as a "good act to perform," it is clear that we are not calling into play implicit standards of judgment as definite and closed to appeal as those for "good knife" or "good Pekingese," and that the meanings of the terms we use do not restrict our attention in a corresponding fashion. Thus, in normal contexts, judgments of something as a "good act to perform" have a conclusive relation to what we should do; judgments of something as a "good knife" normally do not.

5. Ethical judgments conclusively determine what we should do, not what we in fact do. People often make judgments of what is right and wrong, and then avoid what they judge is right and pursue what they say is wrong. Nevertheless, ethical statements, if sincere, normally correlate with the way the people who make them *try* to act. An individual may sincerely say that something is good or right, and then be overcome by temptation and behave in a manner opposite to what we have been led to expect. But if that individual is especially easily overcome by temptation, or manifests no regrets, hesitations, or feelings of guilt, we can question his or her sincerity.

Let us suppose, for example, that a man says that the most rewarding moments in life are those spent listening to great music in the concert hall, that he fully agrees with G. E. Moore's evaluation of contemplation of the beautiful, and that we then discover that he avoids attending concerts. Now, it is easy to imagine a man who sincerely says that the best experiences are to be found in the concert hall, and yet never attends concerts because of laziness, stinginess, or chronic alcoholism, which confines him to his home. The sincerity of his ethical judgment will be marked by the presence of some motivation to attend concerts, even if that motivation is overridden by others. But if there is no such motivation, if, given every opportunity, the man avoids concerts or proves indifferent to them, we must then conclude that his ethical statement was not sincere.

A more extreme case is the man who says, "Murder is wrong," indicating that this is not merely a report of the prevailing judgment but is his own opinion, and who then cheerfully, remorselessly commits murder. Such a man may be mentally disturbed, in which case we might say that he did not fully mean what he said. His ethical statement would be classified neither as sincere nor insincere. If the man is, let us say, a Cesare Borgia or a Stalin, we may say simply that his ethical statements were hypocritical. In any case, if a man sincerely says that murder is wrong, we normally would feel entitled to infer that he is strongly motivated not to commit murder.

We can state generally that someone who says something is right, wrong, good, or bad will normally be taken to be *pledging* conduct along corresponding lines. Such judgments also will normally have the character of guiding, attempting to guide, or being able to guide the conduct of other people.

As has been remarked, other kinds of evaluative judgment have this feature to some extent. They too guide conduct. When we speak of one play as aesthetically better than another, we are saying that, all things being equal, the first one is the one to see. But "all things being equal" covers nonaesthetic grounds: it includes not only an equal ability to appreciate the two works, but also the morale of the playwrights, the financial needs and worthiness of the theaters, and so on. Similarly, the better car is, all things being equal, the one to drive. But "all things being equal" here includes not only equal cost, but also that one car does not pollute the environment more drastically than the other, is not more needed by some handicapped person, and so on. Because only ethical judgments have a conclusive relation to conduct, only ethical judgments can be unqualified guides to conduct.

6.   Ethics is cognitive.[4] That is, we normally assume, and are entitled to assume, that there are correct and incorrect answers to ethical questions, and that people sometimes have a right to be confident of their ethical views and sometimes lack this right. This does not imply, of course, that any claim to ethical correctness or ethical knowledge is ever demonstrable or absolutely certain, although some seem nearly so. If someone says, "It is desirable to torture as many people as possible," our normal linguistic bent is to say that we *know* this is incorrect. Further, almost all of us can supply reasons, or cite experiences, that put us in a position to be confident that torture is wrong.

Most types of evaluative judgments arguably share this feature. One can know that Haydn's *Missa Sanctae Caeciliae* is a great composition, or that one knife is much better than another. Arguably, however, not all types of evaluative judgment are cognitive. It would seem inappropriate to speak of knowing that one brand of ice cream is nicer than another, or that warm baths are nicer than cold showers.

The foregoing six features constitute a portrait of what we would normally consider ethical discourse. How many are essential is open to argument. I myself feel confident that 1-4 must be features of anything we would call ethics. No. 5 is more difficult. The difficulty can be grasped if we try to imagine a society of satanists, who make judgments of good, bad, right, and wrong much as we do, but then say, "Evil be thou my Good," and behave in a manner opposite to what one normally would associate with their judgments. Or one might try to imagine a society of "indifferentists," to coin a word, whose conduct had no correlation, positive or negative, with their purportedly ethical judgments of right, wrong, good, and bad. If the satanists and indifferentists, at the same time as they made their judgments, announced openly what their conduct was going to be (so that we could not accuse them of hypocrisy), could we judge that their judgments of right, wrong, good, and bad were ethical judgments?

One may *try* to imagine societies of satanists and of indifferentists, but it is open to question whether the pictures arrived at are entirely consistent. It is clear that a group of satanists or indifferentists could exist within our own society. I would judge that we would recognize their uses of "good," "bad," "right," and "wrong" as being ethical language, although the uses certainly would be considered abnormal. It is also clear that an entire class of ethical judgments can be pronounced within a society in a way unrelated or inversely related to conduct. There are some matters on which everyone may be a hypocrite. In sum: it is possible that for some people all ethical judgments may not be a guide to conduct, and it is possible that for all people ethical judgments of some specified kind may not be a guide to conduct. But is it possible that for all people in a society the full range of ethical judgments can be not a guide to conduct? If we encountered a tribe whose members applied "good," "bad," "right," and "wrong" to much the same objects and actions to which we apply the words, but for whom judgments using the words had no role as guiding conduct, we would, I think, deny that the tribe had an ethical language. What this suggests is that satanists or indifferentists can use ethical language not as a guide to conduct only within the context of a society in which these words normally are used in guiding conduct. They capitalize on the fact that their use resembles (in other features) the use which most people give to the terms they employ. The terms can count as ethical, by virtue of their normal use, but not as guides to conduct by virtue of the use the satanists or indifferentists give them.

We can, I think, imagine an entire society whose purported ethical judgments lacked feature 6—a cognitive aspect. The judgments are not put forward as cognitive, and they are considered to have the same subjective character as judgments of the niceness of brands of ice cream. Are these ethical judgments? Here I am somewhat hesitantly inclined to say that, if the purportedly ethical discourse of these people had features 1–5, we would judge them to be ethical even if they lacked feature 6. The absence of feature 6, however, would give us pause. Also, even if a noncognitive way of talking about right, wrong, good, and bad became common (and even if this was accepted as ethical discourse), ethics would still be cognitive in this sense: it would always be possible to reintroduce a cognitive pattern of ethical discourse.

Why We Have Ethics

Why do we have ethics? Having characterized what ethics is, we are now in a position to answer this question. Conversely, our answer will help to sharpen our understanding of what ethics is. In human discourse, just as in architecture, form frequently follows function; so that when we know what the function of ethics is, we can have a better understanding of its form.

The primary function of ethical judgments is to provide conclusive guidance to human conduct. The person who makes an ethical judgment is, in effect, telling himself or herself what to do, and also providing advice for others. Other kinds of judgment provide advice. "X is a good play" provides advice to someone who is about to plan an evening at the theater. "That is a good knife" provides advice to someone who is about to select a knife in order to cut something. But, as we pointed out, ethical judgments have a special character in that they conclusively tell us what we should or should not do, seek or avoid, rather than concentrating on particular, specialized facets of the situation. Some ethical judgments tell us in a very general way what we should do in planning our entire life. This is what Aristotle was doing when he recommended the contemplative life.

Ethics exists, first of all, because our world is not a world of hermits. Neither are we all self-sufficient nor do we automatically function in a certain way. We have ethics because we have problems to confront and choices to make, and because we interact with one another in such a way that advice can be given and taken. Ethics makes sense only against the background of a social world of choices that have to be made, in which people sometimes want to influence the choices that others make, and some people genuinely want advice as to what they should do. If any of these factors were missing, ethics as we know it could not exist.

It is possible to lose sight of this when we examine ethical decision as a rational process. People often think hard about what is right and wrong. It is also possible to approach the codifying of ethical judgments as an intellectual problem. Yet the root remains in conduct, and ethical judgments take their form from the function of providing guidance in matters of conduct.

Ethics is not always so gentle as we have made it sound. Ethical judgments are used to advise others, but sometimes they also are used to pressure others. A philosopher can recommend the contemplative life in a spirit of "Take it or leave it." Another philosopher might make the same recommendation with a clearly expressed suggestion that it would be contemptible not to lead the life he recommends. Some ethical judgments may carry with them an even stronger negative verdict on those who make what is judged to be the wrong choice. We can reflect on this when we examine an especially prominent region of ethics: morality.

Morality

Morality is a subspecies of ethics. In order to understand this, one must realize that certain judgments generally classified as moral (e.g., "Torture is wrong"; "We ought to save lives where we can") fit the characterization we have given of the ethical, but so do judgments that would not generally be classified as moral (e.g., "One should develop one's intellectual abilities"; "It is better to help others out of love than out of a sense of duty"). Virtually no one who makes the latter judgments would claim that it is *morally* wrong not to develop one's intellectual abilities, or to help others out of a sense of duty rather than love. Not all issues which fit traditionally within ethics are moral issues. There are plenty of things that we think people conclusively should do that we do not consider it immoral for them not to do. Thus ethics, which includes all of our judgments of what people conclusively should do in their lives, is broader than morality, and it is worthwhile to see the difference.

To move from the species ethics to the subspecies morality, we may add three more features to our portrait.

7. Moral grading must often, although not necessarily always, be taken with great seriousness. We would not call a method of grading a morality if its adherents generally took its determinations very lightly, and if it had little effect on feelings about the actions or persons graded.

This is not to say that moral grading must be taken more seriously than any other form of grading. Some people, for example, take aesthetic judgments very seriously, and scorn bad taste more than they do immorality. It is possible to imagine a whole society that functioned in this way. There would be some temptation to remark that these aesthetes were rather moralistic about aesthetic matters; but if their aesthetic judgments lacked other general features of moral judgments, there should be little difficulty in identifying them as aesthetic, rather than moral, judgments.

Ethical judgments that are not moral also may be taken very

seriously. Indeed, people ought to take seriously Aristotle's praise of the contemplative life. However, the seriousness of ethical, nonmoral judgments is a degree more dispensable than the seriousness of moral judgments. This is a fine point, and deserves to be elaborated.

It is possible for individuals, and for groups within a society, to make moral judgments but take them very lightly. Someone may be judged to be immoral but yet welcomed as freely as always, and be treated and discussed in much the same manner as always. Anyone who treats his moral judgments so lightly uses moral language in an abnormal way; but it is hard to deny that he is using moral language if his words constitute what is considered moral language in the society, and if in most respects his use is the common one.

Nevertheless, an entire society, or self-contained group, cannot be like this. Suppose that we heard of the existence of a tribe which used the English words "morally right" and "immoral," applied these words in the very cases in which most of us would apply them, but seemed lighthearted and unconcerned in their attitudes toward those persons and actions classified as immoral. We would not, I think, say that these people were using moral language, or that their views constituted a morality. Suppose, now, that we heard of a tribe whose members agreed that the contemplative life was best, but who did not have a strongly negative attitude toward those who chose not to follow the contemplative life, and generally did not feel badly if they themselves did not pursue the contemplative life. We would not be strongly inclined, on the basis of this alone, to deny that the tribe was using ethical language in speaking of the excellence of the contemplative life.

Relating this to our previous discussion of the role of ethical judgments in guiding conduct, we can say that it is possible for an entire society to treat ethical judgments of a certain kind as not a guide to conduct. But not only is this in fact more common with respect to nonmoral ethical judgments than with respect to moral judgments, but also the logic of moral judgments makes a tighter demand on a role in guiding conduct. If too large a class of purportedly moral judgments were taken throughout a society as not guides to conduct, we would deny that they formed part of a morality. Either they are not moral judgments, but certain other judgments made in the society are; or the society lacks a morality.

Further, the logic of moral judgments demands a "heavier," or more seriously felt, role in guiding conduct than does the logic of nonmoral ethical judgments. This requires not only that moral judgments normally function as guides to conduct, but also that they normally be able to be taken as pledges of really serious effort to behave accordingly on the part of those who make them. Some people within a society can be exceptions to this, but not the entire society.

A consequence of this is that the concept of guilt, or something like guilt, is closely linked to morality. Those who do what is said to be morally wrong must usually be strongly blamed. If an individual sincerely says that an action is morally wrong, and performs it while continuing to say sincerely that it is morally wrong, we expect that person to feel strong qualms or to blame himself strongly.

Again this is not to say that everyone who makes moral judgments feels guilty if his or her own actions violate these moral standards. But for there to be a morality there must be a common pattern of this sort. Suppose we encountered a tribe that used the English words "morally right" and "immoral," applied these words in the very cases in which most of us would apply them, but did not feel at all guilty or uneasy when they did not do what they sincerely said was immoral. We would deny that this usage constituted moral discourse, or that the views expressed constituted a morality.

8. Morality normally has a social role: it applies pressure to malefactors, and encourages the upright. The very use of moral language may count as a sanction. A society that thinks in moral terms will normally distinguish between matters that are moral (i.e., open to severe social pressure) and matters that are a person's own business.

In other words, the function of morality is to provide conclusive guidance in certain matters of conduct that has enough weight, normally, for it to amount to pressure. To those who want to do what is right, morality provides advice in matters of special importance. To those who may do what is wrong, morality serves notice as to what counts as the wrong choice, and also that wrongdoing is taken seriously.

A society of entirely well-meaning people might develop morality as a system of urgent advice. It is possible to imagine a society in which morality was used to advise but never to exert direct pressure. In our world, however, morality generally does reflect a need for pressure. Our world contains some people who are not always well-meaning; and it contains people who are afraid (or envious) of wrongdoing, and who feel a need for wrongdoing to be minimized by creation of an atmosphere in which people are strongly encouraged not to behave in certain ways. Morality, as a social device, creates this atmosphere.

Thus we cannot understand morality, in the forms in which it has developed in our world, without realizing that guidance can amount to pressure, and that there is a strong social need for pressure in some areas of life. It is because it is not uncommon for human beings to steal or murder that we teach children that it is immoral to steal or murder. And we cannot understand the character of moral judgments concerning theft and murder unless we grasp the general resentment against those who, after all the indoctrination, steal or murder.

Morality in our society singles out a significant but not very large area of conduct for pressure. Individuals, of course, can favor a different arrangement, and develop their conceptions of morality in different ways. It is also possible to imagine societies with different arrangements. Three such arrangements especially deserve mention.

(1) Morality could be the whole of ethics. Then every judgment that something is good or bad, right or wrong, more or less desirable is subject to be accompanied by the pressure characteristic of moral judgment. In such a society, if it is judged that a person would spend her time better seeing *King Lear* than the latest musical comedy, she is liable to be severely blamed, and to feel guilty, if she sees the musical comedy. To waste time will be treated in the same manner as breaking promises and cheating. Calvinistic societies come somewhat close to adopting this model. Certainly in Calvin's Geneva morality was a larger part of ethics than in our present society. However, only an omniscient totalitarian society could adopt a conception of ethics in which all of ethics was morality.

(2) In the opposite direction, it is possible to imagine a society in which morality was a far smaller part of ethics than at present. (Our future society may have this character, if either we come to worry less about the actions now classified as immoral, or an extreme value comes to be placed on an individual's not being pressured by society.) A wide range of actions at present classified as morally wrong might in such a society be regarded as mistaken but a person's own business, and thus would not be subject to the pressure associated with morality. Such a society would have a morality as long as there were *some* actions subject to this pressure.

(3) It is possible to imagine a society whose morality was treated as extremely discreet and intimate. People never voiced moral judgments of actual persons; moral language was taught to children by means of hypothetical instances. Such a morality could arise in a society that greatly disliked personal conflicts. In such a society morality would not have quite the social role of applying pressure that it customarily has. However, this pressure could not be too thoroughly attenuated if the society could be spoken of as having a morality. If

unspoken judgments had virtually none of the normal burden of blame and guilt, then we would not speak of them as constituting a morality. If unspoken judgments had some of this burden, it is hard to imagine people's being unaware of one another's unspoken judgments, and there would be some social pressure connected with morality.

It should be added that not only is the place of morality within ethics subject to social variation, but also different individuals may give different roles to morality within their ethics. Some people are very "moralistic": they use moral language with especially great weight and treat a wider than usual range of matters as moral. At the opposite extreme, some people use moral language both sparingly and lightly, and are inclined to treat as a person's own business many matters normally treated as moral. At the root of this are contrasting attitudes toward morality. It is possible to be strongly in favor of, or in awe of, the general functioning of moral judgment, regardless of the particular morality one endorses. A great philosopher who is notably pro-moral is Kant. It is possible also to be strongly opposed to the general functioning of moral judgment. Some people nowadays take this attitude because they think of morality per se as illiberal and intolerant. The nineteenth-century German philosopher Nietzsche opposed morality because he considered it repressive of individualism.

Now, some of what we have been saying may seem very puzzling. How can a philosopher be said to be *notably* pro-moral, if what is morally right ipso facto is what is right? And how, without logical contradiction, can a philosopher oppose morality, as I claimed Nietzsche did?

The answer is that morality involves a *way* of making certain ethical judgments (or, one might say, a form of life). In order to be a moral judgment, a judgment must fulfill the formal conditions for ethical judgments. It also must be a judgment that normally would carry with it a heavy weight, and that therefore could be used to appeal to social pressure.

Thus a philosopher may make ethical judgments without wishing to make any of these judgments in the way characteristic of morality: he eschews heavily felt guidance with its potentiality for social pressure. He may regard morality as a loathsome social game. This was Nietzsche's view. Of course, what is morally right ipso facto is right. But Nietzsche's view implies that the things that others consider morally right either are not right at all, or are right in a way that is not moral (or, in the light of Nietzsche's characteristic wariness of ethical generalization, in some cases are one and in other cases are the other). Kant, on the other hand, believed that the moral way of making ethical judgments calls forth admirable self-respect and self-discipline. He was unusually enchanted by the process of moral judgment.

9. In line with the preceding feature, morality normally has special objects. Some entirely private acts (e.g., drug taking and suicide) may be considered matters of morality. But normally, by and large, morality will be concerned with blaming the acute and visible harm that people do to one another. It is normally true that the appeal to social pressure characteristic of morality has as a primary goal the harmonious functioning of society.

This will do as a first generalization. But of course the truth is far more complicated. We shall now explore in much more detail how the line gets drawn, and can be drawn, between what is a moral matter and what lies outside of morality. We shall do this by the analysis of two hypothetical cases: that of a man who works too hard, and that of one who takes drugs. When we have done this, we can replace feature 9 of morality with a more complicated account of the domain of morality.

Two points should be made about the analysis to follow. One is that it is complex. The boundaries of morality are irregular. We must not expect to find some simple formula for what falls within morality and what does not. At most we can get an idea of what is relevant to such a classification. Later in the chapter we give a list of nine factors that seem especially relevant.

Secondly, the boundaries of morality also are fluid. What is considered a moral matter today may not be considered a moral matter one hundred years from now. Even today there is considerable debate about the classification of some issues. Accordingly, it must be clearly understood that the boundaries of morality that we shall determine are merely current boundaries. Also, since "morality" and "moral" are English words, we shall be concerned with the current boundaries of morality within our own culture. This inevitably leads to some remarks about Western ethical traditions, which have set these boundaries.

Earlier we pointed out that moral grading must often, although not necessarily always, be taken with great seriousness. This is essential to anything that we would call morality. But it is possible that something could exist in a hundred years which we would call morality if we could see it now, but which would not involve social pressure to quite the same degree that morality does now. It is possible also to imagine something which we would call morality, but which had different boundaries from the present ones. There are limits to how different the boundaries could be, if we now would still speak of what they enclosed as morality; but it is clear that there is considerable room for change. What we are exploring now is primarily our current concept of what morality is concerned with. But we shall say something at the end about what we would be willing to consider morality.

Throughout the discussion, we shall brush against the question of whether the boundaries of morality should be redrawn, which is itself an ethical question. I do not propose at any point to answer it. However, anyone who wishes intelligently to answer it must first get a clear conceptual picture of why certain matters are usually included in, or excluded from, morality. This is what our analysis provides.

We may begin by considering the two cases, and examining their relations to the boundaries of morality.

Two Cases Near the Boundary of Morality

The first case is that of a man who, in order to increase his income and prestige, works extra hours at his job. He has a wife and children, of whom he is somewhat fond; however, his hard work drains his energy, occupies his attention, and takes his time, so that he has little time and energy left to share activities with, or pay attention to, his family. The wife accepts this, and experiences momentary pleasure at each increase in rank and salary. She, however, has very little to occupy her life, takes up inconsequential diversions, but finds them not entirely satisfying, and is generally lonely. The children experience also a kind of loneliness, and feel dissatisfied with their parents and with their own lives, without being able to articulate why.

This is in fact a common pattern in our society nowadays. If one were giving advice to the man, one would need many more details of his life. For example, if the man stood an excellent chance of finding a cure for cancer, one might say, sadly, that all his time on the job was worth it. If he were writing music as great as Bach's, one might say the same thing (although Bach himself did not have to make such sacrifices). If he were an executive of a corporation which made things nobody badly needed, or was busy writing second-rate books and journal articles, one might respond differently.

Further, it is especially illusory in cases of this sort to suppose there are merely two or three discrete alternatives. Many variations, significantly different among themselves, are possible on any course upon which an individual decides. Style, the manner in which one carries out basic choices, may be all-important.

Also, generalization is especially risky. Some wives are highly independent, whereas the wife in our example is not. (Some, indeed, might find fault with the wife for being so dependent.) Not all children respond to paternal neglect in the same way. And so on.

However, our question is not "What should the man do?" but rather "Does his case as described embody a moral problem, and if not why not?"

There is one obvious argument for considering this case a moral matter. If morality is concerned primarily with preventing harm, and with the well-being of society, this case (and other cases involving bad relations within a family) could be argued to be well within the boundaries of morality. First, the harm that may be done by the behavior described far exceeds the harm involved in most acts generally considered immoral. Stealing a few dollars, and breaking a promise to do a piece of work, are morally wrong; but much less harm is done by them than is done frequently by unfelicitous patterns of family life. Who does more harm to others, a petty thief or the mother of the protagonist in Philip Roth's *Portnoy's Complaint*?

A second argument might go as follows. If morality concerns harm done to others, this case would seem to fit within morality. The hard-working man (in this case we suppose) inflicts psychological damage not only on himself but also on his family. Thus society, it might be said, has a special obligation in this case to exert the pressure characteristic of morality.

A third argument is that the welfare of society is peculiarly at stake in the case of the hard-working man. If behavior of this sort becomes extremely common, and large classes of intelligent people are emotionally crippled, this may have a serious effect on the development of society. Arguably, it is more serious than the effect of a similarly widespread occurrence of suicide or lechery (both of which often are considered within the purview of morality).

Nevertheless, this case, I think, would generally not be placed within the boundaries of morality. It would be unusual to say that it is morally wrong for a man to behave in the manner described. Even people who were clearly aware of the effects of the man's actions would be unlikely to speak in this way.

There are two major reasons why this case would not be considered a moral matter.

1. The harm that the hard-working man does is acute, but its visibility is not. Some onlookers may not see it at all. If someone steals

or breaks a promise, we can readily perceive the immediate injury—the loss of property or the disappointed expectation. But the damage done by the hard-working man is not so immediately apparent. It consists of a series of subtle and gradual effects on the personalities of the people around him. It requires some sensitivity to perceive these effects. Even if the man's behavior ultimately results in something both crystallized and dramatic—for example, the suicide of a member of his family—it will not be obvious and unquestionable that this act is a direct effect of his actions.

This uncertainty is related to an opacity in the nature of what the man does. One might say broadly that he neglects his family. But what counts as "neglect" is subject to different interpretations and may be far from apparent to many people. Concepts such as "theft" and "murder" are not precise, but in most cases they appear far more precise and easier to apply than the concepts we have to apply to the case of the hard-working man.

It may seem unreasonable that harm which requires sensitivity to be perceived should be less a moral matter than harm which anyone can perceive, or that the relative imprecision of concepts should provide an escape from moral scrutiny. But we must remember that morality normally is designed to exert social pressure. Effective social pressure presupposes a clear common vision of the occasion of the pressure. There cannot be social pressure against thieves unless we are usually able to agree when stealing has taken place. In cases as open to interpretation as that of the hard-working man, this clear common vision cannot be achieved. Were it achieved—were the nature of what the hard-working man does as clear to almost everyone as the nature of most thefts—there would be an increased tendency to consider this case a moral matter.

2. What the hard-working man does cannot without artificiality be regarded as determined by a single decision. It may be that the man did decide at a certain point in his life that he would favor his career over his personal relations. Even so, the manner and degree of this preference are crucial, and they are determined on a day-to-day basis. One might say that the man's behavior is the product of dozens of decisions each day, which together form a pattern.

The diffuseness of his choice is perhaps not a reason why the case of the hard-working man *should* be placed outside of morality. It is true that the matters we normally consider within the domain of morality (e.g., murder, theft, adultery, false promises) can more comfortably be regarded as crystallized in a single decision, or a small number of decisions. (That this comfort is a matter of degree can be seen if we ponder Buddha's claim that "All that we are is the result of what we have thought.") But it is not essential that morality be concerned just with matters which can comfortably be regarded as crystallized in a single decision or a few decisions.

Nevertheless, this is the traditional Western image of morality, and it influences what all of us currently tend to regard as matters of morality. Morality traditionally is thought to concern itself with single, distinct decisions between discrete alternatives. This no doubt is closely related to views that stress the importance of will in moral decision. It is plausible to suppose that someone can avoid committing murder or adultery simply by an effort of will. It is implausible to suppose that someone can avoid having sterile personal relationships simply by an effort of will; a change of outlook and sensitivity also is needed.

We should again remember that morality normally is a vehicle of social pressure. Pressure may be more immediately useful in the cases of people who are considering whether to kill or steal than in the cases of people reviewing the entire patterns of their lives. More fundamentally, pressure may be directly useful in cases where mainly will power or a reminder of the general standards of society is required; its usefulness will be less direct when it is less easy for the agent to specify his behavior in advance.

In any event, given our traditional view, we are disposed to place outside of morality any behavior determined by a long series of decisions rather than by a single decision or a few decisions. The relevance of this to the case of the hard-working man is as follows. Suppose that the man, rather than gradually and subtly neglecting his personal relations, decides abruptly that he will never again see his wife and children since this conflicts with his career. We would be more likely to regard this decision as a moral matter, and to raise a moral question as to whether his decision was right.

Let us now examine our second case. A man regularly takes a drug, which to some extent impairs his fitness for the ordinary business of life. The drug is habit forming; after the third or fourth occasion of use it becomes extremely difficult not to take it. Let us suppose that the man has no close personal relationships which are affected significantly by his drug taking. Let us suppose also that, unlike the vast majority of drug addicts, he is independently wealthy, so that his drug habit does not cause him to commit crimes to provide money for drugs.

As I have stated the case, there might be some debate as to whether the man was right or wrong to take the drug (or whether he was "making a mistake"). Probably most people would say that he was wrong. I myself tend to share this view, although I would want to know more about how the drug impairs his fitness for the ordinary business of life (and which parts of ordinary business were impaired) and also about the supposed advantages of taking the drug. If a drug turned one into a Rembrandt for an hour a day, then taking it might conceivably be worthwhile. Unfortunately, it is much easier to have a second-rate vision of things, which in an abnormally relaxed mood one thinks superior, than to have a superior vision. It is much more likely that a drug would paralyze a person's critical faculties, so that the mediocre is conceived as sublime, than that it would provide something truly sublime.

Reflectively we can ask not whether the man is right, but whether the issue of whether he is right is a moral one. Here there will be considerable debate. Many people who think the man is wrong or mistaken to take the drug will argue also that he is not *morally* wrong (it is his own business). Probably, though, it is still true that a majority of people would consider drug taking (even in this case) a moral matter.

At yet a higher level of reflection, there is the question: What makes the majority classify as it does? What would incline people to treat the case as a moral matter? What factors also would incline some to treat the case as not a moral matter?

First we may take the arguments that the case is not, or should not be, a moral matter. There are two major arguments. One is that the effects of the man's actions are primarily on himself and only very indirectly on others. The assumption here is that we tend to classify within morality actions which directly harm others, and we tend to classify outside of morality actions whose direct and major effect is on the agent.

The second argument starts from the claim that drug taking is a private matter and moves to the point that a society that exerts pressure on its members in their private lives is, in some sense, less free than a society that does not. Most people who argue this way concede that there are areas in which society should exert on individuals the pressure characteristic of morality, but they would like to restrict these areas to those in which serious harm is done to others. Some would like to exclude from morality all cases in which serious harm is done to another who is a consenting adult; some would like to place within morality cases in which serious harm to a consenting adult is physical (e.g., torturing a willing victim), and exclude cases in which the harm is psychological (as in some destructive intimate relationships); still others would like to draw the line in different ways.

The preceding two arguments are also sometimes presented to exclude suicide from the province of morality. It is argued that the effects of suicide are primarily on the agent, so that it is a private matter. It is argued also that a society that exerts pressure on people who wish to commit suicide is more repressive than a society that does not.

Let us now consider the factors that contribute to most people's classifying cases like that of the drug taker as moral matters. There are, I think, three major factors.

One is that it is widely believed that drug taking is conducive to other forms of behavior which most people classify as immoral. Many people would speak of sex. This attitude is related to the fact that the great majority of people who place drug taking within the boundaries of morality also place sexual relations between consenting adults within these boundaries; generally people who place drug taking outside of morality also place sexual relations between consenting adults outside of morality. However, many people would also say that drug taking might have the effect of lowering resistance to temptations to steal, to make false promises, and so on—matters whose status as moral is less controversial.

This factor distinguishes drug taking from suicide. Virtually no one would claim that the desire to commit suicide is conducive to immorality. Thus it appears likely that many people would be less reluctant to consider suicide not a moral matter than to consider drug taking not a moral matter.

The second factor is this. If drug taking became extremely widespread, so that the great majority of people were addicted to drugs, the effect upon society would be very great. (This would be true also if there were an extreme epidemic of suicide, and, perhaps to a lesser extent, if there were an epidemic of sexual promiscuity.) Now, this suggests that even if the primary effect of drug taking is upon the agent, there is some effect, potentially a great one, on other people. This suggests that the distinction between drug taking, suicide, and sexual relations between consenting adults on the one hand, and theft, murder, and making false promises on the other is less sharp than it might appear. *All* of our actions affect others, if only by changing the "climate of opinion" or changing others' expectations with regard to us; and we have some tendency to regard the actions whose effects are most serious as moral matters. Some people would add to this the claim that society has a right to protect itself against what they would regard as drastic changes for the worse, and that this justifies moral pressure against one who takes drugs.

The third factor is that the drug taker's behavior can be regarded as simply the expression of a small number of decisions. Some would regard the crucial decisions as those to take drugs the first few times; others would consider that every day the individual makes one or two crucial decisions. In any event, the pattern of decision-making does not seem as diffuse as in the case of the hard-working man. It also does not seem as diffuse as in the case of someone who is extremely lazy. It may be that the effects of extreme laziness are as serious as those of drug taking. Even if this is so, few people nowadays would classify extreme laziness as a moral matter. This third factor surely is crucial here.

The Boundaries of Morality

Let us summarize what we can perceive about the current boundaries of morality within ethics. We shall list nine factors that appear to have considerable weight in affecting whether something is classified as a moral matter. It should be clear that these nine factors (or even the first seven) do not constitute a list of necessary and sufficient conditions. What follows is simply a catalogue of factors that count within our current concept. These factors provide an expanded and more complex view of what was noted in point 9 of our portrait of morality. The nine factors, accordingly, will be numbered 9a through 9i.

9a. We are much more likely to consider some behavior a moral matter if serious harm is involved—if whether serious harm occurs depends on what is done. If murder and theft are generally classified as moral matters, it is because we normally take seriously the loss of life or property. We might waver, though, in considering as a moral matter theft of one penny (to complete what was needed for subway fare). We tend not to consider a moral matter false promising of a very trivial kind (as when a man promises to wear a suit to a party but wears a sports jacket instead). We might say that the seriousness of harm at stake in an action is relevant to its classification as moral, but that so is the usual degree of seriousness of harm at stake in acts which we normally would place under the same very broad description. It may be that some acts of theft or false promising are not moral matters; but probably less has to be at stake for acts of this kind to be classified as moral matters than for acts of some usually innocuous kind to be classified as moral matters.

9b. We are more likely to consider some behavior a moral matter if other people are seriously harmed or helped by it than if the benefit or harm is primarily on the agent. Thus we have a tendency (which has some exceptions) to regard what people do to ruin or improve their own lives as not a moral matter. We normally do not consider advice on how to be happy as moral advice.

9c. If some behavior harms or benefits other people, we are more likely to consider it a moral matter if the harm or benefit appears direct rather than indirect. Some of the harm done by theft or false promising is direct and immediate. When a person commits suicide, this may sadden or disturb others; and it certainly is likely to impair the general morale. But these effects are relatively indirect; the direct effect of this act is simply the agent's loss of life. Thus we may be somewhat less firmly inclined to treat suicide as a moral matter than we might be to treat as a moral matter something which had much the same effects on others, but had them more directly.

9d. If some behavior harms other people, we are less likely to consider it a moral matter if the affected parties consented than if they did not. There may be, for example, a few cases in which the long-run effects on a woman are much the same whether a man has seduced or raped her. But, even in such cases, there would be much more widespread reluctance to consider the seduction a moral matter than to consider the rape in that light. If someone willingly is tortured by another, there would be strong sentiment to consider the behavior of the torturer not merely wrong but also morally wrong. But there would be more hesitation in arriving at this judgment than there would be if the victim were unwilling.

Many people regard children and mentally ill adults as special cases, and deny that they can be said to consent to anything (in the normal sense of "consent"). Thus many people are much readier to regard behavior which harms a child as a moral matter than behavior which harms a consenting adult who is not mentally ill.

9e. We are much more likely to consider a kind of behavior a moral matter if the welfare of society would be seriously impaired or aided if that behavior is widespread. If it could be shown that widespread suicide would have very little effect on the general workings of society, we would be less likely to consider suicide morally wrong than if it were shown instead that the effects would include pervasive depression and discouragement that would cause society to break down.

9f. If the character of some behavior is easy for almost everyone to recognize, we are more likely to consider it a moral matter than if many people often find the character difficult to recognize. Thus various forms of inflicting damage through sterile personal relationships are not generally considered moral matters. There may be extreme cases of this, however, in which the character of what is done is unusually noticeable. If a man neglects his family to the extent of sleeping at the office, seeing them once a month, and forgetting their names, some may be inclined to consider this a moral matter.

The recognizability, in the general run of cases, of the *type* of behavior that a specific case might be said to exemplify is also relevant to whether that case is considered a moral matter. Thus ·borderline cases of theft and murder are usually considered moral matters, even if it is difficult to decide whether an individual act was theft or murder. If, for example, a worker takes tools for a short time from the factory to use at home, a great many people may be in considerable doubt as to whether this constitutes theft. Theft in this case is not easily identifiable. But it is generally easy to identify. Thus issues involving theft are generally considered moral matters, and the question of whether the worker was wrong to take tools home would be considered a moral matter to the extent it was considered possibly a matter of theft. Someone, of course, who strongly believed that what the worker did was not theft would also be unlikely to consider whether the worker was wrong a moral question.

9g. We are more likely to regard something as a moral matter if it can be viewed as the result of a small number of decisions than if it must be viewed as the result of a very large number of continuing decisions, or simply as the expression of a general way of life. This corersponds to a traditional Western image of morality that is both dramatic and comfortable. Moments of moral decision are regarded as crises both highlighting and determining our general worthiness. In between these moments (which for most people do not happen all that frequently), the pressure is off, and we are free to pursue our happiness. To the extent that the part of ethics which is not morality has been neglected, or has been facilely equated with prudence, this dominant Western tradition has been singularly unhelpful in enabling people to deal with the day-to-day character of their lives.

The following two factors are deeply involved in current divisions concerning the boundaries of morality.

9h. We are less likely to consider something a moral matter if we consider unfortunate the effect on society of applying in relation to it the pressure of morality. Many people feel strongly that the best society is one in which people are left alone in their private lives. Someone with this view is less likely to regard sexual relations between consenting adults as a moral matter than is someone with an opposite view. Someone who takes an extreme view, believing that moral pressure should never be put on people whatever they do, may come to feel as Nietzsche did that nothing should be viewed in moral terms.

It is worth remarking that classification of something as a moral matter is related to, but distinct from, its classification as a legal matter. Many people who feel that sexual behavior between consenting adults is not a moral matter also strenuously oppose all the old laws which have forbidden certain forms of sexual behavior between consenting adults. However, it is quite possible to consider sexual behavior between consenting adults as a moral but not a legal matter, and it is possible (although unlikely) that some people might consider it a legal but not a moral matter. There are some forms of behavior, for example speeding on the highway, that are legally forbidden but would not generally be called morally wrong (except perhaps in cases in which extreme danger may result). Someone who took the extreme position that stealing should not be considered a moral matter would not thereby be committed to supporting the abolition of laws against theft.

9i. Many people consider anything a moral matter if they consider it sufficiently disgusting. Moral philosophers themselves are generally free from these attitudes, and it is not surprising that this factor has been overlooked by philosophers who have linked somewhat too closely the concepts of morality and harm. Now, it is true that people who consider a practice disgusting usually will claim that it does subtle harm to those who engage in it; but this is not invariably the case, and there is no logical inconsistency in someone's maintaining that an act is extremely disgusting, and therefore immoral, but that it does no harm to anyone.

There are deep divisions in our society on this issue. Many people claim that practices which used to be widely condemned as disgusting and immoral are neither disgusting nor immoral. Others consider some of these practices disgusting but argue (on lines connected with 9h above) that they do not fall within the purview of morality. Still others retain the old view. Thus it is still disputed whether the extremely disgusting character of a practice is ever grounds for considering it a moral matter.

It is true not only that the boundaries of morality are controversial, but that they have changed, and can change further. We may ask now how flexible the boundaries of morality are.

The question can be put in another way. Suppose that we discovered a tribe that had a pattern of discourse in some respects similar to our moral discourse, but which used this discourse to praise and blame a set of actions and behavior that were different from what we praise or blame morally. What differences in objects would we consider so significant that we would deny that the moral-like discourse of the tribe in fact expressed a morality?

We may remind ourselves that we would not consider that the tribe had a morality if their putative morality was generally taken very lightly. If tribe members' putative moral judgments generally involved virtually no appeal to social pressure, we would also deny that they constituted a morality. Thus, in discussing the present question, we may assume a tribe which makes judgments like our moral judgments in usually being taken seriously and in normally conveying some degree of appeal to social pressure. We may assume, also, that these judgments have all the essential features of ethical judgments (1–5 in our list), and that they are treated by the tribe as cognitive.

All these assumptions do not guarantee that the putative morality of the tribe would indeed be considered by us to be a morality. We may imagine the following case.[5] The moral-like discourse of the tribe is entirely focused on actions involving the clasping and unclasping of hands: clasping and unclasping, done in the right way, is praised; done in the wrong way, it is condemned. These judgments are made in a consistent and universalizable manner.

The background of belief that we can supply is crucial here. Incorrect beliefs can provide the starting point for a morality. If the members of the tribe seriously believe that unclasping one's hands in the wrong way can discourage the sun from rising, then discourse centered entirely on clasping and unclasping hands becomes intelligible as a morality—even if we know that no serious harm is at stake. But let us suppose that no belief of this sort lies behind the tribe's attitudes toward styles of hand clasping and unclasping. The tribe gives reasons for its judgments, but these reasons (having to do with what is considered a noble arrangement of the hands) seem to us frivolous. There is no claim that clasping or unclasping hands in the wrong way does serious harm to anyone.

Clearly we would not consider this a morality. Nor would we, if we were careful, speak of the tribe as "morally condemning" certain forms of unclasping hands, although we would say that they regard such actions in a moralistic manner, or that they regard such actions much as we regard immorality.

It is important to distinguish this extreme case from less extreme ones. Consider, for example, the case in which the tribe makes only a few of its putative moral judgments about hand clasping; most of the judgments concern such matters as taking other people's property or killing. This is significantly different from the case in which hand clasping is *the* focus of what is putatively morality. I am inclined to say that in this less extreme case we could discern a morality, even if the reasons given to support the tribe's judgments of hand clasping contained no suggestion that what was condemned was harmful.

In order to see this, we must remember that many people in our society consider anything immoral that is sufficiently disgusting. We may remember also that there is no logical inconsistency in someone's maintaining that an act is extremely disgusting, and therefore immoral, but that it does no harm to anyone.

Anything, even hand clasping (or, conversely, abstinence from hand clasping, or particular types of hand clasping), is capable of being considered extremely disgusting. Thus a morality in which hand clasping is the object of some judgments could, I think, be comprehensible, even apart from beliefs relating hand clasping to harm. As long as the morality's main focus was on actions that did serious harm, it would not be, so to speak, different beyond recognition from morality with which we are familiar.

It may be objected that, by my remarks about the extreme case, I am treating matters of substance as if they could be settled by appeals to language—in this case by appeal to what we are willing to call "morality." My reply is simple. Even if linguistic conventions did govern whether we could consider all acts of hand clasping moral matters (which is a stronger claim than I have made), they would not determine whether hand clasping is wrong. Whether hand clasping is wrong is a separate issue from that of what category of wrongness (if it is wrong) we are to place it in. Issues of rightness and wrongness are substantive. Nothing that I have said implies that they can be settled by means of appeals to language.

Obligation

The map of ethics that we have been drawing emphasizes not only the part of ethics that governs moral choice—those highly dramatic moments in which we may or may not perceive our duty, or resist temptation—but also the part of ethics that governs the rest of life, including those matters too subtle, or too concerned with general goals and directions, to be included in morality. This is a highly traditional picture of ethics, and would not have seemed surprising, I think, to Aristotle. But to many philosophers it will present an unfamiliar image. Much philosophical work on ethics in recent decades has concerned itself less broadly with ethics, and instead has centered on obligation, and especially on moral obligation. Thus it is fitting that we conclude our survey of ethics by saying something about obligation and especially moral obligation. This also serves as a bridge to chapter 4, which takes up the problem of political obligation.

We first may note that some obligations are normally considered moral, and others are not. The obligation of a strong swimmer to help a drowning person is a moral obligation. So is our obligation not to kill our neighbors just because we do not like their taste in music. The obligation we have to thank someone for a present is hardly a moral obligation; there is nothing *morally* wrong in being rude. Similarly, it might be said that an instructor has an obligation to erase the blackboard after the class for the benefit of the next instructor using the room, but this is not a moral obligation.

The most striking thing about obligations is the way in which they bring out the impulse to generalize. This is especially true of moral obligations. Almost always, moral obligations are discussed in relation to moral rules. Thus what gets discussed, typically, is not a particular obligation of one person to another under certain specific circumstances, but a general obligation that anyone will have under certain very broadly defined circumstances.

This is not surprising if one considers the social role of morality, or of another great source of obligations—manners. Both morality and manners are designed to be taught at large to virtually everyone in a society. They are taught even to the highly unintelligent and to children. They represent a minimum social expectation with respect to our conduct, and it is important for the security of all of us that the moral message generally get across. The result of this effort is that everyone except for imbeciles, lunatics, and small children is expected to have mastered moral precepts. Indeed, it is said commonly of the core of morality that everyone except for imbeciles, lunatics, and small children "knows right from wrong."

Is it any wonder that the basic precepts of morality (as also of manners) are formulated in general rules, and in the West have been so since the time of the Ten Commandments? General rules are good mnemonic devices; and they are the easiest ways to convey quickly, with little possibility of radical misunderstanding, a framework of expectations. Most general rules of morality have imaginable exceptions; for example, perhaps a strong swimmer should not have saved a drowning Hitler. But this detracts little from their general usefulness.

Given our impulse to generalize, we should not be surprised that many philosophers have attempted to approach the topic of moral obligation by means of extremely abstract generalizations. If we ask "How can we know in a particular case that we have a moral obligation?" such philosophers will answer by proposing a theory. A classic example is the utilitarian theory, held prominently by the English philosophers Jeremy Bentham and John Stuart Mill, which holds that we should do what produces the most favorable balance of pleasure over pain. In Chapter 5 of his *Utilitarianism*, Mill suggests that this involves moral obligation in those cases in which the wrong choice would deserve punishment of some sort. One source of punishment is public opinion.

But to answer "How can we know in a particular case that we have a moral obligation?" by giving a theory is just to push the question to a greater level of difficulty. For now we can ask how do we know the theory is correct. Part of Mill's theory is the contention that the best action to perform is that which has the best consequences, but Mill gives scarcely any argument for this contention. Nor have any other highly general ethical theories had much more success. One might ask: Why do we need highly general theories in ethics? It is clear why we need the level of generalization involved in familiar moral rules: for teaching purposes, so that everyone in society will have a rough idea of minimum expectations. But we do not need highly general theories in ethics for this purpose. The parallel between ethics and the sciences, in which highly general theories regularly are sought for, is seductive. But in the sciences highly general theories serve predictive purposes. There is no close counterpart to this in ethics. Further, even in the sciences no one has arrived at a single unified theory that explains all phenomena, which is what Mill claimed to have done in ethics.

If we continue to ask "How can we know in a particular case that we have a moral obligation?" it seems more promising to investigate the actual circumstances in which people come to recognize that they have moral obligations. A full answer would require a detailed examination of the moral life, for which there is no room in these pages. We may, however, point out the following. We most frequently accord people the right to be confident that they indeed have a moral obligation in cases in which (1) they derive the obligation from a familiar moral rule, and (2) they can convince us that they have used their judgment to ascertain that the particular case is not an exception to the general rule. In most cases requirement 2 amounts merely to their having the sense that there was nothing extraordinary or peculiar in the case at hand. The topics of how people can have the right to be confident of the general usefulness of a familiar moral rule, or of how a moral reformer reasonably can arrive at a new moral rule (or reject an old one), or of how, in some cases, we can be confident that we have an obligation even if there is no familiar rule that governs it, are all extremely complex. To explore them is to explore the ways in which we normally appeal to reason, to experience, and even to authority in our moral discussions. Perhaps the best course here is not to answer the questions—which cannot be given a simple or a brief answer—but to indicate that there is no reason to expect that the answers will consist of some neat formula or other.

There is one further thing that needs to be said. It echoes feature 6 of our six general features of ethics. Even though our way of knowing *that* we have a moral obligation varies from case to case, it is built into our language that claims that we have moral obligations can be correct. In short, we have moral obligations, even if there is no simple formula to tell us what they are, or how we can know about them.

Thus the fact that ethics, including morality, is needed to perform certain social roles does not preclude some ethical views' being more correct than others. Ethics is a tool for giving advice or exerting pressure, but it is more than just a tool. The advice would never be worth taking were it not that some things are better than others and that certain actions are right and others are wrong.

Notes

1. In asking this question, as in much of this chapter, I am indebted to P. F. Strawson, "Social Morality and Individual Ideals," *Philosophy*, Vol. 36 (1961).

2. See J. Kupperman, "Aesthetic Value," *American Philosophical Quarterly*, Vol. 9 (1972).

3. For a classic attempt in this direction, see J. O. Urmson, "On Grading," *Mind*, Vol. 59 (1950).

4. For extended argument, see J. Kupperman, *Ethical Knowledge* (London: George Allen & Unwin, 1970).

5. I am indebted for this example to Philippa Foot, "Moral Beliefs," *Proceedings of the Aristotelian Society*, Vol. 59 (1958).

SUGGESTED FURTHER READING

The following works are the major classics of modern ethical philosophy that a beginning student would want to read. They are both concerned primarily with establishing the foundations of morality; that is, the logical basis or system of evidence on which a moral judgment can be based. But both are also especially germane to this chapter in that they suggest views on how the boundaries between morality and the rest of life are to be drawn. Kant does this in his distinction between categorical and hypothetical imperatives; Mill's analysis is contained in his Chapter 5, in his discussion of the boundary between "morality" and "expediency."

Kant, Immanuel. *Foundations of the Metaphysics of Morals*, trans. Lewis White Beck. New York: Library of Liberal Arts, 1959.

Mill, John Stuart. *Utilitarianism*. Many modern editions.

The following contain classic ethical systems.

Plato. *Dialogues*. There are many good translations. The beginning reader might start with the *Gorgias* or the *Republic*. Plato places a good sense of value at the root of ethics. Those who, given an opportunity, choose evil do so because they have never known what is most valuable in life.

Aristotle. *Nicomachean Ethics*. There are many good translations. This contains a carefully qualified defense of the "contemplative" life as being the most desirable.

Confucius. *Analects*. The translations by W. E. Soothill and Arthur Waley are especially recommended. Confucius's ethics is not unlike Aristotle's. The best way of life requires a careful and harmonious balance within oneself. External events are subject to chance; but what you are is most important, and is not subject to chance.

Buddha. *The Teachings of the Compassionate Buddha*, ed. E. A. Burtt. New York: Mentor Books, 1955. Buddha claims to offer an escape from all suffering. If you attach no value to things and relationships, you will not suffer when you lose them. This is not as purely negative as it may seem; a positive joy grows out of detachment and clarity of vision. Like Plato, Aristotle, and Confucius, Buddha believes that someone with the proper values will, as something that follows from this, adhere to an acceptable morality, and that this adherence is more deeply dependable than that of someone who does what is morally right in order to conform or to stay out of trouble.

Nietzsche, Friedrich. *Thus Spake Zarathustra*, trans. Walter Kaufmann, in the *Viking Portable Nietzsche*. New York: Viking Press, 1954. Zarathustra anticipates the "overman," whose values Nietzsche will not and cannot specify, since the essence of the overman is to be independent and no one's follower. Nietzsche offers a vision of psychological strength, integrity, and toughness as being far more valuable than what is praised in traditional morality.

The following provide some overview of ethics.

Frankena, William. *Ethics*. Englewood Cliffs, N.J.: Prentice-Hall, 1973.

Harman, Gilbert. *The Nature of Morality*. New York: Oxford University Press, 1976.

MacIntyre, Alasdair. *A Short History of Ethics*. New York: Macmillan, 1966.

3 What Is Art?

What is art? Here again we are looking for something like a definition. We are engaged in attempting to find principles of classification. What makes it appropriate to call some things "art," and not appropriate to call other things "art"?

Traditionally, investigations of this sort were construed as searches for definitions. The goal would be some dictionary equivalent of the word "art." Many philosophers, most notably Socrates as presented in the *Dialogues* of Plato, have assumed that one did not know what one was talking about, in using a word, unless one could provide a definition of the word. Thus, from Socrates's point of view, one does not know what goodness is unless one can define "good," what knowledge is unless one can define "knowledge," and what art is unless one can define "art."

This view has fallen into disfavor since the publication in 1953 of the *Philosophical Investigations* of Ludwig Wittgenstein, probably the most influential philosopher of the twentieth century. Wittgenstein casts general doubt on our ability to define terms used in ordinary language. He uses the example of "game." An acceptable definition of "game" would provide necessary and sufficient conditions; that is, conditions such that activities that meet those conditions, and only activities that meet those conditions, will count as games. But any characterization that applies to tennis will have difficulty in applying both to chess and to ring-around-a-rosy, unless it is made so broad that it applies to activities that we normally do not consider to be games. "Energetic activity in which there is winning and losing" applies to tennis but not to chess and ring-around-a-rosy, and it applies to war as well. If we drop the requirement that the activity is energetic, we include chess but we still include war; if we then require that the activity be playful instead of dead-earnest, we eliminate war but we eliminate pro football championship games as well. If we try to include ring-around-a-rosy by speaking of "rule-governed playful activity, in which there is not necessarily winning or losing," we include also certain forms of singing or dancing which we normally would not term "games." Thus "game" cannot be defined.

Wittgenstein suggests that the meaning of a word can be explained in terms of "family resemblances." Members of a family can resemble one another in a variety of respects, so that perhaps every member of the family resembles some others in some respects although there is no one feature or set of features that all share. In much the same way, every game resembles some other games in some respects, although there is no feature or set of features that games and only games have. If this is correct, a child learns the meaning of the word "game" not by mastering a definition but by becoming familiar with some paradigm cases—that is, outstanding examples—of what are called "games," and learning that any activity similar enough to one of the paradigm cases counts as a game.

If we apply this reasoning to the word "art," we can arrive at the following hypothesis. "Art" cannot be defined: there is no set of conditions such that objects that meet the conditions, and only such objects, count as works of art. But there are characteristics that make it appropriate to call certain things works of art. Anything that in major respects resembles, say, the *Mona Lisa*, or Beethoven's *Fifth Symphony*, or Shakespeare's sonnets will count as art. Analysis can take us further. It can show what features of a thing make us likely to consider that it importantly resembles paradigm cases of works of art. Thus analysis can give us not a set of necessary and sufficient conditions for "art," but a set of what might be called "art-making" features—features such that the possession of a number of them makes a thing likely to be considered "art," the likelihood rising as the number increases. This tells us as much about art as a list of the characteristic features that constitute the "family resemblances" of the Smith family tells us about that family.

Such an analysis of "art" is consonant with what Wittgenstein says about "game," but certainly would not follow from it. We cannot rule out the possibility that "art," unlike "game," is a term that lacks descriptive meaning. It could be a purely honorific term, like "a sight" in the language of tourist guides, applied only to objects that we are prepared to like in a certain way; furthermore, there could be no pattern, or set of rules, that could be fitted to our bestowal of the honor. Thus art could be just what we, or a group of people in an especially privileged position, choose to call art. There might be no more to it than that.

Let us call this possibility, that "art" is just an honorific term with no descriptive meaning, the skeptical possibility. In what follows we can examine the ways in which the term "art" is applied, always bearing in mind this possibility.

The Line Between Art and Non-Art

We can point out first that we commonly do make a distinction between plays, films, stories, and pictures that we consider works of art, and plays, films, stories, and pictures that we do not consider art. *Hamlet* is art; a light comedy playing on Broadway is commonly not considered art. Eisenstein's film *Ivan the Terrible* is often considered a work of art; films of the character of *I Was a Teen-age Vampire* commonly are not. A story by James Joyce or F. Scott Fitzgerald is considered art; most magazine fiction of the sort that would appear in, say, *Field & Stream* is not. A caricature by Daumier is art; a *New Yorker* cartoon, or a political cartoon in a newspaper, typically is not.

Two points about this distinction may be noted in passing. One is that it is fluid. The Fitzgerald short stories perhaps were not considered art when they were published, but they are now. Whole classes of objects may pass over from non-art to art; connoisseurs now speak of certain old barns as "anonymous art." Interestingly enough, there is little movement in the opposite direction; what once has been considered art rarely is later considered non-art. Secondly, the line we draw between art and non-art has something to do with value, achievement, or distinction; but this turns out to be far less simple than it might appear. To the extent that an object even of a humble, utilitarian sort is finely and attractively made, to that extent it is likely to be considered art. There is some feeling that non-art is by and large less substantial and impressive than art. Yet there is some very bad art. The worst paintings in art galleries often are very bad indeed. *If* they were comparable to *New Yorker* cartoons (which on the whole they are not), one might be tempted to rate them lower. There may be some temptation to say that the *New Yorker* cartoons would be art if they were as good as Daumier's (although a reply might be that *for what they are* they are as good as they could be), but there is no temptation at all to say that they would be art if they were as good as that very bad painting, *The Death of Chatterton*.

Now, one very obvious point about the difference between art and non-art is this. It is usually the case (as teachers of literature and the arts are fond of pointing out) that some effort is required, at least in initial approaches, to appreciate what we call works of art. This is not usually the case with those forms of non-art that would be called "amusements." Wittgenstein is said to have gone, after strenuous philosophizing, to the front row of a nearby movie theater. He scarcely would have fled to the front row of performances of *Hamlet* or to theaters where "art films" were being shown. A second obvious point is this. We often demand different things from art and from amusing non-art. A film that we consider amusing but not art may entertain us during repeated viewings, but we do not hold it against that film if it is less amusing in the second viewing and if we lose interest in seeing it a third time. Excellence in art, on the other hand, is often connected with "inexhaustibility," and, even in speaking about works of a middle rank, we are inclined to discount attractive features if they do not contribute to a second or third experience of the work.

If there is a distinction to be made between art and amusement non-art, it plainly is not going to be precise, rigid, or easily formulable. In such a position, it is useful to look for hints. A good source of hints is a work of the eighteenth-century German philosopher Immanuel Kant—*The Critique of Judgment*. In this book Kant offers a characterization of the aesthetic. Since the experience of art is normally what would be termed "aesthetic experience," any characterization of aesthetic experience, or of aesthetic judgment, can shed light on what art is.

Kant's View of the Aesthetic

A word should be said about this use of Kant. Kant is the greatest modern philosopher who wrote about aesthetics. It seems to many readers that he did not always express himself as straightforwardly as he might. But what he said, interpreted patiently, is of unique value. In discussing what the "aesthetic" is, Kant's views must be considered.

Four points stand out in Kant's discussion of the aesthetic. We can summarize these using Kant's language and then explain them at some length in an untechnical way.

(1) Aesthetic judgment is essentially disinterested. A judgment of

taste "in which the least interest mingles, is very partial and is not a pure judgment of taste."[1] (2) Kant distinguishes between the beautiful and aesthetically excellent on the one hand, and the charming or merely pleasant on the other. "A judgment of taste in which charm and emotion have no influence . . . is a pure judgment of taste."[2] Charm is contrasted to form.[3] Pleasure in the beautiful is not a "pleasure of enjoyment" (in respect of which we are passive), but is a pleasure "of reflection."[4] (3) In aesthetic experience an essential element is the experience of purposiveness without purpose. The "inner purposiveness in the relation of our mental faculties in judging certain of its products . . . cannot be a natural purpose." Kant speaks of an "idealism of purposiveness," and compares this to the ideality he had propounded earlier in his *Critique of Pure Reason* of the objects of sense as phenomena.[5] (4) In aesthetic experience representations are referred to "cognition in general." Kant speaks of the "free play" and the "harmony" of the cognitive faculties.[6] These presumably provide aesthetic satisfaction.

All four of these points deserve both explanation and to be related to the question "What is Art?" We shall discuss them in turn.

1.   When Kant speaks of aesthetic judgment as essentially disinterested, it is important not to confuse, as many people do, the words "disinterested" and "uninterested." To be disinterested is to be free from bias and from the influence of selfish interest; one can be "disinterested" and yet very interested. A spectator at a football game can be disinterested, in the very strong sense of not caring which side wins, and yet very interested in the game.

To say that aesthetic judgment is disinterested is not to rule out the possibility of, say, an aesthetic judgment of a play by a person with a financial interest in its success. What is required is just that the personal bias be put aside in making the aesthetic judgment. A woman with a financial interest in the success of a play can judge the play as if she had no financial interest in it. If she praises the play because she has a financial interest, her judgment is not disinterested and cannot qualify as aesthetic. If she praises the play on grounds that have nothing to do with personal bias, this judgment is capable of being considered aesthetic.

Kant's point about disinterestedness can be applied to the question "What is art?" as follows. We tend to classify as "art" not just things that we particularly admire but things we particularly admire in a disinterested way. Our admiration of something because it is useful, or suits our purpose in some way, or we can imagine its suiting our purpose in some way, does not make it art. The car we would like to own is not thereby art.

2.   To speak of pleasure in the beautiful as a "pleasure of reflection" rather than a "pleasure of enjoyment" does seem to capture the difference between going to a good movie which we do not consider "art" and going to a Shakespeare play. We use our minds more in attending to the Shakespeare play. This is one reason why the good movie is so much more relaxing. It is also why a commentary or scholarly essay upon the good movie that is not a work of art may seem not only pompous and pedantic but also entirely beside the point. If we try to analyze how the good movie that is not art makes us like it, "charm" may be generally as good a word as any. The kind of movie we are inclined to classify as "art," on which we do not mind critical enlightenment, might be said to have "form."

Perhaps Kant draws too sharp a contrast between charm and form. Even works of art can be charming and owe some of their merit to their charm; usually the kind of light comedy we do not consider art will not be formless. The contrast that Kant is drawing, however, cannot be made precisely, and his use of the words "charm" and "form" helps to call our attention to differences that it is difficult to articulate in much more detail. Certainly we tend to take formal elements more seriously, by and large, in what we call art; and by and large a movie that is charming will be considered art only if it has much more than charm to recommend it.

Kant may have underestimated the role of emotion in the appreciation of art. Many scholars argue that emotion plays an important role in the appreciation of Greek tragedy, and was a very large part of the experience of tragedy for the original Greek audiences. Some modern works of art, such as the play *Marat/Sade*, also have an emotional content as an important intrinsic part of their meaning. To attribute the appeal of works of this character to purely formal considerations may be narrow-minded. It is true that the merit of a work of art cannot be attributed to its emotional *effect* on us; otherwise, in time works of art could be replaced by pills. But the emotional *character* of works of art cannot be disregarded, and in some cases it contributes significantly to the merit of the works.

3.   When Kant speaks of "purposiveness without purpose," he is making two connected claims. One is that art is without purpose. This is true in two senses. Art is without purpose in that, as art, it is not to be judged as satisfaction of some practical interest. The beautiful is distinguishable from the useful; even if the same object sometimes turns out to be both beautiful and useful. Art is also without purpose in the sense of having no objectively compelling, determinate structure that one simply reads off from the work of art. That is, a work of art does not have a correct meaning written on its face. Thus the second claim is that we create structure in our experience of art as part of our reflective activity. The meaning we create is not an entirely free invention; it is based on facts about, or evidence in, or markings in, the work of art. But it is created actively, not registered passively. Thus one can speak of an "idealism of purposiveness," meaning that the structure of an aesthetic experience is projected outward by us. Kant had earlier claimed that the structure of the reality we experience comes from us rather than from the world; here he makes a similar claim about the structure in our experience of beauty.

The degree of "idealism of purposiveness" helps to distinguish art from the beautiful in nature. It may be true that, as the twentieth-century Italian philosopher Benedetto Croce has said, "As regards natural beauty, man is like the mythical Narcissus at the fountain."[7] That is, it may be that the structures which enable us to perceive parts of nature as beautiful are essentially arbitrary, and are contributed by us, so that what we get out of the experience is what we put in. A great artist such as Rembrandt can paint a side of beef hanging in a slaughterhouse in such a way as to suggest that he could find beauty in it; perhaps our finding beauty typically in mountains and the seaside but not in ordinary city streets or sides of beef in the slaughterhouse has something to do with conventional expectations, and with our willingness to infuse formal structures in some cases and not in others. This makes the experience of beauty in nature seem entirely active and creative. The experience of art is active but not so entirely creative. We can see the mountains or the side of beef any way we like, but we are not at quite the same liberty to see *Hamlet* or a Rembrandt painting any way we like. Any view of *Hamlet* that makes Claudius the innocent victim of his crazy nephew, or any view of the Rembrandt painting that does not see certain darker areas as shadows, has missed something. It makes no sense to speak of *the* correct interpretation of a work of art (new interpretations of great art are always forthcoming), but it is clear that some interpretations of works of art are impermissible. There are constraints in our experience of art, as there are not in our experience of the beauties of nature, so that we must be guided and limited by markings in the text, the canvas, the musical score, and so on.

4. When Kant refers representations in aesthetic experience to "cognition in general," he may be making the general, correct point that experiencing art in an adequate way, or experiencing beauty in nature, involves intelligence; such experiencing is not simply a matter of letting feelings sweep over you. The "free play" of the cognitive faculties presumably refers to the experience we have of providing the structure of our aesthetic experiences, of rising to the challenge of the purposiveness without purpose. The discussion thus far suggests some qualification of Kant's claim that the appreciation of the beautiful involves the free play of the cognitive faculties. Insofar as "free play" suggests utter lack of constraint, we must point out that there are elements of constraint in appreciating art even if there are none in appreciating the beauties of nature.

If our cognitive faculties create a satisfying experience of the aesthetic, this must have something to do with what Kant calls a "harmony" of the cognitive faculties. That is, the appeal of what is beautiful must have to do with the arrangement of something within us that creates the experience of beauty. If it is true that Kant underestimated the role of emotional faculties in the experience of art, then it might have been better if he had spoken of a "harmony" of the cognitive *and* emotional faculties.

Good art presumably is especially conducive to a harmony of the cognitive and emotional faculties. Bad art does not provide the markings and indications of structure to stimulate such a harmony; and if such a harmony is created out of the experience of bad art, we are apt to say that someone has experienced "more than is there." In other words, good art stimulates harmonious experiences; if we get these from bad art, we are plain lucky. But good art not only stimulates harmonious experiences; it contains within itself justifications of them, elements that can be pointed to as making them appropriate. This does not suggest a characterization of "art," but it does suggest a characterization of good art.

From a suitably amended version of Kant's various insights on the aesthetic, we can construct a view of what good art is. Good art provides, at least for the proper audience, a harmony of the cognitive (and, we would want to add, the emotional) faculties. It may be that certain intellectual products, such as mathematical theorems or scientific theories, also provide a harmony of the cognitive faculties. (This may be why mathematical theorems and scientific hypotheses are sometimes described by words such as "beautiful" or "elegant.") But what distinguishes good art from these intellectual products is what Kant calls "purposiveness without purpose": our relative freedom in creating our experience, and the fact that the structure experienced is in a sense our own product. This freedom is greatest in experiencing the beauties of nature, only moderate in experiencing good art, and virtually nonexistent in relation to mathematical theorems and scientific hypotheses.

It may be that good art is what provides harmony of our faculties, within experiences of the kind of limited freedom we have been discussing, for the proper audience. I am inclined to think that it is. There are some difficulties with the formulation of this view. It is not clear what a "harmony" is or whether we should call what some turbulent and disturbing works of art provide a "harmony." It is not clear either what is to count as a "proper" audience for a work of art. But within the limits of reasonable and normal interpretations of what it states, the preceding paragraph seems to provide a plausible view of what good art is.

We are still left with the question of what art is, however. Many paintings in museums, many pieces of music, and many published poems do not by any reasonable standards provide a harmony of the cognitive and emotional faculties. What enables them to be called "art"?

The Skeptical View

Let us consider the skeptical view again: that "art" is a purely honorific term (like a "sight" in tourist guides), applied only to objects that we are prepared to like in a certain way, and that there could be no pattern or set of rules that could be fitted to our bestowal of the honor. This view is not inconsistent with the conception of good art developed above. It could be said that good art is what we are not only prepared to like, but also deserves to be liked—in that way which involves appreciating the induced harmony of the cognitive and emotional faculties. "Art" thus is what is regarded as a candidate for aesthetic appreciation, of the somewhat constrained sort distinguished above from the appreciation of the beauties of nature; good art is what deserves to be a successful candidate.[8]

Some plausibility is lent to the skeptical view by recent developments in the arts. "Pop art" has replaced replicas of Campbell's soup cans in museums; giant trenches have been claimed to be art; and music has been performed whose notes were randomly selected. One is tempted, observing these phenomena, to say, "Anything can be art." And, indeed, that may be one of the points that the producers of these works have been attempting to get across. Some of them may feel that, as a lapel button produced by the New England Thing Company asserts, "Art is all over." We are entirely surrounded by art, in this view, as we can see if we just look properly.

To many people this view is anarchic. It looks like a repudiation of standards. There is, however, a positive side to it which is not so easily understood. It is worth explaining that side before we criticize the skeptical view.

The positive side of the view that art is simply what we choose to call art is this. There is, arguably, a set of characteristic attitudes, a kind of frame of mind that we put ourselves into when we enter a museum, or when we look at sunsets in the mountains. The aesthetic attitude characteristically is disinterested and reflective, as Kant pointed out. It also tends to unify and structure its subject matter.[9] And, presumably, when we are in the museum, the cathedral, or the concert hall, we tend to concentrate more on what we are seeing or listening to than we normally do.

The question arises: Why can we not be like this all of the time? Many people would dismiss this question by saying we cannot spend all our waking day in museums and concert halls, or that the practical demands of life require that our states of mind normally be nonaesthetic. But this answer is not conclusive. If we were willing to make demands on ourselves by exerting ourselves aesthetically, at the same time worrying less about the practical needs of life, we could make most or all of our experience aesthetic. This aesthetic appreciation is one of the goals of such movements as Zen Buddhism. There is abundant testimony that it can work, although it requires considerable sustained effort. The reward of this effort is a more thoroughly aesthetic waking life, and also, of course, tranquility and a thoroughly collected mind.

Zen Buddhists, along with many avant-garde artists, would say we are arbitrarily reserving our aesthetic experiences for certain objects and certain moments. If a sunset in the mountains deserves an aesthetic experience, why does not an ordinary tree with snow on its branches also deserve one? Why exclude the sky on an ordinary day, or trash cans waiting for collection, or the side of beef that stimulated Rembrandt to paint it? Why exclude, to take an extreme case, a urinal? This may have been the line of thought that led to the exhibition of a urinal entitled *Fountain* in a Dada art exhibit early in this century. If works of art are those man-made objects that provide aesthetic experience, then a urinal could be a work of art, because it—like anything—can provide aesthetic experience.

This is the positive side of the skeptical view of "art." In the interests of a fuller aesthetic life some people have denied that "art" denotes special kinds of objects that are objectively marked off from the rest of the world. When they say that anything can be art, they are really saying that anything can be an object of aesthetic experience.

It is true that anything can be an object of aesthetic experience. It looks true, indeed, that anything can be an object of valuable experience. It is plausible to suppose, for example, that Rembrandt had a valuable aesthetic experience of the side of beef that he painted. If he had looked at the urinal in the Dada exhibit, presumably something comparable might have happened.

It is not clear, though, that the claim that anything can be the object of aesthetic experience implies that anything can be art. Even objects in nature that are generally considered beautiful, such as the Alps or the Bay of Naples, do not thereby qualify as works of art. An easy way of attempting to explain this is to say that they are not works of art because they are not man-made, but this explanation turns out to be too easy. The case of a man-made exact replica of the Alps would present difficulties. If the same community in Arizona that imported a London bridge also created a duplicate of the Bay of Naples, would that duplicate thereby be a work of art?

A better, although more difficult, explanation is this. Works of art have meanings; the Alps and the Bay of Naples do not. That is, there are constraints in interpreting paintings, cathedrals, musical compositions, and poems. Not just anything can be regarded as the melody of a piece of music, or as the repetition of a theme, or as the emotional character of the music; in this sense one can speak of the meaning of a piece of music. Similarly, certain eye movements are appropriate in looking at a painting and others are not; certain shapes are appropriately discerned. We have some latitude in creating a structure of our experience, but not complete latitude.

This assertion is clearly based on the man-made origin of what we normally call works of art. Their meanings, we normally assume, are placed there by their creators. The Bay of Naples, or a man-made replica thereof, cannot have this source of meaning.

In any case, however, the goodness of a work of art obtains in virtue of its meaning. That is, a good work of art is one that can provide a harmonious experience in virtue of the structural constraints that it contains. The structure of the experience that a prepared audience has of the work is not in any sense "read off from," or a duplication of, the meaning of the work; rather, it is made possible by the meaning of the work, which provides the material and the guidelines for a harmonious structuring of the cognitive and the emotional faculties.

The Bay of Naples may be the occasion for a harmonious structuring of the cognitive and emotional faculties, but it does not provide the guidelines. Neither does a side of beef, or the urinal in the Dada exhibit. Neither, for that matter, does an advertising jingle, or the average concrete and glass office building. As the Zen Buddhists have shown, anything can provide the occasion for a harmonious structuring of the cognitive and emotional faculties for a finely tuned perceiver. But not every object earns this response in virtue of its own structure of meaning. The crucial distinction here is not between objects that have objective meaning and objects that do not. The advertising jingle has meaning, as does in some sense the concrete and glass office building. The crucial distinction is between objects that have a structure of meaning that requires, if properly understood, some harmonious structuring of response, and objects that do not have meaning of this order. Artifacts that are not good art fall on the same side of this distinction as do beauties of nature.

Thus the claim that anything can be the object of valuable aesthetic experience does not also mean that anything can be good art. To see that not everything is good art, even in some potential way, is to see that not everything is art. If the Bay of Naples is not good art, there is no reason to adopt the alternative of calling it bad art. The appropriate thing to say about the bay, the advertising jingle, and the sterile office building is that they are not art at all. Perhaps we should view them and everything else aesthetically; but they are not art.

A Solution

What is art then? Is the urinal in the Dada exhibit art? There is one very strong reason to say it was: namely, that it was a man-made object put forward as a special candidate for aesthetic appreciation. It had one important thing in common with the *Mona Lisa:* it too had been exhibited in a museum.

But is this degree of resemblance enough? It is difficult to claim that the urinal ever became more than a borderline case, a case in which we could not confidently say "It is art" or "It is not art." Few people, I think, would unhesitatingly say that the urinal became, by being placed in the exhibit, an unquestionable work of art in some straightforward sense of the word "art." The more natural response is that the urinal was promoted to the status of an object about which one does not know what to say. This is to say that the word "art" has a meaning which, as normally interpreted, prevents the urinal from being art. Perhaps the urinal ceased to be non-art, but its status as a work of art was highly ambiguous. That very urinal displayed in any city would be a "sight," as anything can be that is talked about in the right way; but being a work of art is something of a different order.

This is a crucial case. If the urinal could be made art by being treated as art, then anything, or at least any artifact, could be made art. If this were the case, then "art" indeed would be an honorific term, and the skeptical view would turn out to be correct. If the urinal did not become art in some straightforward and unambiguous way, then the skeptical view is not correct. The term "art" may well have honorific aspects, but it cannot be viewed as purely honorific.

The following seems a plausible view of the meaning of "art." Certain objects have a structure of meaning that requires some harmonious structuring of response if properly understood. These are good works of art. Just as the outstanding examples of what a knife is are likely to be good knives, so also the outstanding examples of art are good works of art. If we survey what we normally count as works of art, we see that the bad works of art in every case resemble some good works in some major respects. The bad poems resemble good poems in some respects of meter or rhyme, and in some signs of literary pretension—properties of language or structure which seem to say, "Take me seriously." In much the same way, we are likely to call any ugly painted canvas that is framed and hung in a museum a work of art, provided only that there is some evidence of artistic pretension, some artistic attempts at color and form. Much the same distinction obtains between a building that is a bad work of art and a building we would not term art at all; the former bears evidence of artistic pretensions. In some cases neither pretensions nor success may be obvious at first but may become evident later, which is why certain old barns or Fitzgerald short stories could cross the line from non-art to art.

If the foregoing reasoning is correct, it solves a philosophical question that is both venerable and crucial to the pursuit of philosophical aesthetics. The question "What is art?" provided an example of a case in which we both knew and did not know what we meant. We knew what we meant in that we could use the words properly and confidently, classifying some things readily as art and others readily as not art; we did not know what we meant in that we could not provide an explanation. Here philosophy can perform the important task of enabling us, in both senses, to know what we mean.

The plausibility of our solution can be seen if we look at the realistic dimension of our problem behind the meaning of the word "art." What is there in the world that makes us distinguish between art and non-art? The answer consists of three points.

1.   Certain artifacts provide very satisfying experiences when we look at them or read them in a certain way, and certain sound sequences provide very satisfying experiences when we listen to them in a certain way. In other words, we would not be concerned with distinguishing between art and non-art if there were not things important to us that, once we made the distinction, we could call good art.

2.   We are not prepared to look at, read, or listen to everything in the way that we look at, read, or listen to good artistic works. A reason for distinguishing art from non-art is that our capacity for aesthetic attention is normally limited. We want to separate from the rest of life a zone within which artifacts can have special attention.

3.   Just as bad knives sometimes are used effectively for cutting, so also bad paintings sometimes give satisfaction to people who look at them aesthetically. We cannot agree among ourselves in every case whether a painting, musical composition, or novel is good; and in any case, we do not always arrive at these judgments quickly and easily. Because of these facts, we do not reserve the word "art" for highly successful paintings, musical compositions, novels, and so on. If we attempted to do this, the results would be controversial and arrived at with difficulty. Therefore we are normally willing to call the general run of paintings, musical compositions, novels, and so on, "art."

We cannot understand fully the meaning of the word "art" without grasping the facts of human life that it reflects. If no artifact gave us great aesthetic satisfaction, or if we lived differently, the word "art" would have a different meaning or would not exist at all. And if every object contained meanings that justified a valuable aesthetic response, then anything could be art.

Notes

1. Immanuel Kant, *The Critique of Judgment*, trans. J. H. Bernard (New York: Hafner Press, n.d.), sec. 2, p. 39.

2. Ibid., sec. 13, p. 59.

3. Ibid., sec. 42, p. 141.

4. Ibid., sec. 39, p. 134.

5. Ibid., sec. 58, p. 196.

6. Ibid., sec. 9, pp. 52–53.

7. Benedetto Croce, *Aesthetic*, trans. D. Ainslie (New York: Noonday Press, 1958), p. 99.

8. For a somewhat similar definition of art, see G. Dickie, "On Defining Art," *American Philosophical Quarterly*, 6 (1969), 254.

9. Cf. J. Kupperman, "Art and Aesthetic Experience," *British Journal of Aesthetics*, Vol. 11 (1975).

SUGGESTED FURTHER READING

The following works develop major alternative views of the nature of art and aesthetic experience.

Aristotle. *Poetics*. There are many good translations. This is the classic statement of the view that art is imitation.

Collingwood, Robin. *The Principles of Art*. Oxford: Clarendon Press, 1938. Collingwood concentrates on the expressive function of art.

Croce, Benedetto. *Aesthetic*, trans. Douglas Ainslie. New York: Noonday Press, 1958. Croce's view is that art is "intuition." The cutting edge of this comes from the sharp distinction between what is artistic and what is conceptual.

Dewey, John. *Art as Experience*. New York: Minton Balch, 1934. Dewey is concerned with undermining the frequently assumed division between aesthetic experience and the rest of life.

Kant, Immanuel. *Critique of Judgment*, trans. J. H. Bernard. New York: Hafner Publishing Co., 1951. This work is concerned with more than aesthetics, but it does contain Kant's view of the distinctive features of the experience of the beautiful.

Richards, Ivor. *Principles of Literary Criticism*. London: Routledge & Kegan Paul, 1924. Richards is particularly good on the difference between what good art does (to us), and what bad art does.

Tolstoy, Leo. *What Is Art?* London: Oxford University Press, 1930. Tolstoy's view of the function of art has highly controversial implications. It in effect extols folk art, and depreciates the "high" art that appeals only to connoisseurs.

These works provide overviews of aesthetics.

Aldrich, Virgil. *Philosophy of Art.* Englewood Cliffs, N.J.: Prentice-Hall, 1963.

Beardsley, Monroe. *Aesthetics from Classical Greece to the Present.* New York: Macmillan, 1966.

Dickie, George. *Aesthetics.* Indianapolis: Pegasus, 1971.

4 Political Obligation

Governmental authorities command, and people, by and large, obey. In most circumstances people feel they ought to obey. But why ought one to obey? If a policeman tells you, at a certain moment, not to walk across the street, you are likely to take this admonition more seriously than if a friend tells you the same thing. The policeman has, as we normally say, authority. But why should this make a difference? And even if it does, are there any limits to the difference it should make? Should one do anything that a properly constituted authority requires?

These are the central questions of political obligation. They are philosophical as well as practical and personal questions. We shall examine them philosophically, bearing in mind as well their practical and personal dimension.

One good way of approaching the issues is through established positions. Let us examine two established answers to the question "Why should one obey properly constituted authority?" Why should one obey laws and established regulations? One answer is that laws and regulations have moral weight because we have promised to obey them. A second, opposed, answer is that there is no general reason why one should obey properly constituted authority, and that laws and established regulations have no moral weight.

Social Contract Theory

The first answer is associated with social contract theory, which is the creation of such great thinkers as Richard Hooker, Hobbes, Locke, and

Rousseau. It has been a strong tradition in Western political thought from the late Renaissance onward. At its core is the concept of the social contract—an agreement of men to follow the laws and play their part in the social order. Without laws and the social order men are in a "state of nature"; the social contract brings them from the state of nature into civilized society. The agreement makes possible greater security, especially greater protection from one's fellow man, than is possible without laws and police in a state of nature. It also makes possible all the advantages of the cooperative enterprises of civilization. What is given up is sovereignty, or a part of one's autonomy. In Hobbes's version one agrees to let a government make certain decisions for one and to abide by these decisions.

How necessary the social contract appears to be depends on both one's view of human nature and one's opinion of the advantages of civilization. Social cooperation, which requires that one be able to depend on others, makes possible such things as electricity supplies and highways. But someone who believes that a simple life, with little mobility or technology, is better than the highly complicated life most of us lead today would say that these benefits of the social contract are at best mixed blessings. If, as Hobbes thought, man in a state of nature is selfish, competitive, and aggressive, then the state of nature would be so insecure and miserable that any kind of government in contrast would seem a blessing. Someone who took the view that man is naturally benevolent, and that selfishness and aggression are fostered only by social structures, might consider the social contract less desirable than Hobbes did.

In any event, the social contract is not something that any of us is likely to have entered as a result of a conscious decision; it is part of the world we were born into. Was it entered into by our caveman ancestors? The conception of a group of cavemen, weary of constant battling, nighttime raids, theft of food supplies, and so on, deciding to end all this by establishing a government is engaging, but historically implausible. It is not clear that there ever was a state of nature as political philosophers have described it; and, if there was a transition from a state of nature, fundamental transitions in history do not, as a rule, happen all that neatly. In any event, Hobbes, for one, can be interpreted as not claiming that the social contract was an actual historical event, but merely that human society exists *as if* there had been a social contract.[1] According to this view, whether it was Hobbes's or not, the social contract is an explanatory myth. The nature of human society makes sense if we think there has been a social contract, which is to think of society as a mutually advantageous understanding among its members.

This understanding certainly exists. We do generally assume, except in special cases with concrete evidence to the contrary, that other people will conform to the requirements of socially ordained law and morality. In the United States we assume that when a car turns onto the road, it will drive on the right side. We assume that most people are not thieves, although our confidence is not so great that we are apt to leave money lying about. We assume the police will usually enforce laws, with certain possible exceptions; so that someone who does violate the laws risks punishment. The fabric of society is not very tight; we cannot entirely depend on others. But the presence of the fabric can be felt if we imagine living in a world in which laws generally were violated and were generally not enforced. This world would be dangerous and chaotic. It also is not our world.

Even if our ancestors did not sign a contract pledging to obey society's laws and to play their social role, and even if we did not sign such a contract, it could be argued that we implicitly agreed to be full-fledged members of society. After all, we reap the benefits of the social order in the security we enjoy while growing up, and most of us do not announce our withdrawal from this order. This perhaps is not the same as our signature at the bottom of a contract; but, in the eyes of others, it carries almost the same weight. We reap the benefits of the social order; we participate in it as if we were signatories; and for all practical purposes we are signatories.

From this we can infer that we have much the same obligation to fulfill our part in the social contract that we have to keep our promises. With regard to our membership in the social order, it is as if we had promised to maintain it. This means we ought to obey its laws; we ought not to cross the street if a policeman forbids us. Once we are aware of our implicit promise to adhere to the societal order, we become aware of the ground of political obligation.

Even if this is true, though, it does not always commit us to comply with laws and established regulations. After all, it is generally recognized that there are cases in which promises should be broken for overriding reasons. We should not give a man his rifle we promised to return if he has become a maniac and will certainly commit murder with it. Something analogous is true in the political sphere. Most people nowadays agree that there are cases in which one should not do what is required by regularly constituted authority, although there is considerable disagreement as to where the boundary is to be drawn. Many official commands in Hitler's Germany should have been disobeyed. Perhaps the officials who gave the commands were not in fact regularly constituted authority; in other words, there is room for argument as to the legitimacy of Hitler's power. But even if Hitler and his officials were, by any normal standard, regularly constituted authorities, it is hard to see how this makes much difference. Many of their commands still should have been disobeyed and many of their laws should have been disregarded. Thus, even if we have promised to obey the laws, this does not imply that we always should do what we promised.

Further, it is not clear that a promise, or some promise-like episode, is generally part of the story at all. Native-born citizens, who thus have not been naturalized, may never have promised to uphold the laws at all. It may be argued that there is an implicit promise involved in our reaping the benefits of the social order while we are growing up, without protesting. But consider what happens if we live not far from the border with another country and wander across the border to visit the neighboring country. We had not promised to uphold the laws of that country, even implicitly; they made no direct contribution to our welfare while we were growing up. And yet most people would, I think, feel much the same obligation to obey the laws of, say, Canada, as they would the laws of their own country. This suggests strongly that political obligation cannot be adequately explained or justified in terms of a social contract. If we are not Canadian, there is no social contract at the root of our obeying the laws of Canada.

Now, one might assume in all of this that the laws of Canada are fairly reasonable laws, and that the things they forbid, such as murder, theft, or torture, are things that one would have independent moral reasons for not doing. This may suggest that it is generally appropriate to obey a set of laws, or commands, of regularly constituted authorities if and only if these are good laws or commands. We have agreed that the wicked commands of a Hitler should not be obeyed; it may seem to follow that we have to make some evaluation of the goodness of laws and commands before deciding whether we should obey them.

Wolff's Anarchism

If we hypothesize that only good laws or commands should be obeyed, then does it make any difference that these have "official" sanction in the lawbooks or as commands of regularly constituted authorities? If the action is good, it should be performed whether or not there is a legal or official basis for it. If the action is bad, it should not be done. If this reasoning is correct, then it may seem that the existence of laws and regulations is never a reason for doing something required by regularly constituted authority. The only valid reason for doing something is that it is a good thing to do.

This is close to R. P. Wolff's argument *In Defense of Anarchism.* Many people think of anarchism as endorsing an absence of order, but this is a mistaken conception. Anarchists favor voluntary order. Institutions are possible, and perhaps even necessary, but they should have the ongoing consent of all of those who participate in or are affected by them. The philosophical anarchism that Wolff espouses is centered on the complementary idea that institutions which lack this character, such as governments, cannot claim the unquestioning obedience of those who fall within their domain.

At the root of Wolff's argument is a particular interpretation of the ethics of Immanuel Kant. Kant's ethics proclaims the infallibility of the categorical imperative as a test for moral maxims. In its most famous formulation, the categorical imperative decrees that it is wrong to act on a maximum (i.e., a personal principle) which is such that either (1) it could not be a universal law for rational beings, or (2) if it could be a universal law, this would involve a situation which one could not possibly want to see. For example, to make a false promise is morally wrong because it would be literally impossible for everyone to make it a principle to make false promises. Even if one set out to have a world in which everyone made false promises, in such a world no "promises" would be believed, the words "I promise" would lose their meaning, and, in short, there would no longer be promises, false or otherwise. Thus the maxim involved in making a false promise is shown to be morally unacceptable by the fact that it cannot be a universal law. A world in which everyone followed the maxim "I shall not help others in need" would be possible, but we could not want there to be such a world, since there are imaginable circumstances in which we should want help ourselves. Therefore it is immoral to act on the maxim "I shall not help others in need."

What makes morality possible, in Kant's view, is autonomy. Autonomy is the capacity of each rational being to adopt personal principles which can also take on the character of universal laws. Each of us can be, so to speak, a lawgiver. The implication of this is that morality is rational, thus being within the scope of any rational being's thought; morality is not, in Kant's view, a matter for appeals to experience or authority. We can decide moral questions in the way (broadly speaking) in which we decide questions of mathematics—in our own heads. Autonomy also involves taking responsibility for the rightness of what we decide.

Building upon this notion of autonomy, Wolff asserts that "for the autonomous man, there is no such thing, strictly speaking, as a *command*."[2] There may be "commands" in the environment of an autonomous person, which she or he may well take into account, as facts about the situation, in deliberating what to do. But these "commands" cannot be viewed as having binding moral force. One may do what the policeman says out of a sense of the general convenience of having an orderly traffic pattern; the command is not right just because the policeman makes it. The commands of authorities may be viewed as suggestions and taken on their merits, but there is no legitimate political authority.

It is worth noting that Kant himself in his various political writings drew very different conclusions, and in particular was much more reluctant than Wolff is to countenance rejection of the demands of political authorities.[3] It could be argued, of course, that Kant was inconsistent, that his political theory was more conservative than his ethics would warrant. On the other side, there is an argument for obeying the commands of regularly constituted political authority parallel to the Kantian argument for not making false promises.

If one adopts a maxim that endorses disobeying commands of regularly constituted authority, then one must ask oneself about a world in which everyone disobeyed the commands of regularly constituted political authority. In this world, of course, there would be no political authority, any more than there could be promises in a world in which people generally did not keep them. Thus, from a Kantian point of view, disobeying commands of regularly constituted authority, like making false promises, has a self-contradictory quality. There cannot be a universal law to disobey the commands of regularly constituted authorities.

It is not entirely clear how much this argument is worth, but at least it is Kantian. It does not, however, represent the side of Kant that interests Wolff. It is Kant's concept of autonomy that interests Wolff. We can therefore ask: Is there no legitimate political authority, assuming that moral autonomy is of the greatest importance? Wolff's answer is "yes." It is in this way that he bases his view on Kant's ethics.

The temptation to agree quickly with Wolff is strengthened for many people by events in living memory. It seems abundantly clear that an awareness of moral autonomy would have enabled Germans to take the commands of Hitler for what they were worth. Many Americans feel much the same way about some of the commands of their government during the Vietnam War.

However, in philosophy it is important not to be blinded by examples, explicit or implicit. If we consider the full range of laws and regulations, and of commands issuing from regularly constituted political authority, we may get a more complex picture of what is at stake. We also will be in a position to apply some fundamental distinctions.

The most fundamental distinction relevant here is between moral decisions and decisions that are not of a moral character. The character and grounds of this distinction were discussed in chapter 2. The boundaries of morality run straight through the area of governmental involvement in our lives. Some matters on which the government requires certain behavior of us would be generally classified as moral, and others as nonmoral. An example of the former would be not torturing people or committing murder. An example of the latter would be not parking in a no-parking zone or speeding on the highway (in conditions that do not involve unusual or blatant hazard to others). We normally label torture or murder as morally wrong and visit moral condemnation (as well as legal punishment) on those who are guilty of them. Those who park in no-parking zones may be legally punished as well, and we tell them they ought not to do it (especially if it seriously inconveniences others). But it would be very unusual—and, indeed, odd—to tell someone that it is morally wrong to park in a no-parking zone.

As was pointed out, one of the differences between the two categories of wrong actions is seriousness. Murder is a far more serious business than parking in a no-parking zone. If one parks in a no-parking zone deliberately so as to cause death or serious injury to someone (say a blind person walking that way and expecting there to be an empty space), then the action takes on the character of something morally wrong.

The seriousness of an action or a decision can be viewed in more than one way. Some would argue that what is important is the principle at stake. Plainly, though, this is not the whole story. Promises normally are of some importance, but it is hard to regard a promise to repay one penny or to wear a red necktie as involving a serious issue. The importance of the consequences of an action also has to do with how seriously we take it. We take seriously actions that lead to death, or major injury, or intense pain.

We take seriously also actions that contribute to major changes in social relationships. If breaking a promise is likely to contribute significantly to people's not trusting promises thereafter, then we are much more likely to take the breaking of the promise seriously. If an action contributes significantly to breaking down people's ability to rely on social order, and if we regard the ability to rely on social order as important, then we are that much more likely to take the action seriously.

If we bear this in mind, we can see that whether a regularly constituted political authority requires something may affect our classification of the decision whether to do that thing as moral or nonmoral. That is, a decision to do X may be in itself a nonmoral decision; however, if a regularly constituted authority requires us to do X, and the consequences of our refusing to do X include a significant contribution to the breakdown of established social order, then the decision of whether to do X may come to be counted as a moral decision. It should be stressed that the existence of a requirement by a regularly constituted authority is not enough automatically to make a decision a moral one: the wrongness of parking in a no-parking zone is not normally moral wrongness even if a policeman or a traffic sign tells us not to do it. The point is that there are *some* imaginable situations in which the existence of a requirement by a regularly constituted authority is enough to convert what would have been a nonmoral decision into a moral one. If we live in a city in which police authority has been seriously undermined and, with a crowd watching, a policeman tells us to wait before crossing the street, the decision whether to wait before crossing may be a moral one. If a riot is brewing, a great many decisions that normally are not serious enough to be moral may become moral decisions.

The reverse is unimaginable. That is, we cannot imagine a decision which would be a moral one if there were no requirement by a regularly constituted authority, but which is converted into a nonmoral one by the requirement of a regularly constituted authority. If the issue is serious enough to be a moral issue, there is nothing a regularly constituted authority can say which will make it less serious.

This gives us three possible classifications for any given decision. The decision can be moral whether or not there is a requirement by a regularly constituted authority. It can be nonmoral whether or not there is a requirement of a regularly constituted authority. Finally, the decision could have been nonmoral had there been no requirement of a regularly constituted authority; however, as a consequence of this requirement, it counts as moral.

The point of spelling out these classifications is this. If Wolff's argument has any force, it is only with regard to decisions in the first classification. It is only in this classification that moral autonomy has a voice which might be compromised by heeding the call of political authority. In the second classification moral autonomy is not involved at all, because the issue is not a moral one. In the third classification moral autonomy does not have any voice if the call of political authority is not taken into account, since the issue becomes a moral one only in the light of the demands of political authority. It cannot be argued that we should do what moral autonomy would have us do, because moral autonomy would not have been involved in the case.

Thus respect for our own moral autonomy can provide no reason for violating the requirements of regularly constituted authority in cases which do not involve moral issues, or in cases in which there was no moral issue antecedent to the involvement of political authority.

This still leaves open the question of whether there is some positive reason to do X in virtue of the fact that a regularly constituted authority requires X. Let us agree that the great majority of requirements of regularly constituted authorities do not involve moral issues. Some have an obvious point to them; others are silly and perhaps downright stupid, although they are not requirements to do something morally wrong. We might wonder: Why follow the silly and stupid requirements? Why follow any at all, other than those which have us do something we would have considered it reasonable to do in any case?

There are some laws and regulations which are relatively easy to justify. These introduce an expectation of order instead of harmful chaos. An especially clear case is the rule in many countries that one drive on the right side of the road. There is nothing immoral per se in driving on the left; but there is, arguably, something morally wrong about deliberately driving on the other side of the road from everyone else, thus deliberately causing hazards to life. What is important is coordination: ensuring that everyone drives on the same side of the road. There is an obvious usefulness here both in the rule's being made and in its being followed.

In many cases, the usefulness of laws and regulations is more debatable. Nevertheless, we can separate two questions: (1) how useful is it that the law or regulation was made and (2) how useful is it to fulfill the requirements once it has been made? These two questions can have different answers.

Ideally, every decision a government makes is for the good of its citizens. However, governments, especially in the modern world, are very complex, ill-coordinated operations. The people who make crucial decisions are often not very well informed and in any case are fallible. It might be argued that part of the problem is that government does too much, that it is overextended. If governments made fewer decisions and issued fewer commands, then, it is argued, they would make fewer mistakes, asking less that is the opposite of useful. This may in fact be correct, but there is no reason to assume that it must be correct. For the refusal to act and to issue commands is also a decision of sorts, and it too can be the opposite of useful. To institute an irrigation project over a large area calls for extensive coordination and many governmental commands; but it also can provide great benefits that could not have been provided by the separate efforts of the individuals involved. For a government to refuse to act in matters such at this could be harmful.

What is at stake when we decide whether to fulfill a requirement of a regularly constituted authority to do X, when doing X in itself (i.e., if not required by a regularly constituted authority) involves no moral issue? Part of what is at stake is the success of a policy—the government's policy of having people like us or with circumstances like ours do X. If we fulfill the requirements, we presumably increase the chances of success of the policy (except in cases in which the policy is extremely ill-conceived); if we refuse to fulfill the requirement, we undermine the success of the policy. If this were all that was at stake, a reasonable rule of thumb might be to fulfill intelligent requirements (thus increasing the chances of success of intelligent policies) and violate silly or stupid ones (thus undermining silly or stupid policies).

However, there are two difficulties with this. The obvious one is that our judgment of whether a policy is intelligent, silly, or stupid may be wrong. An intelligent policy may be judged by us to be silly or stupid; there may be cases in which an intelligent policy seems silly or stupid to almost everyone. If bureaucrats are fallible, so are we. If bureaucrats are harried and occupied with too many matters, they are still likely to have thought longer about the reasonableness of a policy than we have.

The second difficulty is this. Our choices of whether to do what is required by regularly constituted authority are likely to influence the "climate of opinion." These effects will go beyond the effect on the implementation of a particular policy. If we do not do what is required by a regularly constituted authority, this failure to obey is likely to contribute a little bit to a climate of opinion in which people feel extremely free about violating rules that look silly to them, and in which authorities cannot count on general compliance with what is ordained.

Whether this general effect is good or bad is a matter for individual judgment. It could be that, in some societies, it would be desirable to undermine authority in this general way. This could be argued in relation to Hitler's Germany; perhaps even driving on the wrong side of the road could have been justified as undermining a generally bad system. There might be other, less extreme cases in which a fundamentally beneficent bureaucracy had got out of hand, and it appears desirable to undermine its expectations of compliance with silly or frivolous directives. If an arm of the government becomes excessively bureaucratic, for example, it might be useful to refuse to reply to some of its questionnaires.

In general, however, if the structure of government is working not too badly, then actions which tend to undermine the authority of government are prima facie undesirable. In general, actions which tend to undermine social structures that are on the whole desirable should not be performed unless there is some overriding reason in their favor. Even silly commands of regularly constituted authorities ought generally to be obeyed. But there can be cases in which there is a clearly good reason for disobeying a silly command; and if what is commanded is not merely silly but immoral, there is thereby a compelling reason for disobeying the command.

This amounts to a fairly guarded conclusion about the extent of political obligation. Instead of a sweeping judgment about our obligations to do what is required by political authority, we have a judgment that we should normally do what is required by political authority. But the judgment tells us there are special cases which call for reflection. For example, we have to consider how useful is the existence of the regularly constituted authority, how seriously would we undermine the authority if we refused to do what it required, whether the requirement is immoral, and so on. This leaves us with a guideline to case-by-case reflection, rather than an easy generalization. But perhaps this corresponds fairly to the intuition most of us have about political obligation, which is that there are exceptions to the most important rules.

What about the ground of political obligation? In cases where we truly ought to obey regularly constituted authority, what is the ground for this obligation?

We have already dismissed the claim that the ground lies in some primeval promise to obey, or in some implicit promise to obey that we made (perhaps unwittingly) while growing up. We can dismiss anything that implies some simple general rule that applies to, and decides, all cases in which we might inquire about political obligation. This suggests that the question "What is *the* ground of political obligation?" is radically misconceived. It is like that very silly question, "What is the secret of the universe?" What is looked for is some very general answer, when what is really the case does not admit of this kind of generality.

We have supplied *a* ground for political obligation that states, if it is useful to keep a social structure strong, then it is useful not to undermine it by our actions. But it would be foolish to suggest that this is the only reason for doing what is required by regularly constituted authorities. In some cases, the effect on us (our future character or our relations with others) of what we do is at least as important as the effect on the strength of social structures. In some cases the major reason for obeying regularly constituted authority coincides with the major reason for giving these commands—that some good can be accomplished or evil averted. There may be a moral obligation to obey a command quite apart from its official sanction. There may also be a moral obligation because the actions that are commanded will lead to some great good. In some cases it may seem that a major reason for obeying regularly constituted authority is a sense of gratitude or responsibility to the society in which one grew up. Socrates cited this sort of reason for his decision not to violate the laws of Athens by fleeing to avoid certain death.

Thus there are many grounds, whose strength varies from case to case, for political obligation. Political obligation has been viewed by some as if it were like the conclusion of a theorem. But our investigation suggests a more complicated, less rationalistic view.

In the last analysis, political obligation, like obligation in general, is a matter of what is the case. For example, our experiences of human suffering and of the benefits of social organization tell us that we are obligated to do various things: to help those in dire need, to avoid causing the deaths of innocent people, and in certain cases to do what is required by regularly constituted political authorities. In the end, some judgments of obligation seem well-founded and correct.

One is tempted to speak of facts, of ethical facts of obligation. But the word "fact" is misleading here, suggesting there is some scientific way of determining our obligations, or some special sense that discovers our obligations. To say that we have certain obligations does not imply that these can be determined scientifically or through some special sense.

Nor need one claim that there is some general formula for these obligations or some one general way of finding out about them. Reasons and arguments can be helpful, as can experiences of various kinds; but none of these constitutes an entirely general method, or anything like proof. Here as elsewhere, philosophers wish to impose a rationalism on their problems, viewing political obligation as derivable within a closed system. But, here as elsewhere, it seems that reality, or something like judgments of reality in being unprovable and correct, interposes itself. We have certain political obligations whether we realize them or not; in arguing about our obligations we are trying to find out what is the case, rather than trying to reach some abstraction or arbitrary conclusion.

Notes

1. See Thomas Hobbes, *Leviathan*, ed. M. Oakeshott (Oxford: Basil Blackwell, 1957), chap. 13, p. 83.
2. R. P. Wolff, *In Defense of Anarchism* (New York: Harper Torchbooks, 1970), p. 15, italics Wolff's.
3. See Immanuel Kant, *Metaphysical Elements of Justice*, trans. J. Ladd (New York: Library of Liberal Arts, 1964), pp. 84, 86, 138.

SUGGESTED FURTHER READING

The following works are classic statements of the social-contract theory.
Hobbes, Thomas. *Leviathan*. Many modern editions.
Locke, John. *Two Treatises of Government*, ed. P. Laslett. Cambridge: Cambridge University Press, 1964.
Rousseau, Jean Jacques. *The Social Contract*. Many modern editions of acceptable translations.

The following works contain good statements of anarchist positions.
Krimerman, Leonard, and Lewis Perry, eds. *Patterns of Anarchy*. New York: Doubleday Anchor Books, 1966.
Wolff, Robert. *In Defense of Anarchism*. New York: Harper Torchbooks, 1970.

The student interested in recent political philosophy might consider the following.
Quinton, Anthony, ed. *Political Philosophy*. Oxford: Oxford University Press, 1970. A strong collection of essays by contemporary philosophers.
Rawls, John. *A Theory of Justice*. Cambridge: Harvard University Press, 1971. This book is concerned with the just distribution of resources. It is

possible for someone reading Rawls to get the impression that money and material resources are of more ultimate value than they really are, but Rawls offers a brilliant and unparalleled theoretical justification of liberal social policies.

Nozick, Robert. *Anarchy, State, and Utopia.* New York: Basic Books, 1974. Nozick does for libertarianism what Rawls does for welfare liberalism. The result is a masterly development of what might be considered a right-wing position, but not a standard right-wing position by any means.

5 Do Physical Objects Exist?

Philosophers who have asked "Do physical objects exist?" have, in the great majority of cases, assumed that physical objects do exist *in some sense* (as we all know). What they worried about was the *kind* of existence physical objects had. Thus the question usually formulated as "Do physical objects exist?" could be stated more accurately as "What kind of existence do physical objects have?" The link between the two formulations is that many philosophers have denied that physical objects have the kind of existence that most of us ascribe to them. Thus these philosophers have denied that physical objects exist *in the way most people think that they exist.*

The reader may find this puzzling. How can there be kinds of existence or ways of existing? Either physical objects exist or they do not, and plainly they do.

One way of considering the problem is to examine the view of a major philosopher who raised it, Bishop Berkeley, the eighteenth-century Irish philosopher, who denied that physical objects exist in the way most people think they do. Berkeley's insistence that the existence of physical objects is really mental makes him a leading representative of the school of thought known as *idealism.* Following our examination of Berkeley, we can examine an opposing position, known as *realism.* Then we can see what kind of case can be made for realism.

Berkeley's Idealism

Berkeley's idealism centers on the view, briefly stated, that physical objects exist only as ideas in minds. God exists and is omniscient; so objects unperceived by human beings yet can have existence in God's mind. A table exists as your idea of it when you perceive it, and the ideas of others when they perceive it; however, when the room is dark and deserted at night, the table still exists, since God continues to have an idea of it. The table does not exist as a thing separate from your mind, the minds of others, and God's mind; its existence is constituted by the ideas of it. The only things that exist are minds and ideas in minds.

In Berkeley's analysis, our experience of the world consists of ideas in the mind. When we experience something, it is in the form of images or something like images. From this claim it is a short step, although one that can be challenged, to say that these ideas are what we experience. What you see, for example, when you look at a table is your image of the table. If all this is correct, then what you experience is in fact something mental. If all that we experience is mental, then there is no possible reason to think anything exists that is not mental; that is, if we just stick to what we know, we will speak only of mental realities. Indeed, if what we think of is mental, it can look impossible for us even to entertain meaningfully the possibility that something nonmental exists. For if all that we can think of is mental, how can we even think of something existing that is not mental?

Thus Berkeley concluded that it did not make sense to suppose that physical objects existed independently of minds. Physical objects do exist, however.

The table does exist—as ideas in minds. We can speak of what Berkeley denied as "extramental existence." Berkeley denied the extramental existence not only of physical objects but also by implication of physical phenomena such as light, rainbows, magnetic fields, and so on. For the sake of brevity we can speak of the "existence of physical objects" when we mean "existence of physical objects and occurrence of physical phenomena." Our concern includes not only chairs and tables but also light, rainbows, magnetic fields, and the like. All these Berkeley relocated in minds.

Even though Berkeley maintained that physical objects exist only as ideas in minds, he was ready to say the familiar things about them. As his representative Philonous remarks in the *Dialogues*, "I cannot for my life help thinking that snow is white and fire hot."[1] (This for

Berkeley is a way of saying that our idea of snow includes the idea of whiteness, and our idea of fire includes the idea of heat.) This insistence on being able to say the commonplace thing is part of Berkeley's general policy: "to think with the learned and speak with the vulgar." "The common use of language," he claims, "would receive no manner of alteration or disturbance from the admission of our tenets."[2]

Despite this strategic conformity, Berkeley's view is bound to seem unusual to most people. The most obvious question to ask is, "Is it correct?" In due course this question will be taken up. But first we should consider a more reflective and at least equally difficult question: "What kind of question is the question 'Is Berkeley's view correct?'"

A very strong tradition dictates a choice of two answers to this question: "conceptual" or "factual." (The word "linguistic" will be used interchangeably with "conceptual" in what follows.) Given this dichotomy, we classify as conceptual any question that can be resolved by an analysis of language, or simply by a decision as to how language should be used. Questions of historical truth, scientific data, the acceptability of scientific theories, and so on, are classified as factual. Some on the fringes of this tradition might wish to speak also of special metaphysical or ontological facts, although this is highly controversial. The status of ethical questions, too, has given rise to sharp controversies.

Examples at this point might help. A standard example of a conceptual question is "Are all bachelors unmarried?" One might take statistical samples in order to resolve this question, but that would be foolish, for "unmarried" is built into the meaning of the word "bachelor." One need go no further than the meanings of the words. One could imagine a social scientist, for some special purpose, deciding to broaden the term "bachelor" so that it applied also to married men who were separated from their wives. Given this use of the term, we would have to deny that all bachelors are unmarried. Alternatively, we might challenge the social scientist and say that he was wrong *because* he was misusing language. But the issue would remain conceptual as long as it was taken for granted that there were at least some married men in the world who were separated from their wives. We would not have to look beyond language.

Thus the question that I am raising is this. Is Berkeley's claim about physical objects just a highly sophisticated and subtle analogue to the social scientist's claim that not all "bachelors" are unmarried? Is Berkeley just constructing his own version of language in order to yield surprising results? Or is his claim instead like a historian's claim that America was in fact discovered by Madoc the Welshman, or a scientist's claim that the earth is surrounded by a band of ether: a claim that may be true or false, but in any event is a claim of fact?

It is easy to establish that Berkeley's central claim is not factual in the way in which claims professionally made by scientists are factual. No experiment will decide between Berkeley and his opponents. The result of any experiment or observation can be put by Berkeley in his own terms; as revealing the truth about ideas and about the connections among ideas. If putting your hand next to fire results in real pain or a real scar, this can be expressed in terms of a connection between the idea of the hand's being next to the fire and a succeeding idea of pain or of a scar. The experimental evidence thus is neutral between Berkeley and his opponents.

One possible view of the character of what Berkeley has to say is this. The "metaphysical" side of Berkeley (the side that involves abstract-sounding claims about reality) is not detachable from the "conceptual" side; so the issues raised by Berkeley's account of reality are at bottom conceptual issues. At bottom the issues concern language. This is suggested by one recent commentator on Berkeley, G. J. Warnock. Warnock remarks on Berkeley's "own personal, extraordinary vision of the true nature of reality."[3] But it may be, he remarks, "that Berkeley's 'version of the world' . . . should be represented, not as an ontology conjoined with and detachable from a programme of analysis, but as a single 'version' having, according as it is 'read,' *both* ontological and conceptual implications."[4]

Warnock, it is clear, regards the conceptual here as fundamental. There is nothing to suggest that he considers the question of whether Berkeley's view is correct to be at all a factual one. The focus is on Berkeley's use of, or analysis of, language. Berkeley emerges as a philosopher primarily concerned with espousing an unusual interpretation and use of language. What is primary in Berkeley's philosophy in this account is that language works differently for him than it does for us.

It is arguable that Berkeley thought differently of his own work. In the passage already cited in which he recommends thinking with the learned and speaking with the vulgar, Berkeley uses the analogy of Copernicans who cheerfully speak of sunrises. In other words, even though they are convinced that the earth in fact revolves around the sun, they maintain the old way of speaking, which had been appropriate to the belief that the sun revolves around the earth. Berkeley's use of this analogy suggests that he thought of his conformity in "speaking with the vulgar" as like that of the Copernicans, which in turn suggests that he may have thought of his philosophy as, fundamentally, revealing a previously unrealized factual character of the world, with conceptual modifications to follow from this and linguistic accommodations to be worked into the fabric. Berkeley's concern with his unusual interpretation of, and use of, language then was not primary. Like Copernicus, he was primarily concerned with the nature of reality.

The evidence for this is certainly not decisive. In any event, our question here is a different one: not whether Berkeley thought the central issue was conceptual or factual, but rather whether the central issue indeed is conceptual or factual, whatever Berkeley may have thought about the matter. Warnock can be right in treating the issue as conceptual, even if Berkeley thought otherwise.

A major complaint that Warnock makes against Berkeley is worth discussing as shedding light on the character of the issues. Warnock gives the example of a jury foreman who, when asked to give the verdict, says, "We are sure that all the evidence produced in court, and also any other evidence that might be or might have been produced, supports the view that the accused committed the offense." This, Warnock points out, is not to give the verdict.[5] To confuse the verdict with the summation of evidence is a logical error. But Berkeley, he says, makes an analogous error in confusing the reality of physical objects with ideas of them. This is a conceptual error. The ideas do not add up to a real physical object any more than the sum of the evidence equals the verdict. Reality is not the sum of appearances. And we can understand this conceptual point merely by understanding the meaning of the word "real." Once we understand that, according to Warnock, we can see that Berkeley is wrong.

In considering this objection, we have to realize that Berkeley has two senses of "real." There is what might be called the "bedrock" sense, in which what is real is only minds and ideas in minds. This is Berkeley's basic view, after all. The table exists as ideas in minds (our minds and God's mind). If we see a pink elephant in a hallucination, or while drunk, the pink elephant also occurs as an idea in our mind; therefore, in Berkeley's bedrock sense, it is real as an idea in a mind.

There also is the sense (which we may call, punning, "the common sense") in which Berkeley can say that "the distinction between realities and chimeras retains its full force."[6] Berkeley recognizes that in common speech the word "real" is used in such a way as to distinguish between ideas that normally are repeatable, and can be expected to be shared by others, such as our idea of the table, and ideas that normally are not repeatable and likely to be shared, such as the idea of the pink elephant. We call the table "real" and the pink elephant "not real": in Berkeley's view both are ideas in minds, but what we mean is that the idea of the table has relations to the rest of our experience, and to the possible experience of others, that the idea of the pink elephant lacks; the idea of the table also is more lively and distinct. In Berkeley's view, this is all we can mean.

Most people would say, of course, that the basic difference between the table and the pink elephant is that the former really exists "out there" and the latter does not. Berkeley would deny the claim that is intended by this; in his view objects are just ideas in minds, and neither the table nor the pink elephant exists "out there." But our criterion for distinguishing as we do between the table and the pink elephant is the relation that one has and the other lacks to the rest of actual and possible experience, and this Berkeley can accept. Thus he too can adopt a sense—his "common sense"—in which he can speak of the table as real and the pink elephant as not real. Only what he means by this is simply that the former (as an idea) has relations to experience that the latter (as an idea) lacks.

This, of course, is speaking with the vulgar. There is an ordinary distinction between veridical experience on the one hand and illusions on the other, which Berkeley is determined to capture in his account. We must continue to distinguish the ideas of sense from those of imagination. "The ideas of sense are more strong, lively, and distinct than those of imagination; they have likewise a steadiness, order, and coherence, and are not excited at random . . ."[7]

In this sense of "real," an object that only I can see is not real. God, of course, cannot be deluded. But there is nothing in Berkeley's works to suggest that he considered it impossible that a very large group of human beings could all be mistaken about what is real. Thus suppose that I report that I and friends X, Y, and Z seem to see an object in the room, and then consider whether to say that the object is (in the common sense) real. For Berkeley these are two distinct judgments. There is a logical gap that cannot be bridged simply by bringing in more friends.

How could Berkeley put the difference between reporting that it seems to us as if the object were in the room, and judging that (in the common sense) the object is real? It is not clear what he would have said, but there is no reason to assume that he would have to reject Warnock's analogy. Warnock's analogy with verdicts and evidence does not conflict with what Berkeley says about the real—in the common sense of "real." It does conflict with Berkeley's other sense, the bedrock one; but what of that? Berkeley could say, "You have accused me of failing to capture the distinction between evidence and reality; but I have captured the distinction, in my analysis of the common sense of 'real.' I have another sense of 'real,' for expressing truth of uncommon importance. It is not that I have missed something which is part of general knowledge; it is rather that I have added something." If Berkeley is to be faulted, then it is on whether the addition is justified. He can make the same distinctions between reality and appearance that we all do.

Is Berkeley's central thesis after all, at bottom, purely conceptual? The pattern of evasion that I have sketched for him, in response to Warnock's objections, rests on adroit manipulation of conceptual constructions. This suggests that the question of whether Berkeley's view is correct is a conceptual one, as, indeed, Warnock's study on the whole appears to assume. We can see whether this is so by examining a view opposed to Berkeley's, namely, realism.

Realism

Berkeley at one point remarks that "it is indeed an opinion strangely prevailing amongst men, that houses, mountains, rivers, and in a word all sensible objects have an existence natural or real, distinct from their being perceived by the understanding."[8] We may take this "strangely prevailing" opinion as a first formulation of the realist position. I shall explain why Berkeley's wording does seem more promising as a first formulation of realism than one alternative. Then we can formulate realism somewhat more fully.

The crucial words in Berkeley's formulation are "distinct existence." The realist holds that physical objects have an existence distinct from experiences. Now, there is a related matter on which some philosophers have focused attention. Do objects exist when we do not perceive them? Does the furniture go out of existence when the room is deserted for the night? We have a propensity to believe that things continue to exist when we do not perceive them, although it may not be entirely clear what rational basis this could have. Is not this continued existence the nub of realism?

This is close to the issue of whether realism is correct, but there are reasons why a formulation in terms of "distinct existence" cuts closer to the philosophical joint.

For one thing, Berkeley does believe that the furniture continues to exist when we leave the room. It continues to exist because God perceives it. On much the same basis, Berkeley could imagine the existence of a world in which there was no life.

Conversely, it is possible for someone to be a realist, holding that physical objects exist "out there," and yet hold that they do not exist when we do not perceive them. We could imagine the following fantastic and highly implausible possibility. Suppose that physical objects are controlled by a law yet unknown, the Principle of Conservation of Reality. This Principle conserves the resources of the universe. For physical objects to continue existing while unperceived is wasteful. Accordingly, under the Principle, physical objects "blink off" while unperceived. Or, to put it another way, the objects are destroyed every time they are no longer perceived, and then created anew when perception is forthcoming.

The implausibility of this hypothesis is not so extreme as to amount to logical contradiction. The hypothesis is compatible with the realist position as it has been traditionally understood. Objects could exist "outside the mind": that objects are periodically destroyed and created would not render them within anyone's mind, any more than the light we turn off when we leave a room is thereby in our minds. But under the hypothesis, objects would not exist unperceived. Therefore realism can be satisfied by a case in which objects do not exist when they are not perceived.

It has to be added, of course, that if realism is correct, there would be no reason to suppose that objects do not exist when not perceived in much the way that they exist when perceived. But what we are concerned with now is not states of affairs, but rather formulation of a position.

Another element in realism, besides the thesis that physical objects have an existence distinct from being experienced, is this thesis: no collection of statements about actual or possible human experiences jointly entails a statement that a physical object or objects exist (or do not exist) in the manner the realist claims. Thus a realist holds that, no matter how many people think they see an object, or no matter how many people (under various circumstances) *would* think they saw the object, it would remain conceivable that the object was not there.

This second thesis has been challenged by the contemporary philosopher A. J. Ayer, among others. In *The Problem of Knowledge* he maintains that in "the limiting case" of an infinite set of observations all running the same way, conjunctions of statements about what would be experienced do imply statements about physical reality. "It surely would follow," he says, that an object did not exist "if there were no circumstances whatsoever in which it would seem to be perceived." Conversely, it would logically follow that an object existed if "in what appeared to be the relevant setting the object would always seem to be perceived, no matter what further experiences were obtainable."[9]

If Ayer's claim is to be significant, it must be a claim about infinite sets of possible experiences constituted as follows. Possible experiences are experiences that would occur if certain causal conditions obtained—if an observer were in a certain position, and if certain factors were operating on him or in the environment. The only factors that cannot be varied in constituting a possible experience are factors dependent only on what is being talked about. That is, in talking about the possible experiences of seeing an elephant, we can vary the character, condition, and placement of the observer, the content of what people are saying to him, the character of the light, and so on; but we must hold constant the physical properties of that part of space possibly occupied by the elephant. Thus possible experiences of the elephant would include cases in which the observer was under the control of a hypnotist, but also cases in which the observer was not hypnotized; they certainly would include cases in which the observer was peering in dim light, or under the influence of LSD.

We could render Ayer's thesis, then, as follows. If the infinite set of possible experiences (treating "possible" in the manner just outlined) vis-à-vis an object is all positive, then logically the object must exist. If it is all negative, then logically the object cannot exist.

The difficulty now is this. There are no sets comprising all of the possible experiences relevant to the existence of an object X that are all positive or all negative. In any case in which the existence of X is at stake, we can include the possible experience of a susceptible observer who has been hypnotized to experience X, and also the possible experience of a susceptible observer who has been hypnotized to experience not-X.

The point is not merely that there are no appropriate sets of possible experiences that are all positive or all negative, but that we cannot coherently set up a case in which there would be any. Our failure to find cases is not bad luck; what we are concerned with, after all, is possible facts. To ask whether a set of all possible experiences vis-à-vis the object, all positive, would logically guarantee the existence of the object is like asking what would follow logically from the existence of round squares. In speculating about the character of what turns out to be a meaningless case, Ayer does not thereby say anything to refute the thesis of logical independence.

Let us now review the realist position. It consists of two theses:

1. Physical objects have an existence distinct from actual or possible experience. The information which we convey by speaking about physical objects is not just information about the way things seem or would seem.
2. Statements about the (distinct) existence of physical objects are not entailed by collections of statements describing actual human experiences or the experiences that would occur in various descriptively specifiable circumstances.

We may call these, respectively, the theses of distinct existence and of logical independence.

Now that we have outlined two opposing positions—idealism and realism—we can return to our questioning the nature of the issue between them. Is it factual or conceptual?

It is important to realize that the question "What kind of issue is that between realism and idealism?" is not totally separate from the bottom level question, "Is realism correct or not?" How one answers either question has a great deal to do with how one answers the other.

Let us suppose that we render an anti-realist verdict by rejecting the thesis of logical independence. This then implies that the issue is conceptual; after all, the issue must be conceptual if a correct answer can be given on the basis of logic. Conversely, if we give a positive verdict and accept the thesis of logical independence, then it becomes difficult to maintain that the issue is primarily conceptual. Unless we invent new categories for what must be supplied, it looks as if we would have to say that knowledge of facts is needed to supply what we have admitted our logic does not provide. If both theses are affirmed— if one accepts both the thesis of logical independence and that of distinct existence—then it appears difficult not to say that the issue of the distinct and independent reality of physical objects is a factual one.

Not only does a stand on the issue of realism prejudge the kind of issue it is, but also a judgment of the kind of issue it is goes at least some way toward prejudging the issue. If we hold that the issue is conceptual, then we must claim by denying the thesis of logical independence that the issue can be resolved conceptually. To hold that the issue is conceptual is to take an anti-realist stand.

If we judge the issue to be factual, the situation is more complicated. We would have to say that if physical objects had extramental existence, it would be independently of actual or possible experience, and it would be distinct existence. But there is room for a skeptical decision. We could simply deny or doubt that physical objects in fact do have extramental existence. Thus to take the issue of realism to be factual need not commit one to a realist position. But it does commit one to rejecting the standard anti-realist positions, and carries one some way in the direction of realism.

If the foregoing is correct, it is disturbing. Philosophers often like to think that questions of method are independent of questions of results, but here there appears to be an uncomfortably close relation between philosophical assumptions about method and the results that will be obtained. This suggests two further worries. First, we appear to be at an impasse with regard to realism. If we cannot even determine the kind of problem it is without (at least partially) begging the question, how can we proceed? Secondly, how do we arrive at our judgments of character of philosophical problems? In the case of the nature of the problem confronted by Berkeley and the realists, we are again at an impasse.

In what follows I shall attempt to break both impasses. This will involve presenting a case for realism—a case that is also a case for considering the question answered by realism to be a factual one.

A Case for Realism

We will present one argument each for the two theses that constitute realism. These arguments are designed to create a presumption in favor of realism. In chapter 1 the distinction was mentioned between grounds that make it reasonable to accept a conclusion and grounds that prove a conclusion to be correct. The arguments presented here have the former character. They amount to a case for realism, not a proof of it.

Let us begin with the thesis of logical independence, which claims that statements of the existence or nonexistence of physical objects as we normally conceive of them (i.e., as extramental) are not logically derivable from statements about actual or possible experiences. The thesis states, in effect, that we cannot achieve entire theoretical certainty about what really is the case on the basis of what the result of a finite, or even an infinite, set of observations would be. This has obvious links with doubt of the kind the seventeenth-century French philosopher René Descartes made famous. Descartes at one stage in his work considered it possible that he might be wrong in all his everyday judgments. This phenomenon is called, after him, Cartesian doubt. Clearly, a case for the thesis of logical independence is a case for Cartesian doubt regarding physical objects.

Consider this. Psychologists have had some success in stimulating experiences directly by means of wires to the brain. Let us suppose (as is certainly conceivable) that by the twenty-fifth century psychologists will have had far greater success. They can stimulate a full array of sensory experience by means of wires to the brain, and by means of computers they can ensure that the experiences stimulated will be congruent with imagined actions (speech, movement, etc.) of experimental subjects. Thus it will be possible to create an entire world of experience for a subject who has no ordinary sensory input.

Let us suppose that psychologists do this. One of their research projects is to reconstruct some of the details of what life and attitudes were in the twentieth century. Thus an infant in the twenty-fifth century is taken at birth, deprived of ordinary sensory input, and made (by wires to the brain) to have a complete set of experiences that seem appropriate to the twentieth century.

As described, the case seems to involve thoroughgoing and complete delusion. If the psychologists are really efficient, there is no way that the experimental subject can contrive to find out the truth. The question "Am I really living in the twentieth century?" of course would express an absurd doubt. But even if the question occurred to the subject (the psychologists in a cruel moment might contrive to have the subject "read" a philosophical essay which raised such a doubt), there would be no way for the subject to go about finding the right answer.

Nevertheless, we can give some experiential sense to the notion that the subject is deluded. We can imagine the psychologists, after thirty or forty years have elapsed and their research grant has been exhausted, removing the wires from the brain of the experimental subject and restoring normal sensory input. The subject then might realize that he is living in the twenty-fifth century.

I say "might realize," because it is difficult to say what would happen in fact, or even what a thoroughly reasonable person would conclude. When the wires are removed, the subject might reasonably think the reality exposed was a dream or (more plausibly, since dreams do have special characteristics) the reflection of mental breakdown. Even after months of exposure to life in the twenty-fifth century, he might be in a position comparable to that of the ancient Chinese philosopher Chuang Tzu, who, after he dreamt that he was a butterfly, could not be sure whether he was a man who had dreamt that he was a butterfly or a butterfly now dreaming that it was a man.

Thus if we take some statement describing what we think of as physical reality (e.g., "The Eiffel Tower still stands" or "There is a goldfinch near me"), this statement is not entailed by statements about actual or possible experiences. The psychologists may have fooled us, and there may be no way of finding out.

This is a fairly artless reintroduction of Cartesian doubt, which needs to be refined. The refinement can take place in the context of consideration of objections. Four objections especially are likely to be made. We shall consider them in ascending order of philosophical importance.

First, it could be argued that the case of the deceitful psychologists, among its other defects, does not even establish what it is supposed to. It is supposed to establish what we have called the thesis of logical independence, that statements about physical reality are not entailed by conjunctions of statements describing actual experiences or the experiences that would occur in various descriptively specifiable circumstances. But if we include among our descriptions of experiences a very large number of descriptions of experiences that would occur when the wires are removed, then (the objection runs) we can arrive at a conjunction that would entail certain statements about reality.

The reply is this. Even if we have the wires removed, and then have a long and internally consistent succession of experiences, we still cannot have entire theoretical certainty about reality. How can we eliminate the theoretical possibility that we are deceived in some other way? Perhaps we have escaped the psychologists with their wires but are under the influence of a hypnotist. The objector may reply that he can specify a conjunction of experiences in which neither wires nor hypnosis is a factor as grounds for entire theoretical certainty about reality. But suppose there is yet some other means of deception, about which we at present know nothing. In order for the objector to make a case that there is a conjunction of possible experiences that would entail judgments about reality, he must show first that we can have entire theoretical certainty that we can specify all the possible ways in which we might be deceived; that is, that there is a set of descriptive conditions we can specify such that a statement that these conditions obtain entails that we are not deceived. It appears highly doubtful that an objector can do this, especially since there seems nothing incoherent in the idea of a mode of deception one of whose features is that the deceived person cannot think of it as a possibility.

A second objection might go as follows. Perhaps the case of the psychologists' wires does establish that judgments about the Eiffel Tower, goldfinches, and so on, are logically independent of statements of experience. But the general judgment that physical objects exist is in a special category. Once we are warned about the possibility of psychologists of the twenty-fifth century tampering with our brains, we can see that the general run of our judgments about reality lacks complete theoretical certainty. But still, we can be certain at least that some physical objects exist, even if they are not the ones that we think. After all (the objection might continue), the very case presented was formulated in terms that presupposed the existence of physical objects (e.g., "wires," "brain").

The more general part of this objection, that some physical objects must exist even if we may be mistaken about their character, is taken up in discussion of the third and fourth objections, which raise this point in a philosophically more acute way. Let us now deal with the specific part of the objection at hand, that some physical objects must exist because even the hypothesis of entire deceit must be framed in terms of physical realities.

The reply is this. The hypothesis of the psychologists and their wires was used for pedagogical purposes, because it represents the kind of deceit that many people find increasingly easy to imagine. It lacks the obscurities of Descartes's original version, which involved a deceiving evil demon. However, if the reader's mind is opened to the possibilities of doubt, the psychologists' wires can be replaced by something more abstract and less appealing to the imagination. We may say simply, "Suppose that there are no physical objects (having extramental existence), and that another bodiless being is deceiving us into thinking that there are." Details of this case are far more difficult to imagine convincingly than are details of the case of the twenty-fifth-century psychologists. But why should that count against it? If we are deceived, why could not the deception encompass our inability to imagine the circumstances of our being deceived? As long as there is no logical contradiction in the notion of a bodiless being's deceiving us into thinking that physical objects exist, the hypothesis must be taken seriously. And it is hard to see what logical contradiction there could be, unless there is a fundamental contradiction involved in the mere thought that physical objects do not exist.

Let us consider, then, the two objections that provide arguments for saying that there would be such a contradiction in physical objects not existing. One is as follows. We do think that physical objects exist; we have the idea (taking the word "idea" in a sense as general and as different from those of seventeenth- and eighteenth-century philosophy as one likes) that physical objects exist. But consider this analogy. We cannot have the idea of a color unless we have experienced the color, and we cannot have experienced a color unless something (perhaps merely some light, or perhaps even merely something in the eye) has or has reflected on it that color. In the same way, we cannot think that physical objects exist unless, in fact, some physical objects do exist.

This argument is difficult to state with precision and without an archaic semblance. Nevertheless, it has very high initial plausibility. It sounds grossly implausible to suggest that we could have an idea of some fundamental kind of reality without there being something of the appropriate kind to serve as the source or occasion of the idea.

Having conceded plausibility to the argument, let us concede also some limited force. Even if everything that has preceded this has made sense (and, of course, the anti-realist may deny that), it still, one might say, would be strange if on the one hand we continually had experiences that gave us the idea of physical objects having extramental existence, and on the other hand no physical objects existed thus. Anyone wishing to create a case for the extramental existence of physical objects would certainly want to appeal to the experiences that give us the idea of physical objects.

Nevertheless, this is not proof. In weighing the objection, we have to ask this. The objection rests on the assumption that we cannot have an idea of such a thing as extramental physical objects unless at least the ingredients of the idea are given in experience. How do we know that this assumption is warranted?

This question is, I venture to say, unanswerable. When we deal with problems as central and fundamental as that of realism, we constantly encounter primitive assumptions—assumptions concerning meaning or the sources of thought. We also encounter philosophical views that rest on unargued assumptions. Descartes is often derided for his reliance, at crucial gaps in argument, on his "light of nature." But Professor Ayer could not have written his anti-metaphysical classic, *Language, Truth, and Logic,* without his own light of nature. And only an appropriate light of nature can tell us that the assumption underlying the present objection is correct. This is to say that the objection lacks a firm foundation. Unless it can be clearly *demonstrated* that it is impossible to have ideas of physical objects (having extramental existence) without something corresponding to the ideas, theoretical doubt about the extramental existence of physical objects cannot be eliminated in this way.

A more profound and argued objection can be found in Immanuel

Kant's *Critique of Pure Reason*. This is the "Refutation of Idealism." The Refutation centers on the contention, first, that "All determination of time presupposes something *permanent* in perception," and, secondly, that "perception of this permanent is possible only through a *thing* outside me. . ." Consequently, "the determination of my existence in time is possible only through the existence of actual things which I perceive outside me."[10] In other words, there cannot be human experience unless external objects are items of experience.

This is an important and valid argument. But what does it prove? In order to see the difficulty, consider first the most obvious objection to Kant here. The objection is that the conceptual requirement for experience can be fulfilled if there merely *seem* to be external objects. It is not required that the objects actually exist.

This could be elaborated in a shell of Cartesian mythology as follows. Suppose that the demon is charitable rather than evil. He is Kantian, and he knows that if the world as it is—*sans* extramental physical objects—is presented to us, we will fail to attain experience, thought, or, indeed, humanity. Therefore he makes it appear that there are extramentally real physical objects. If we ask how the demon himself has managed to be able to think, there are alternative replies. Perhaps physical objects once had extramental existence (during the youth of the demon), but then went out of existence. Or we might appeal to a miracle of self-creating thought. Alternatively still, we might expunge the demon, and hypothesize that it simply is a fact about the world that there seem to be extramentally real physical objects but are not.

In any event, the obvious objection to Kant appears to be that experience does not require the existence of persistent and reidentifiable objects in space, but merely their appearance. This objection, I am convinced, is not telling. In order to see this, we must appreciate how it is that Kant can say so confidently beforehand that "the required proof must, therefore, show that we have *experience*, and not merely imagination of outer things. . ."[11]

The key element that must be supplied is a realization of what kind of existence of outer things Kant is proving—existence within the framework of experience. Once we see this, the opposition Kant claimed between himself and Berkeley appears much less sharp. Kant demonstrates the existence of outer things, but Berkeley too maintained the existence of outer things such as chairs and tables. Kant distinguishes between experiencing things and merely imagining them; but as we saw in the discussion of Berkeley's "common sense" of "real," Berkeley can make a comparable distinction.

Thus we have to say that Kant's "Refutation of Idealism" demonstrates the existence of physical objects in a sense in which no one, not even Descartes (and certainly not Berkeley), had doubted their existence.

Because of this, Kant's "Refutation of Idealism" will not serve as an objection to doubt of the extramental existence of physical objects. Neither will a modern argument similar to Kant's. This is the argument that we have language, which is in its nature shared with other people, but that language requires shared experience, and hence existent physical objects. The doubter, it is contended, contradicts himself, since his doubt is expressed in language. The reply, again, is that language, and shared experience, do not require that physical objects have extramental existence. There could be language even if Berkeley is right.

If none of the objections is entirely telling, then there is no firm obstacle to our admitting the theoretical possibility of Cartesian doubt. This serves to support the thesis of logical independence. Physical objects satisfy the thesis of logical independence if and only if it is not possible to attain entire theoretical certainty about their distinct existence on the basis of the (actual or possible) sensory evidence. It may seem paradoxical that the realist position must include an argument for, or incorporate, doubt. But the realist position must incorporate a logical gap.

We must point out that, even if the foregoing presentation of doubt were more than a strong argument and were a proof, that would not refute all anti-realists. For one thing, some anti-realists such as Berkeley deny the thesis of distinct existence without clearly denying the thesis of logical independence. It would not be inconsistent with Berkeley's position to agree that, on the basis of actual or possible human experiences, there might be room for doubt about what characteristics a given physical object has, or whether it is present at all. Consequently, an argument for realism must include an argument in support of the other half of realism, the thesis of distinct existence.

The thesis of distinct existence traditionally has been thought extremely difficult to argue for. After all, it was thought, if we are directly aware of one kind of reality (our experience), how can we argue from this to the distinct existence of another kind of reality (extramental physical objects)? The argument to be presented is unoriginal, and may seem tenuous; but at least it to some degree sidesteps this difficulty.

The argument begins from the assertion that traditional thought on this subject, including some traditional realism, misconceived the nature of ordinary waking experience. It used to be thought that when we were awake and looking at something, what we were looking at would imprint an image on our minds, from which image we might infer the existence of its cause. However, an impartial examination of ordinary waking experience discloses something very different. When we look at a table, there is nothing closely comparable to what we have when we close our eyes and visualize the table. What we have when we visualize the table is an image; phenomenological examination (that is, examination of the nature of experience) discloses that what we have when we see the table is something else.

Early in the twentieth century that erratic but gifted phenomenologist G. E. Moore realized this very clearly. In analyzing the experience of seeing a blue object, he remarked, "That which makes the sensation of blue a mental fact seems to escape us: it seems, if I may use a metaphor, to be transparent—we look through it and see nothing but the blue. . ."[12] Elsewhere Moore says, "When we try to introspect the sensation of blue, all we can see is the blue: the other element (consciousness) is as if it were diaphanous."[13]

The point is, as Moore again says, that there is no difficulty about getting outside the circle of our own ideas and sensations. "Merely to have a sensation is already to *be* outside of that circle."[14] We are immediately aware that what we perceive presents itself as having, or being connected with something that has, a distinct existence. (The point is put in this cautious wording for two reasons. First, it is important to see that the examination of experience does not prove that there *is* a distinct physical reality, but merely enables us to realize that sense experience occurs *as if* there were a distinct physical reality. Secondly, while Moore's own analysis can lend itself to the view that we directly experience physical objects themselves, it is possible to accept his insight without identifying what we are aware of with the physical object itself or any part of the physical object.)

Thus one might say that sense experience provides a prima facie case that there is a distinct physical reality. It is this element in everyday experience that makes most people believe immediately that Berkeley is wrong.

How far does this realist argument take us? And does it have any value at all? We can deal with the latter question first.

The argument may seem vulnerable in one important respect. It is an appeal to what is experienced, but not to data of experience in the sense in which we speak of "scientific data."

This objection will carry weight with a great many people. But it ultimately rests on a view of meaning which asserts that evidence either will be scientific or will count as evidence in virtue of its role within a deductive logical system. This view of meaning may be at stake in the present investigation; it certainly is very difficult to maintain except in conjunction with an implicit anti-realism. Therefore there is something circular in an appeal to it.

Further, one can reply to the objection as follows. Scientific data are by their nature particular findings—findings that distinguish one set of events from others. The outward-pointing character of sense experience is a general finding. It constitutes a general feature accompanying all data of the physical sciences, and not just data about certain kinds of physical events. Thus, of course, the outward-pointing character of sense experience cannot occur as a *scientific* datum. But to insist because of this that it is a worthless finding is to dogmatize on the basis of, again, a challengeable theory.

Distinct physical reality does make a difference, not perhaps in the special features of isolated experiences with which the sciences deal but in the continuing character of experience. It is difficult to express fully the difference made by the fact that sense experience presents itself as if there were a distinct physical reality. But that the difference made by this feature of sense experience is so all-encompassing does not make it any less real. Thus the nonscientific character of what Moore says does not provide a warrant for ignoring it.

If the argument is not to be discarded, how much weight is it to be given? Here we should give a balanced answer. On the one hand, the argument is merely a point about how things seem, about how they present themselves as being. We have already said in the discussion of Cartesian doubt that this falls far short of proof. But, on the other hand, the argument must be taken seriously. It is the only starter in a field of nonstarters.

Consider, after all, where the debate between realists and their opponents stands. Appeals to language and *a priori* arguments work only if the issue is conceptual. But why suppose that the issue is conceptual? If this were the case, there ought to be some clear way of demonstrating the correct answer, or of demonstrating that there is no correct answer. It appears that no one has been this successful in the debate surrounding realism.

The major reason for insisting that the issue is conceptual is a theory of language. But this theory of language itself is at stake in the debate. It cannot be treated as not subject to revision, or as automatically the last word on the matter.

If the issue is factual, what facts do we have to go on? Traditionally, philosophers such as Berkeley began with the fact, which appeared to verge on a tautology, that experience involves a mental event, thus seeming profoundly "interior." But this, if Moore is right, is a very one-sided presentation of what is the case. The fact is that sense experience is outward-pointing and has a character that gives people the opinion "strangely prevailing" that physical objects have a distinct existence.

Notes

1. George Berkeley, *Third Dialogue*, in *Works*, ed. A. A. Luce and T. E. Jessop (London: Thomas Nelson & Sons, 1949), Vol. 2, p. 230.

2. Berkeley, *Principles of Human Knowledge*, sec. 51, in *Works*, Vol. 2, pp. 62-63.

3. G. J. Warnock, *Berkeley* (Harmondsworth: Peregrine Books, 1969), Preface to the Peregrine Edition, p. 9.

4. Ibid., p. 10, Warnock's italics.

5. Ibid., p. 177.

6. Berkeley, *Principles of Human Knowledge*, sec. 34, in *Works*, Vol. 2, p. 55.

7. Ibid., sec. 30, p. 53.

8. Ibid., sec. 4, p. 42.

9. A. J. Ayer, *The Problem of Knowledge* (Harmondsworth: Penguin Books, 1956), p. 130.

10. Immanuel Kant, *Critique of Pure Reason*, B 275-276, trans. Norman Kemp Smith (New York: St. Martin's Press, 1965), p. 245, Kant's italics.

11. Ibid., B 275, p. 244, Kant's italics.

12. G. E. Moore, "The Refutation of Idealism," in *Philosophical Studies* (London: Routledge & Kegan Paul, 1958), p. 20.

13. Ibid., p. 25.

14. Ibid., p. 27, Moore's italics.

SUGGESTED FURTHER READING

Traditional realism is argued for in the following classics.

Descartes, René. *Meditations.* There are many modern editions of acceptable translations.

Locke, John. *Essay on the Human Understanding.* Many modern editions.

Berkeley's idealism is most accessible in the following.

Berkeley, George. *Three Dialogues between Hylas and Philonous.* Many modern editions.

Important twentieth-century works on the same problems, which are especially accessible to beginning students, include the following.

Russell, Bertrand. *The Problems of Philosophy.* Oxford: Oxford University Press, 1959. In this book Russell develops an interesting variant of a realist position.

Ayer, Alfred. *The Problem of Knowledge.* Harmondsworth: Penguin Books, 1956. This is a clearly written but exceptionally subtle development of an anti-realist position.

Commentaries on philosophers discussed in the chapter include the following.

Warnock, Geoffrey. *Berkeley.* Harmondsworth: Peregrine Books, 1969.

Bennett, Jonathan. *Locke Berkeley Hume Central Themes.* Oxford: Clarendon Press, 1971.

Martin, Charles, and David Armstrong, eds. *Locke and Berkeley.* New York: Doubleday Anchor Books, 1968. A strong collection of critical essays.

6 The Nature of Physical Reality

If there is a physical reality independent and distinct from our experience of it, what is it like? Indeed, even if physical reality is not independent or distinct from our experience of it, we still may ask "What is it like?" Questions of the nature of physical reality naturally follow upon the questions answered by realists and idealists. Once we have established the status of physical reality, or have arrived at the right degree of doubt and puzzlement about its status, we can turn to questions of the *nature* of physical reality.

This is not to say that the meanings of such questions will be clear and unambiguous. Our investigations thus far should have taught us that in philosophy there can be as much difficulty in establishing what a question asks as in answering the question. A well-known anecdote of Gertrude Stein has her being asked, on her deathbed, "What is the answer?" Displaying once again a philosophical bent, she murmurs in reply, "What is the question?" In the same way, when we are presented with a philosophical theory or controversy, we should first ask "What is the question?"

In what follows we begin by considering a recent theory concerning the nature of physical reality: scientific realism. Then we consider an older view, that the nature of physical reality is unknowable, and examine what there is to be said for and against this view.

Scientific Realism

Scientific realism is the doctrine that science gives a more adequate, or truer, description of reality than is available outside the sciences. Thus a leading scientific realist, Wilfred Sellars, comparing the manifest and scientific images of man in the world, describes the manifest image as "an 'inadequate' but pragmatically useful likeness of a reality which first finds its adequate (in principle) likeness in the scientific image."[1] Another prominent scientific realist, J. J. C. Smart, conceding the truth of commonsense claims that tables are solid, remarks that "so though most common-sense propositions in ordinary life are true, I still wish to say that science gives us a 'truer picture' of the world."[2]

Expressed in this way, scientific realism sounds as if it centered on a peculiar doctrine of truth. There are degrees of truth: some truths are truer than others. One wants to know then, are these degrees of truth measurable? Is the commonsense claim that an ordinary table is solid only 70 percent true, whereas the scientific account is 100 percent true?

The writings of scientific realists such as Smart and Sellars suggest, however, that it would be wrong to construe scientific realism as primarily a doctrine about truth. Rather it is a doctrine about reality, with appendages (or perhaps merely verbal shuffles) about truth. The table is solid (true), but it *really* is not solid; it *really* is the assemblage of elementary particles in largely empty space that science tells us of. Objects *really* do not have colors.

Even viewed in this way, scientific realism suggests difficulties reminiscent of very different traditions. A scientific realist has to concede that in some sense the table is really solid (the magician appeared to pass something through it, but it is really solid). Perhaps the table is really solid, but it is *really* not solid. What we have here are two levels of reality—an everyday, provisional reality, adequate for ordinary purposes, and an ultimate reality. The most significant philosophical tradition that has developed such a doctrine of two levels of reality is the Indian. Classical Hindu philosophers penetrated to the level of ultimate reality through mystic exercises or contemplation. From the point of view of scientific realism, to penetrate ultimate reality one must be a scientist.

The scientific realist, however, insists that there is one reality, not two. What is the case, he may say, is that there are two ways of talking—the rough-grained everyday way, and the more exact, scientific way. Everyday language, and the truth it contains, always lags behind real advances in our understanding of reality. Long after Copernicus we continued (as Berkeley observed) to say, "The sun rises"; and, given the criteria built into everyday speech, we can see that there were daily occasions on which this was true. But *really*, of course, if we accept Copernicus, the sun does not rise, and this too is true. This truth, though, must be interpreted within a different framework of discourse.

The scientific realist thus may insist that there is no reality in which the table is solid. There is only one reality, and in this the table is not solid. What he will concede is that there are two systems of *discourse*, as opposed to two systems of reality, each with its own built-in criteria for truth and adequacy. In one of these, the statement "The table is solid" meets the standards for truth. In the other, "The table is solid" is false. Further, the second, the scientific framework, has an immediate relation with the nature of reality which the first, the commonsense (or manifest) framework, lacks. It is this more immediate relation between scientific discourse and reality which the scientific realist may attempt to express metaphorically by speaking of scientific accounts as "more adequate" or "truer" than accounts expressed in everyday speech.

How, though, does the commonsense framework of discourse lack an immediate relation to the nature of reality which the scientific framework possesses? For is there not certain evidence in reality that assures us (despite the illusions of the magician) that it is true that the table is solid? Both the "truth" of commonsense descriptions and the "truth" of scientific descriptions are known by means of evidence, which in turn depends on what is real. What is real provides the evidence for the truth (in the commonsense framework) that the table is solid, and for the truth (in the scientific framework) that the table is not solid.

Thus, if the scientific realist answers a question about reality, so do commonsense judgments that tables are solid. If reality gives warrant to the scientific realist, it also gives warrant to these commonsense judgments. Let us put this aside temporarily and continue the effort to formulate the question that scientific realism answers.

A first attempt might be as follows. "What character do objects have?" This question is to be interpreted as a request for a set of descriptions, involving such qualities as solidity (or lack of solidity), color (or lack of color), mass, velocity, and so on. The scientific realist's answer to this question is that objects have the character assigned to them by the best (or the ultimately most acceptable) scientific accounts, and that it is more correct to ascribe this character than to ascribe any other.

Formulated in this way, both the question the scientific realist answers and the answer look straightforward; and, indeed, the scientific realist's answer looks extremely plausible. My contention is that the question is ambiguous, and that when this is seen, the answer looks either uninteresting or implausible.

We can see this by considering puzzles involving the description of objects. Consider, first, a puzzle involving our ordinary ascription of colors to objects. This will be followed by another look at the puzzle of the table which is (from different points of view) both solid and not solid.

Suppose that nuclear explosions have driven humanity underground to live in caverns lit by yellowish fluorescent light. This yellowish light comes to be considered "normal" in viewing objects such as tables and in talking about their colors. What now seems red would then seem orange in "normal" light. What now seems blue would then seem green in "normal" light.

It may at first not be clear what we can say in this case. If blood looks orangish underground, it surely is perverse and reactionary to insist (after several generations) upon calling it red. It surely will become correct to call it orangish. On the other hand, it would be mad to insist that it always had been correct to speak of blood's color as orangish, even before human beings had gone underground. It also seems wrong to say that the change in the circumstances of human life had changed the color of blood. Unless the blood has been dyed or has undergone some chemical change, it is the same color it has always been. But does this mean that it is still red? Either it is still red or it is not the color it was.

In other words, our normal inclination after several generations underground in yellow light would be to say three things, which turn out to be incompatible:

1. Blood is of an orangish color.
2. Blood had been red, before humanity went underground.
3. The color of blood had not changed.

The most reasonable solution to the puzzle appears to be based on the following analysis. When we say, as we normally now do, that blood is red, we are not claiming that blood will appear red in all lights, or even that there are no people for whom blood might appear some other color. On the other hand, we are claiming that the experiences associated with the claim that blood is red do in some sense represent a norm. Bearing in mind the logical possibility of mass deception regarding the color of blood, we can see that it is false that "Blood is red" means blood looks red to most people whom we would term "normally sighted" in light we would term "normal." But unless we are claiming deception, or that the conditions are in some way abnormal, we must assign to blood the color that it appears to have, in "normal" light, to the vast majority of normal observers. This color, as it now stands, is red. In our puzzle it becomes orange. This change, of course, is not a change in some property of blood apart from its relation to our experience. It is not the color that has changed, but rather what seems normally the color (and what we call the color). Thus to speak of the color of blood as "having changed" is misleading, making it sound as if some intrinsic property of blood had changed.

This suggests that descriptive judgments about objects, such as "blood is red," are "perspectival," by which is meant that their meaning, and the standards for their truth, presuppose a set of conditions in which such judgments normally are made. "Blood is red" implies that blood *should* seem red under conditions we now term normal. It does not imply, however, that blood will in fact seem red to most observers.

The tension of the puzzle, then, is caused by three competing realizations. One is that the truth of descriptive judgments depends on perspective. The truth of "Blood is red" depends on what counts as normal light; the truth of "Object X is traveling at velocity Y" depends on the motion of the frame of reference of the observer. On the other hand, there is a very good sense in which what is true does not depend on observers. If all available observers hallucinate, or for some other reason see improperly, this does not affect the truth of judgments of the color of what they are looking at. Thirdly, we have well-established standards for saying that the velocity or color of an object has changed. These are not met if what has happened is merely that the velocity of the frame of reference of the observer has changed, or the character of the light has changed.

When what count as "normal" conditions change, the correct description of an object may change also. However, to say that the correct description of the color of blood might change if people lived under artificial yellow light is not to say that the color of blood itself would change. We speak of qualities as changing only if the correct description would change *within* a perspective. So strongly, indeed, would we resist saying that the color of blood would change if the character of normal light changed that we may be tempted to say defiantly, "The color would remain the same." This most plausibly should be taken simply as a refusal to make the linguistic wrong move of saying, "The color changed." But it *could* also be taken as suggesting that there is a stable nonperspectival color characteristic which, as it were, underlies color perceptions, and which thus plays a role in determining the correctness of perspectival descriptions. How much there would be to *that* claim is considered later.

First we should consider a refinement of the puzzle about the color of blood. Suppose the underground people who speak of blood as orange encounter on some neutral ground a few human beings who had managed to remain in the natural light, and who continue to judge blood to be red. The two groups attempt to iron out their differences. Is blood now orange, or is it red?

The answer depends on a number of factors, including the relative numbers of the two linguistic communities, whether the underground people expect to return to the natural light, the weight of linguistic tradition, and so on. One point in favor of those who insist on speaking of blood as red is that the conditions under which blood appears to be red are in some sense "natural"; and, when we are offered competing standards of normality, we are generally inclined to favor standards which reflect what is traditionally considered to be natural. We can see this if we consider two sub-puzzle cases. In one, half of humanity over a period of several generations has regularly taken a drug which makes objects appear to have different colors from those they appear now to have, blood appearing orange. In the second, half of humanity wakes up to find that objects appear to have different colors, blood appearing orange; this condition stabilizes and continues over several generations. Our inclination to insist flatly that "Blood is red, period" would be, I think, stronger in the first case than in the second.

This brings up two points. (1) Competing perspectives can coexist in a linguistic community. They can represent the practices or special conditions of separate linguistic subcommunities, or they can represent alternative practices for certain individuals (e.g., someone who shuttles back and forth between the region where blood is orange and that in which it is red). (2) Not all perspectives deserve equal weight. Even if they are unanimous and consistent over a long period, the color judgments of drug takers arguably will not have the same weight as those of undrugged human beings.

Let us turn now to the table which is in a sense solid and in a sense not solid. The physicist Arthur Eddington began his book *The Nature of the Physical World* by describing himself drawing up his chairs to two tables. "Yes," he says in a dramatically effective way, "there are duplicates of every object about me—two tables, two chairs, two pens." One is the object of common sense; the other the object revealed by modern physics.[3] Later, the dramatic effect having been produced, Eddington agrees that there is not literally a duplication of objects: the two tables are just "two aspects or two interpretations of one and the same world."[4]

Nevertheless, the problem remains. Common sense and ordinary experience tell us that the table is solid; modern science tells us that the "scientific table is mostly emptiness."[5] There are comparable difficulties, although perhaps not so sharp, with our ordinary judgment that the table is brown. Which account of the nature of the table are we finally to accept?

Before we solve the puzzle, we must determine what the question is. It is very tempting to say, using the words we used in formulating the question that the scientific realist answers, "The question is 'What character does the object have?'" Only this simply will not do. The words "What character does the object have?" can be used to express at least three very different questions. Once we understand this, we can see both why the puzzle of Eddington's table seems so deep and disturbing and also how the question answered by scientific realism has the depth of ambiguity.

If we ask in ordinary circumstances, "What character does the table have?" someone is likely to reply, tapping the table, "Why, solid, of course." Among scientists, the ready reply will be something like "Elementary particles in the midst of emptiness." In each instance the question is interpreted as "intraperspectival." That is, it is interpreted as concerned with the character assignable to the table within a perspective.

If the question "What character does the table have?" is pressed by a philosopher who has already gone on about the differing characters assignable to the table within commonsense and scientific perspectives, the question can take on a different character. (The philosopher can point to this different character by phrasing his question, "What character does the table *really* have?") The question can be taken as inviting a comparison or choice between perspectives. Which answer should be adopted: that provided within the common-sense perspective, or that provided within the scientific perspective?

Thirdly, a philosopher—perhaps a different kind of philosopher— may ask "What character does the table have?" and explain, "I know that the table *appears*, in everyday terms, solid, and *appears* to scientists to be mostly emptiness; but what is it like *really*?" Here the question asked is one we shall consider shortly, one that plays a prominent part in Immanuel Kant's *Critique of Pure Reason* and in such works as Bertrand Russell's *The Problems of Philosophy*. This question goes "behind" all perspectives. The philosopher may prepare us for seeing this as his question by making extended comments on the conceptual infusions in the accounts of the world given by ordinary people and by scientists, or by an extended disquisition on the causal chain that leads to sensory perception (and the implausibility of assuming that what is at one end of the causal chain closely resembles what is at the other end, or resembles the explanatory models that we adopt).

Obviously, a great deal has been said, can be said, and will be said about this third sense of the question "What character does the object have?" We shall see shortly that *if* the question in this form is meaningful, one plausible answer (and one which many philosophers have enthusiastically embraced) is "I don't know."

The question of the scientific realist, "What character do objects have?", similarly can be given three interpretations. (1) It can be interpreted intraperspectivally (in which case it is not a philosophical question): someone might answer by pointing out that many objects are solid, and so on, but some are not; whereas a scientist will say that ordinary objects such as chairs and tables are in fact mostly emptiness. (2) The question can be interpreted as requesting a comparative rating of, or a choice between, perspectives. Or, lastly, (3) the question can be taken as concerned with a reality that in some sense "lies behind" our experience and our scientific data. Even if the first interpretation of the question is excluded as nonphilosophical, the question remains ambiguous.

The Import of Scientific Realism

If the question of the scientific realist is given the third interpretation, then scientific realism is faced with a very difficult task. First, scientific realists will have to show that the question, in this interpretation, is a meaningful one. Since all of our ascriptions of attributes, commonsense or scientific, occur within the context of a perspective, with implicit rules for arriving at correct answers, it is not clear what sense can be given to a question about the attributes of objects which is raised outside of all perspectives. And, of course, even if scientific realists overcome this obstacle, they will have to show that the scientific image corresponds to what lies behind the conceptualizations and causal chains of our experience. Given the inescapable role of concepts in the scientific image, we can say that this task would be impossible.

Suppose, though, that the question of the scientific realist is given the second interpretation. This interpretation, after all, is the more plausible one; it also makes the clearest sense, since it is clear that we can compare and choose between perspectives. (Recall the case of the orange blood and the red blood.) Cannot we just interpret scientific realism as asking this kind of question?

Even if we adopt this interpretation, however, it is far from clear what the scientific realist wants. Clearly, both scientific and common-sense judgments have validity. Those who are narrowly loyal to common sense may be inclined to say, "The table is solid, and that's an end to it," much in the spirit in which Gertrude Stein said, "A rose is a rose is a rose." But this ignores the truth of scientific accounts. Conversely, it simply is true, within the commonsense perspective, that the table is solid.

Are we to choose between the scientific and commonsense perspectives? Where a linguistic community has developed underground for which blood is orange, but a few people aboveground still consider blood to be red, a choice is possible. That is, an individual or an entire linguistic community could reasonably decide to adopt a linguistic framework within which blood correctly can be called red (or, alternatively, one within which blood is orange). Similarly, in the case of the drug takers, one drug taker (or the entire drug-taking population) could determine to assign to objects the attributes which are assigned to them by undrugged percipients; that is, the drug takers could abandon any special perspective of their own.

But in the case of the two tables it looks as if no choice of this sort were possible. There is no clear way in which we can abandon the commonsense perspective and talk exclusively in terms of the scientific perspective. Conversely, no reasonable person would suggest that scientists, in the course of their scientific work, should assign attributes purely within the commonsense perspective, abandoning entirely a scientific perspective.

It is meaningful to compare perspectives, and in some cases we can choose between them. However, if there is no question of choosing between the commonsense perspective and the scientific perspective, what is it then that scientific realists want?

It may be that all they want is for us all to acknowledge the superiority of the scientific perspective. Just as one perspective can be preferred to another because it reflects a more "natural" mode of experience, or has a closer relation to linguistic tradition, so also a perspective might be preferred because it was associated with judgments of greater explanatory power. Clearly, a strong case can be made along these lines for preferring the scientific to the everyday perspective. But preference here involves more a gesture of respect than anything else. In this light, the issue between scientific realists and their opponents dwindles in significance.

Is the Nature of Physical Reality Unknowable?

Let us now examine the view, held by thinkers as disparate as Kant and Russell when he wrote *The Problems of Philosophy*, that physical reality is humanly not completely knowable. This, as we have seen, is an answer to the question "What character do physical objects have?" if the question is interpreted as asking about a reality behind and apart from the perspectives we may bring to it.

As a convenient shorthand, we refer to the position under discussion as "the agnostic position," although we must bear in mind that the agnosticism concerns the character of physical reality, and not the claim that there is a physical reality. Both Kant and Russell, for example, held the "agnostic position" while maintaining that there was a physical reality independent and distinct from our experience of it.

Both the attraction and the repugnance generated by the agnostic position are so deep that it is hard to believe there is any simple and obvious truth in the matter. All we aim for at present is an understanding of the pros and cons of the issue. The first step is to understand how the agnostic position is generated.

The Agnostic View of the Nature of Physical Reality

We can begin by considering the question "What is physical reality like?" in two ways. They correspond to the second and third interpretations, just discussed, of the scientific realist's question "What character do objects have?" We shall discuss the character of physical objects only.

"What is physical reality like?" can be taken as follows:

Q1. "What collection of words is most appropriate in describing physical reality?"

Alternatively, the question can be taken in a more difficult way to explain, asking about something beyond language that language is really about, such as the true colors (or lack of color) and the true conformations of things.

In this form the question is:

Q2. "What extralinguistic properties does physical reality have?"

It may be that both commonsense realists, who hold that the judgments of common sense give us our final judgments of reality, and scientific realists have in many cases failed to distinguish between these two forms of the question, and consequently have failed to make clear in which form they were answering the question. There is no such doubt in the case of the agnostic position. The agnostic position is an answer to Q2.

Someone holding the agnostic position can easily grant that we can speak of tables as solid, and that by ordinary and acceptable criteria our descriptive claims about them are true; and further, that a scientist can describe the table in a very different way, and that by criteria which certainly seem acceptable in the context of scientific work, the scientist's descriptive claims also are true. All of this, which leads to a comfortable reconciliation of scientific and commonsense perspectives, is beside the point addressed by the agnostic position. Unless he or she is a zealot, the holder of the agnostic position does not insist that we deny truth to the commonsense or scientific descriptive claims about physical reality. But there is, holders of the agnostic position insist, as it were a truth beyond truth, or at least a reality outside the whole apparatus of language and truth. Eddington's table *really* may be something other than what the ordinary individual or the scientist pictures it as being; indeed, what might be called the strong agnostic insists that it *has* to be other than what the ordinary individual or the scientist pictures it as being.

If a philosopher doubts not that "The table is solid" is true, but that the table really has the property of solidity, what sense can we attach to his doubt? The only plausible explanation is that he thinks he knows what the word "solid" refers to, and he doubts that the table really has *it*. The alternative explanation would be that he does not know what "solid" refers to, and hence does not know whether the table really has that property or not; but this explanation would make it seem even more puzzling that the philosopher can assent to the sentence "The table is solid," and, besides, philosophers who have held the agnostic position have seemed to think they knew what they were being skeptical of the real possession of.

Thus the agnostic position makes sense only if we have an idea or an experienced awareness of qualities such as solidity and brownness. We know what solidity and brownness are; we know that objects such as tables seem to have these properties, and by accepted standards sentences assigning these properties to tables are true; but in fact we have no reason to believe that objects such as tables really have these properties.

Further, if an agnostic philosopher claims to have an idea of solidity and brownness, if we are to remain sympathetic we cannot construe his or her idea (as many philosophers would do nowadays) purely in terms of dispositions to behave in certain ways, including the disposition to engage in appropriate linguistic behavior. By a disposition is meant a tendency that manifests itself in certain circumstances. The disposition to engage in appropriate linguistic behavior can be present in someone who in fact does not say a word. The disposition can consist of this kind of thing: that *if* someone were to ask "What is the color of the table?" then the person in question *would* say "brown," or would say "pink" in a joking tone of voice but, if pressed in suitable ways, admit that the table was brown. If this is all that ideas of solidity and brownness are, then again the agnostic position cannot make sense, or at least cannot have the sense that its holders have intended. If the brownness of the table is that which it is appropriate to describe in certain words—if *all* that one can mean by the brownness of the table is that the table is the sort of thing one normally speaks of as "brown"—then it cannot make sense to concede the truth of "The table is brown" and yet doubt that the table is really brown.

Agnostic philosophers must mean, then, that there is a content to experience, so that our experience of the table consists of more than behavioral events and dispositions, and includes also a real experience of brownness. They must mean also that we have a tendency to think that the objects we experience have properties that correspond to the content of experience. And they must mean, finally, that this supposition is unwarranted.

Thus the agnostic position, if this view of it is correct, contains or presupposes claims of more than one sort. It presupposes a position in what might be called the "philosophy of perception"—that there is more to sense experience than some views might allow. It contains or presupposes a claim relevant to doctrines of meaning, namely, that even if by acceptable criteria "X is Y" is true, one yet can ask, putting aside the acceptable criteria of familiar linguistic frameworks, whether X really has the property Y. And finally, it suggests a doctrine of reality in which (either very probably, or assuredly) Xs do not have all their familiar Y properties; and a view of knowledge in which we lack knowledge of the answers to the unusual questions which the agnostic insists on regarding as meaningful.

The questions that the agnostic philosopher insists upon asking can be put more technically, in terms of "linguistic frameworks" and "acceptable criteria." By a "linguistic framework" is meant a form of rule-governed discourse in which there are determinate ways of arriving at what are counted (by standards internal to the form of discourse) as correct answers to questions. By "determinate ways of arriving at answers" I do not mean conclusive, error-proof methods, but merely ways of gathering evidence on some questions that have the endorsement of some professional community (or the larger community as a whole), and that would satisfy a reasonable person. It should be noted that the definition given of linguistic framework is such that not all forms of discourse would count as being, or containing, linguistic frameworks. In particular, if there is a special form of "metaphysical" discourse, involving the talk of philosophers about ultimate realities, and if it is true that there are no ways of arriving at correct answers to metaphysical questions that have the general endorsement of the professional community of metaphysicians, then metaphysical discourse does not have or supply a linguistic framework.

A simple example of a linguistic framework is provided by the system of time zones, by means of which there is an objectively correct determination of the time anywhere on the earth. Anyone who has mastered the system of time zones knows how to go about finding the time in New York, Paris, or Tokyo. Most linguistic frameworks, though, are more complicated, and offer more possibilities of there being inconclusive evidence. Physics involves a linguistic framework, and to master physics is to know (among other things) what counts as evidence in answering questions in physics. But we cannot be sure of the correct account of the transmission of light in the way in which we can be sure what time it is now in Tokyo. Any way of talking about problems that contain built-in rules for solving them is a linguistic framework.

It is a mistake to regard the ways of arriving at what are counted as correct answers within a linguistic framework as necessarily static. A linguistic framework, such as that of scientific investigation generally, can be self-correcting. There can be reasonable grounds built into the nature of the discipline for changing our ideas of what counts as evidence. Thus considerations that are internal to the linguistic framework can cause a change in criteria for acceptability of claims. By the "acceptable criteria" of a linguistic framework is meant the criteria which, if one operates within the mode of judgment of that framework, should be accepted and at no point should finally be rejected.

The sort of question the agnostic philosopher wishes to ask, then, can be put as follows:

Q2A. "If one puts aside the acceptable criteria of linguistic frameworks and tries simply to judge the real character of physical reality, what is it in fact like?"

A Case for Agnosticism

We shall now outline a case for agnosticism. (Following this, we shall criticize the case at one vital point.) The case to be presented is strong enough, at least arguably, for agnosticism not to be dismissed out of hand. But it may not be so very strong as to be entirely convincing. The case is a free construction; that is, it should not be viewed as a faithful rendition of the ideas of any particular philosopher or philosophers.

The argument has three steps; there is a choice of routes at the third step. The steps are as follows:

1. There is a content to experience.
2. It makes sense to ask whether objects have properties the same as, or corresponding to, those displayed in the content of experience; one can ask this apart from the acceptable criteria of any linguistic framework.
3a. The content of experience is the result of causal factors which are such that it is totally implausible to suppose that the properties of objects as they are in themselves are in every case the same as those we conventionally ascribe; for related reasons, it is implausible to suppose that their properties are exhausted by those (relational) properties ascribed to them in scientific accounts.

Or:

3b. The content of experience is infused with structural elements contributed by our conceptual schemes or general orientation. There is no neutral given. Therefore it is implausible to suppose that the properties of objects in themselves are those that we conventionally ascribe. For related reasons, it is equally implausible to suppose that objects have those properties, and just those properties, which are ascribed to them in scientific accounts. Scientific work, after all, is hardly conceptually colorless.

Let us now explain this difficult argument in some detail. We shall discuss the steps in order, explaining both what they mean and why they might seem plausible. Then we can explain what conclusion follows from this.

Step 1 asserts that there is a content to experience—an experienced character of what we experience separable from the words we use to describe it. When we see that grass is green, more is involved than just the verbal behavior and associated dispositions involved in saying "green." Rather, we experience something *which evokes* in us the word "green." It would be misleading to regard the color we experience as being projected on some inner screen, and equally misleading to speak (as philosophers early in this century did) of an entity to be called a green "sense datum." But it is also misleading, and in fact downright wrong, to say that the experience of seeing that the grass is green consists just of the behavior and dispositions surrounding the saying of the word "green."

How does one establish the correctness of step 1? The issue here is clearly related to puzzles such as the inverted spectrum puzzle. This puzzle involves two people whose spectrum of color experience is the inverse of the other's, so that when one experiences a colored object as green the other experiences the color that the first would have called "red." If the inversion is entirely consistent, the argument runs, it cannot be discovered. Suppose for example that when Jones looks at grass he experiences a color which the rest of us would call "red," and that when he looks at blood in normal light he experiences a color which the rest of us call "green." Jones's mother, when he is a small child, tells him that the word for the color he sees when he looks at grass is "green," and so when he looks at dollar bills, lettuce, or more grass, he from that time reports the red color he experiences as "green." His mother tells him that the word for the color he sees when he looks at blood in normal light is "red," and so from that time when he sees things that the rest of us would call "red" he too reports seeing them as "red," even though in fact the color he is experiencing is the color that we experience when looking at things we call "green." In other words, Jones always *says* what the rest of us say. His abnormality cannot be detected, and, indeed, any of us can wonder whether we are not in Jones's position.

It has been argued by some philosophers that the questions raised by the inverted spectrum puzzle are meaningless, simply because, as the puzzle is formulated, there is no evidence that can count toward their solution.[6] Most of us would believe intuitively that the puzzle cannot be dissolved in this way, because most of us are aware of the reality of actual experiences of color. On the basis of these experiences we often speak of two pieces of material as being the same, or as being nearly the same, color. The same linguistic competence enables us to say that the color we experience when we look at one piece of material is the same as the color we experience when we look at the other, and enables us to wonder whether our neighbor is having the same color experience that we are having.

It looks as if logic has a limited use in these matters. Some logical principle or other may be appealed to, in order to support the claim that there cannot be unknowable facts of experience, such as the inverted spectrum puzzle appears to allow. But in relation to what happens when we have our eyes open and look at the green grass, this mode of argument seems uncomfortably a priori. What the constituent elements of our sense experience are is a matter of fact, and as such is subject to an appeal to fact, not to an a priori principle.

Thus the question of whether step 1 is correct is not a logical or a linguistic question. Rather, it is a question about the facts of experience, which presumably each of us is in a position to answer. Speaking for myself, I would say that step 1 is clearly correct. An element in my visual experience of grass is a color, the color that I associate with the word "green." It is imaginable that the color that in fact I associate with the word "red" could have been an element in my visual experience of grass, but it is not.

If step 1 raises an issue that is primarily nonlinguistic, this is not true of step 2. In order to ask whether it makes sense to ask the question the agnostic philosopher insists upon asking, however, we first must understand what leads to the agnostic philosopher's question.

It is arguable that the naïve person—which means everyone at an early stage in human history, and a few people nowadays—would assume that the properties of immediate experience simply belonged to the objects which seemed to be experienced. The greenness which was an element in visual experience of grass was a property which actually did belong to the grass.

It is natural to think this until one has become aware of the causal factors in perception, or of the role of conceptual structures in experience. The green that occurs in visual experience of grass is the result of a causal chain: light waves of a certain frequency travel through a certain medium to reach our retinas, from which signals are transmitted to our brains. The light waves themselves are not colored; their properties are geometric rather than color properties. Is there any reason to think that the grass, from which these light waves are reflected, has in itself that very property which we experience as a result of this complicated and circumstantial process?

Further, if what we experience has a great deal to do with the language we speak, and the way we divide up the world, so that beings speaking radically different languages would experience the world in radically different ways, then how can we assume that the objects we experience have just the character in which we experience them? If we view reality through conceptual spectacles, then it is natural to wonder whether the nature of reality somehow matches the prescription of our spectacles.

This is how the question referred to in step 2 arises, and why it seems a meaningful question. It is important to distinguish the claim of step 2 from a much more modest one that might at first seem similar to it. This is the claim that, even if "X is Y" is true by acceptable criteria of a linguistic framework, one can step outside the linguistic framework to judge whether an answer within that framework is to be given much weight. *This* claim appears to be indisputably correct. Even if "The table is solid" is true by adequate criteria built into ordinary discourse, one might have grounds for preferring the scientific view of the table. But this is to step out of one linguistic framework into another. The ontology which is yielded is still relativized to the acceptable criteria of the preferred linguistic framework. Step 2 makes the radical claim that one can inquire about the nature of physical reality in some absolute sense, apart from the acceptable criteria of linguistic frameworks. If step 2 is correct, even after hearing the commonsense and scientific accounts of the table, one meaningfully can ask, "But what is the table really like?"

Thus step 2 is the claim that one can meaningfully ask about the properties of things outside the normal linguistic channels. What seems to be the strongest argument in support of step 2 is this. The original supposition that the color that occurs in our visual experience of grass is indeed a property of grass surely has meaning. It cannot even be regarded as the sophistication of philosophers or of puzzle-mongers. But if the original supposition has meaning, then it has meaning to question (on the basis of the considerations involved in steps 3a or 3b) whether the original supposition, or allied suppositions regarding the properties of physical reality, is correct. Once we have granted meaning to the hypothesis that physical objects have a real nature that is conveyed in experience, we can ask meaningfully whether everyday or scientific tests convey to us this real nature.

A secondary argument could be termed the argument from the possibility of God. If the traditional belief in the existence of God is meaningful, then, whether or not it is correct, we can ask how God would experience physical reality. It becomes very plausible to say, in the language of Newton's *Optics*, Query 28, that God would see "the things themselves intimately, and thoroughly perceives them. . . ." Then the question referred to in step 2 could be given meaning as a question about how the physical world could appear to God (or, perhaps less misleadingly, how the physical world would *be* from God's point of view).

Step 3a results from reflection on the psychology and physiology of perception. Once we become aware of the cues that lead us to think of the table as solid or the grass as green, we become aware of what an involved and indirect process is involved in their transmission; and it becomes impossible to think of perception as some immediate reading off of the character of the object experience. It also becomes highly implausible to suppose that the object, at the far end of the chain of causes that results in signals to our brains, has just *that* set of characters that we experience.

The first thing that must be said about step 3b is that the central insights have, for the most part, been suggested by philosophers who probably would not accept both step 1 and step 2, and therefore might well not follow the agnostic argument to its conclusion. One can hold that our experience is infused with structural elements contributed by our conceptual schemes or general orientation, without holding that there is a content of experience that is so infused; and one can hold that we never experience reality in a neutral way without being impelled to posit a neutral reality behind the nonneutral facts of experience. In other words, a good deal of step 3b is separable from the agnostic position. But, if it is combined with steps 1 and 2, 3b yields an agnostic conclusion.

What is meant by saying that there is no "neutral given," and why is it now a virtual orthodoxy among philosophers to say this? By a "neutral given" is meant an experience that is unaffected by what scientific theory the person who has it upholds, and that is unaffected also by the language, general outlook, or practical concerns of the perceiver. It is neutral because, unaffected by scientific assumptions or general outlooks, it can be used to choose fairly among these.

It used to be thought that there were neutral givens, and that these provided the basis for choice between competing scientific theories. This view has been effectively dispelled by a number of studies, most notably T. S. Kuhn's *The Structure of Scientific Revolutions*. Kuhn shows convincingly that the theory with which a scientific observer is armed has a great deal to do with the observations the observer makes. On a banal level, much the same kind of point has been made by studies that show, for example, that Eskimos, who have many words for different types of snow, perceive snow differently from the way in which the typical American perceives snow. If the world we experience is not a blooming, buzzing confusion, it is because we bring to it a readiness to see certain shapes, make certain distinctions, and notice things which have certain forms. But this is something we *bring* to experience, and what we experience must bear its marks.

This, it should be emphasized, is a matter of fact. It is imaginable that there might have been a neutral given, that sense experience might have been like stamping a form onto a blank pad. But in fact it is not like this.

If we accept everything in the agnostic argument including step 3a but not step 3b, what conclusion do we reach about physical reality? It is that physical reality has properties about which we cannot know. If we accept 3b, with or without 3a, the conclusion is more subtle. It is in one respect more astringent, and in another less astringent, than may at first appear.

Since the boundaries we draw within the physical world reflect our conceptual schemes or general orientation, we are not entitled to assume that objects in themselves correspond in number or location to the objects we outline within experience. The conclusion of the argument might be put, then, as the claim that physical reality, in itself, consists of an unknowable number of things the properties and structure of which we cannot know.[7] The conclusion of the argument might be formulated still more radically if we decided that even terms like "world," "physical," "real," or "exists" reflect conceptual boundaries, and thus can be used only within biased schemes of experience. If we decided this, we would be reduced to saying nothing about the character of what lies outside of the conceptual schemes of our experience. Like the Chinese Chan Buddhists and Japanese Zen Buddhists, who appear to have adopted this more radical line, we would not be able even to say "It exists" or "It does not exist."

On the other hand, even if we can say nothing about the *character* of what lies outside of the conceptual schemes of our experience, it does not follow that we can know nothing about it. It is open to someone who accepts the agnostic argument, including both steps 3a and 3b, to claim that we know a great deal about what lies outside of the conceptual schemes of our experience, namely, that it lends itself to certain scientific accounts more readily than to others. The agnostic argument entails merely our ignorance of the nature of physical reality (or, if even the words "physical reality" seem to import conceptual biases, of the ineffable). But we can know, to borrow T. S. Kuhn's words, that "nature cannot be forced into an arbitrary set of conceptual boxes," and we can know the facts of success or failure of certain boxes.[8]

Despite the strength of the agnostic argument, there seems also to be a strong case for rejecting agnosticism. The step in the agnostic argument that seems to me most questionable is step 2, and without this step the argument falls apart. We shall now, therefore, consider an argument against agnosticism that rests on the rejection of step 2 of the agnostic argument.

A Case Against Agnosticism

It should be emphasized that what follows sets forth just one of a large number of possible ways of dissenting from agnosticism, although it may be the most compelling way. Historically, a number of philosophers (e.g., the German philosopher Schopenhauer and many Indian thinkers) have traveled much of the agnostic route, but then have claimed that there are special ways of knowing the ultimate character of reality. Many philosophers would reject step 1 of the agnostic argument, and the final step (3a or 3b) also need not be accepted. It is also possible to argue against step 2 by querying the notion of "correspondence" or "sameness" as a relation between properties of the content of experience and properties of real objects: what sense could "correspondence" or "sameness" have here? However, the argument against the agnostic position that we shall consider centers on a different matter.

This anti-agnostic case assumes the correctness of steps 1 and 3a and 3b of the agnostic argument, and challenges merely step 2. The challenge rests on this claim: It makes sense to speak of objects as "having" properties in only a sense different from that of the agnostic's question. In order to see this, we have to look at how we ordinarily ascribe properties to objects.

Take, for example, the ascription of colors. The color that an object has is that which to undeceived normal observers it appears to have in normal light. Thus that grass is green means that grass looks green to undeceived normal observers in normal light; that is, we are impelled to say "green"; and I have the sort of color content of experience that I have normally when I say "green," and you have a color content that you normally would associate with "green"; and there is no hypnotist or evil demon involved in the case. To say "Grass is green" means just this is to say—assuming that even an agnostic philosopher will accept the truth (in some lower order of truth) of "Grass is green"—that there is nothing more than "Grass is green" in its normal use could mean. It should be clear that the claim "grass is green" means "grass looks green to undeceived normal observers in normal light" is a tautology. It is true by virtue of the meanings of the terms.

Now, if "Grass is green" means "Grass looks green to undeceived normal observers in normal light," then "Grass is green" reports the color property that grass *presents* under certain circumstances—or, to speak more guardedly, the color property that grass *should* present, and would present in normal light to a properly equipped, undeceived person. We then can say that grass is green, while admitting freely that grass would present other color properties in various kinds of abnormal light conditions, or in normal light to people with various kinds of abnormal color vision.

Once we have admitted that grass can present various color properties in various circumstances, it is tempting to ask, "But what color property does grass really have?" In one way of taking the question, the answer is simple. Grass really is green (even if in this light it looks blue or yellow). But to say this is just to unveil a linguistic convention. We count as the real color of grass that which it presents to normal observers (and part of "normal" does involve the requirement of a certain sort of color vision) in normal light. That is why "Grass is green" is true.

Another way of taking the question "But what color property does grass really have?" is in the spirit of Q2. That is, it can be taken as a question not about correct collections of words or about anything that has to do with linguistic conventions, but rather as a question about real properties, apart from language.

One reply to this form of the question is as follows. "We have seen that grass presents various colors in various circumstances. The whole color being of grass lies in presenting colors. And presentation is always in a context—to a particular person, in particular light. So what sense can there be to asking, in the spirit of Q2, what color grass has? Grass does not *have* a color; it just *presents* colors; and there is no fact of experience which allows any room here to assign sense to a Q2-type of question."

From the anti-agnostic point of view, the facts of color experience could run something like this. At first it naïvely seems to us that grass has the color green. Once we realize the causal factors involved in our experience of color, we can, of course, make an agnostic move; we can say that grass does not have a color, but has properties (some of them unknowable) that are responsible for our experience of color. But it is at least equally plausible to make an anti-agnostic move. We can say that the original notion that grass has the color green rests on a confusion. Those considerations which can persuade the agnostic that grass really has no color can persuade us, as easily, that words such as "has" and "have" are out of place here. And this, it should be emphasized, is quite different from saying that grass is colorless. In discussing questions on the order of Q1, we can say simply that grass is green. In confronting questions on the order of Q2, we can say that grass presents various colors, but that (strictly speaking) it is misleading to speak of grass as "having" or as "being" a color.

Can this be generalized? There may be some temptation to say that color is a special case. What is true of color may not be true of such qualities as shape, mass, or velocity. However, there would appear to be a general argument of some strength that applies to all qualities of objects.

We should bear in mind that, in the case of color, the linguistic framework of ordinary color reports includes what counts as normal light. (If what counted as normal light came to be different, then as a result of this alone we might be justified in ascribing a different color to grass.) The linguistic framework also includes concepts involved in our distinctions among colors, and so on.

The general argument is as follows:

1. Judgments of the properties of things normally are made within some linguistic framework or other.
2. Their meaning is explainable entirely in terms of the existence of acceptable criteria (within the linguistic framework) to determine their correctness.

3. Therefore it makes no sense to ask what properties things have apart from linguistic frameworks.

One way of putting this conclusion is to say, again, that strictly speaking it is misleading to speak of objects as "having" properties (if this implies possession in some absolute sense, independently of linguistic frameworks governing the ascription of properties); rather objects, in the various contexts of experience, "present" properties, and linguistic frameworks determine which of the properties they present count as "real."

To this can be appended a counterargument to the argument from the possibility of God. The counterargument is simply that, once we understand the nature of experience, we can see it to be incoherent to suppose any being, even God, to experience absolute properties of things in themselves. There are no absolute properties, so not even God can experience them. The experience of a possible God can most plausibly be interpreted as containing what can be apprehended from an infinity of perspectives.

Before we consider further this anti-agnostic argument, we should see to what it would commit us. It implies that it is senseless to speak of any truth about physical reality which is independent of linguistic frameworks; what is true is true within a linguistic framework. The argument does not imply:

a. that the reality of an object is ever logically implied by a statement of actual or possible experiences of it;
b. that we know everything about physical reality that there is to know; or
c. that, if we could be in the right positions, and looked sharp, we could know anything that there is to know about physical reality.

The argument does not imply *a* because there is nothing in it that assumes physical reality is not (as we would express it) independent and distinct from our experience of it, or that rules out the possibility that we might be deceived in any of a series of experiences. The argument also does not imply that we know everything about physical reality that there is to know. It makes sense to speak of the possibility of unexperienced realities, or to speak of the world as it would have been if there had been no sentient life. The argument insists merely that any truth about unexperienced reality is located within a linguistic framework. If we posit that there is no linguistic framework (i.e., if we imagine a world without language), then we posit a reality about which there are only potential truths. Finally, it would be open to an anti-agnostic (of the stripe here displayed) to admit the possibility that there are aspects of reality which, because of human limitations, we would be unable under any circumstances to experience. But the anti-agnostic could insist, again, that in the absence of usable portions of a linguistic framework, these are aspects of reality about which there are only potential truths.

An analogy which might be helpful in grasping the anti-agnostic conception here developed, of the presentation of physical reality in linguistic frameworks, is of a piece of music and its interpretations in performance or "in one's mind." It is not a perfect analogy: for one thing, the music, after all, has a score that can be pointed to. But it provides another case in which one might be tempted to look for "the thing itself" and on principle be unable to find it. Someone might ask about the "real" Beethoven's Fifth, apart from Klemperer's or Solti's version. But this is nonsense. Anyone who speaks of the piece of music in itself, apart from interpretations, has committed a logical error. (Notice that this does not mean that all interpretations are of equal value, and it is not just that there are scores that enables us to speak of some interpretations as more faithful than others.)

Is the anti-agnostic argument valid? Step 1 is clearly correct, if we are willing to distinguish philosophical judgments from those that are normally made. Step 2 is more troublesome. Is the judgment that the grass is green meaningful, made by a naïve person (who is ignorant of philosophy and of the scientific facts of perception)? It is difficult to deny that it is. There are criteria—the ordinary criteria—for accepting "The grass is green" as true, which the naïve person implicitly accepts; and it could be argued that indeed in the end the naïve person must accept these criteria or give up talking. But it also could be argued, on the agnostic side, that the naïve person means more by "The grass is green" than just that "green" is the right color word to apply to the grass; and that the meaning of this stronger, more difficult to grasp judgment cannot be fully explained in terms of the conventional criteria. In other words, an agnostic could argue that the confusion of the naïve person consists of, on the one hand, accepting and using the criteria of everyday attributions of properties, but, on the other hand, meaning more by his attributions than could be explained in terms of these criteria. (Once the naïve person realizes this confusion, thus becoming sophisticated, he can self-consciously make more than one kind of judgment—i.e., he can come to mean by ordinary judgments only what could be explained in terms of the criteria, but at the same time adopt the agnostic position on the real properties of the objects he perceives.) Thus step 2 of the anti-agnostic argument can be challenged on the basis of the claim that the naïve judgment of the properties of things, even if it involved a claim that on reflection cannot be maintained, is meaningful in a way that cannot fully be explained in terms of acceptable criteria of a linguistic framework.

Even if the agnostic conceded step 2 of the anti-agnostic argument, he would not be compelled to accept step 3. Even, that is, if all the judgments of the properties of objects that are normally made have meaning that is explainable entirely in terms of the existence of acceptable criteria to determine their correctness, the agnostic might insist that he can produce judgments of the properties of things (e.g., "Things do not have all the properties that we think they have") which would have meaning of a different sort; he may insist, further, that one can meaningfully ask whether such judgments are correct. It would appear, however, that if step 2 of the anti-agnostic argument is conceded, it becomes very difficult to deny step 3. If there is no prephilosophical precedent for the kind of meaning that the agnostic philosopher wishes to give his claims and questions, then it is very difficult not to think of him as just playing with words. An anti-agnostic philosopher can claim, in any case, that the questions of the agnostic philosopher, asked out of the context of any linguistic framework, are on the order of "What time is it on the sun?" When we step out of the linguistic framework of established time zones, questions of what time it is become meaningless. Similarly, the anti-agnostic philosopher may insist, questions as to the real character of objects become meaningless outside of established linguistic frameworks. This becomes almost unanswerable if step 2 is conceded.

But must step 2 of the anti-agnostic argument be conceded? It does seem that people in a naïve state do *think* that they mean more by "The grass is green" than the anti-agnostic (of the stripe presented) will allow. But can they mean what they think they mean? There has been a strong tendency in this century to devise highly general principles to answer questions of this sort. Whether any such principle has been, or can be, entirely satisfactory is itself an open question.

Notes

1. Wilfred Sellars, *Science, Perception, and Reality* (London: Routledge & Kegan Paul, 1963), p. 20.

2. J. J. C. Smart, *Philosophy and Scientific Realism* (London: Routledge & Kegan Paul, 1963), p. 47.

3. Arthur Eddington, *The Nature of the Physical World* (Cambridge: Cambridge University Press, 1929), p. xi.

4. Ibid., p. xiv.

5. Ibid., p. xii.

6. See for example M. Schlick, "Positivism and Realism," trans. David Rynin, in *Logical Positivism*, ed. A. J. Ayer (New York: Free Press, 1959), pp. 92–93.

7. For a plausible account of what we would be left with, see N. Rescher, *Conceptual Idealism* (Oxford: Basil Blackwell, 1973), pp. 152-153.

8. T. S. Kuhn, "Reflections on My Critics," in *Criticism and the Growth of Knowledge*, ed. I. Lakatos and A. Musgrave (Cambridge: Cambridge University Press, 1970), p. 263.

SUGGESTED FURTHER READING

Major works by scientific realists include the following.

Sellars, Wilfred. *Science, Perception, and Reality.* London: Routledge & Kegan Paul, 1963. This book should be mentioned, but it is exceptionally difficult reading for beginners.

Smart, John. *Philosophy and Scientific Realism.* London: Routledge & Kegan Paul, 1963. A clearly written and interesting book.

An opposing view, which might be termed commonsense realism, is developed in the following.

Stebbing, L. Susan. *Philosophy and the Physicists.* Harmondsworth: Pelican Books, 1944. Stebbing is concerned with what she argues to be misleading statements in popularizations written by physicists.

Major statements, in various traditions, of the view that ultimate reality is not what either common sense or the sciences might think it to be include the following. *The Upanishads.* There are many modern editions of the principal Upanishads in adequate translations. This is the root classic of Hindu philosophy.

Lao Tzu. *The Tao Te Ching (Way of Life).* There are many good translations. I prefer the one by R. B. Blakney. New York: Mentor Books, 1955. Short poems expressing the Taoist philosophy.

Chuang Tzu. *The Complete Works of Chuang Tzu*, trans. Burton Watson. New York: Columbia University Press, 1968. This is the second classic of Taoism, and possibly the most beautiful philosophy ever written. It argues that reality is beyond labels.

Kant, Immanuel. *The Critique of Pure Reason*, trans. Norman Kemp Smith. New York: St. Martin's Press, 1963. Kant distinguishes sharply between the world of our experience and the world as it really is in itself.

Schopenhauer, Arthur. *The World as Will and Idea*, trans. E. J. Payne, 2 vols. Indian Hills, Colo.: Falcon's Wings Press, 1958. Schopenhauer is particularly good on the part that desires, fears, and human interests play in our image of reality.

Suzuki, Daisetz. *The Zen Philosophy of No Mind.* London: Rider Books, 1972. A more subtle philosophical exposition than most of the fundamental philosophical ideas of Zen Buddhism.

7 Is There an Irreducible Mental Reality?

In this chapter we shall assume, for the sake of argument, that we and other people have thoughts, and understand, fear, or love various things, and that in at least this sense we and they have minds. But what does having a mind amount to? The question asks whether there is a separate kind of reality into which these, or at least some of these, phenomena fit, or whether, as Nietzsche suggested, the mind is just something about the body.[1]

One way of getting perspective on this issue is to realize its similarity to the issue considered in chapter 5. We saw in chapter 5 that there are philosophers (e.g., Berkeley) who, while they admit that there are objects and phenomena that we normally would term "physical," insist that the reality of these objects cannot be regarded as distinct from, or independent of, the reality of the mental. Some of the philosophers we discuss in this chapter hold the converse position. They admit the reality of entities and phenomena that we normally term "mental," but they insist that the reality of these entities and phenomena cannot be regarded as distinct from, or independent of, the reality of physical objects (such as the brain), or they insist that the reality of the "mental" entities and phenomena must be analyzed in terms of behavior or dispositions toward behavior. In the latter account, having a mental state turns out to be nothing but that we *would* do or say certain things in certain circumstances (and perhaps actually do or say these things).

Dualism

The position which asserts that there is both a physical reality distinct from and independent of mental phenomena, and a mental reality distinct from and independent of physical or behavioral phenomena, is known as dualism. If dualism is right about mental reality, two consequences would seem to follow. One is that we can observe the mental only by a kind of "looking inward." This "looking inward" can be termed introspection, if we are willing to extend the ordinary use of "introspection" (normally applied only to special reflective activity) to the continuous unreflective awareness of our thoughts that we arguably have throughout our waking life. The second immediate consequence is that the connection between the mind and behavior is contingent. This is to say that if dualism is correct, the connection is not necessary: certain behavior (or dispositions to behave in certain ways) may happen always to accompany, or express, certain mental realities, but this does not *have* to be the case, and there is always the theoretical possibility that in some particular instance it will not be the case.

The twentieth century has seen a strong anti-dualist attack in the philosophy of mind, much of which has focused on these two consequences of dualism. If the consequences are false, then dualism is false. It has been argued that it is false that we can be aware of the mental only through introspection; it has also been argued that it is false that the connection between the mental and behavior is only contingent.

In what follows we examine this attack on dualism. We shall see what defense the dualist can offer, and what the logic of the dualist's position requires. In particular this will require exploring how, if the dualist is right, we can talk about the mind. Finally, we shall examine a different kind of attack on dualism, embodied in the currently fashionable view that truths about the mental are all expressible as truths about the brain and the central nervous system.

The Campaign Against Dualism

Understanding, knowing, being in pain, and being in various emotional states are widely regarded as examples of the mental. It is very tempting in the case of each to regard its occurrences as something hidden away in the mind in which it occurs. This is the traditional dualist view: only I can be directly aware of my understanding, knowing something, being in pain, or being in various emotional states; only you can be directly aware of your counterparts to these things. And it is a contingent matter whether the understanding, knowledge, pain, or emotion is expressed, or displayed, in behavior.

There are two major difficulties with this traditional view. First, it makes it sound as if some special inference were required to know whether another person understands or knows something, is in pain, or is in some specific emotional state. But it is not clear what form this inference would take. Some philosophers have suggested that the inference rests on analogy: because X is behaving the way you do when you are in pain, you infer that X is in pain. But it can be argued that to suggest that all your knowledge of other people's minds is based on knowledge of your own mind is to suggest, in the words of the twentieth-century Oxford philosopher Gilbert Ryle, an inference that "would be pitiably weak, for it would be a wide generalization based on a single instance."[2]

Secondly, if understanding or knowing something, being in pain, or being in some emotional state is "inner" and private, and only contingently connected with behavior, it is hard to understand how we can be so immediately certain about another person's understanding, knowledge, pain, or emotional states on the basis of behavior. If a man has been stuck with a pin and is yowling and hopping about on one foot, it seems peculiar to wonder whether one is justified in inferring that he is in pain. If a woman explains some theories in physics meticulously and clearly, answering objections and dealing with difficulties that are presented, it seems peculiar to wonder whether she understands the theories.

Because of these difficulties, it may seem implausible to regard understanding, knowing, being in pain, or being in various emotional states as "inner" or private—in short, to regard them as being within a mind, as the mind traditionally was conceived. Thus traditional dualism looks very implausible indeed.

A likely alternative might seem to be this. We can regard understanding, knowing, and so on, as being constituted by behavior or dispositions toward behavior. A man who understands something may not actually display his understanding (he may be modest, and no one may ask him appropriate questions that would allow him to demonstrate his understanding). But to say that he understands X is to say that if appropriate questions are asked, and if he responds in a forthright and normal manner, he will make responses that embody understanding. Thus, we might say (in this view), his understanding consists of a disposition toward, under appropriate circumstances, the kinds of behavior that lead us to speak of him as having understanding. In the same way, his pain (in this anti-dualist view) consists either of his yowling and hopping, or of a suppressed inclination to do these things accompanied by a disposition to reveal, under appropriate circumstances, that he was in pain. Anger is constituted by either the red face and the angry words, the bitten lip and the painful silence, or the disposition to reveal, again, under appropriate circumstances that one was angry.

Very often in the history of philosophy, the implausibility of one view leads philosophers to gravitate to an opposite view, without considering whether there is a third alternative. Let us agree that it is implausible to hold that understanding or knowing something, being in pain, or being in some emotional state is in essence a hidden "inner" thing which is only contingently related to behavior. Does this mean that understanding, knowing, and so on, must be regarded as constituted simply by behavior or dispositions toward behavior? There are difficulties also in this view. We do think, commonly, that there is more to pain than just hopping up and down and shouting "ouch"; the *feeling* of pain, too, is involved. In many cases, it is hard to claim that understanding or knowing something involves more than our giving the right explanation or answer, or being prepared to give the right explanation or answer. But there are also cases in which we know how to solve a complex problem; and part of what happens to us, a typical although perhaps not an essential part, is an experience of clarity which must account for the high value that Plato placed on what he considered true knowledge. In short, if understanding or knowing something, being in pain, or being in some emotional state is not entirely "inner," it looks as if in many cases it was not entirely "outer" either.

A Dualist Account

Let us consider a third alternative. We can apply it to understanding. *Mutatis mutandis*, a similar account can be given of knowledge, being in pain, and emotional states.

The third alternative is that in many cases understanding, knowing, being in pain, or an emotional state is neither entirely locatable in a mind separate from and only contingently related to behavior, nor is it entirely reducible to behavior or dispositions toward behavior. Rather it can be viewed as an amalgam of two sets of components: various qualities of states of mind (which are distinct from, and only contingently related to, behavior), and also behavior or behavioral dispositions. If we adopt this alternative, we can describe the first set of components as "mental," and give a dualist account of *it*; the second set of components can be characterized as "behavioral." Thus this alternative rejects the traditional dualist view of understanding, knowing, being in pain, or being in some emotional state; instead, it insists that these phenomena are not purely mental, as the traditional dualist view insisted, but rather are (at best) amalgams of mental and behavioral components. But this new alternative qualifies as "dualist" in that it claims that in many cases of knowing, understanding, and so on, there are components the reality of which is distinct from, and only contingently related to, behavior or any physical phenomena.

If we apply this third alternative to understanding, we obtain the following result. Understanding, at least in many cases, consists of both behavior or dispositions toward behavior *and* mental states. In this account we can grant that the qualities of states of mind which (at least in many cases) form a part of understanding may vary from individual to individual, and even for an individual from case to case. Thus we are not committed to claiming that there is an essence of the mental component of understanding; "family resemblances" will do. (The reader may recall, as other examples of family resemblances, the discussions in chapter 3 of the meaning of "game" and of "art.") It is enough if, in most cases, one can get an inkling of whether one understands something, without studying one's own behavior. In fact, we do often have a good idea of whether we understand something without having studied our own behavior; this does support the view represented by the third alternative.

Where other people's understanding is concerned, of course, one has to base one's judgment on their behavior; although, in the case of highly intelligent and generally trustworthy people, the verbal behavior contained in their statement of whether or not they understand something may be all the evidence one needs to judge whether they understand it. If certain behavioral dispositions are generally connected with the mental components of understanding, then it is not surprising that these behavior patterns come to be part of what we mean by "understanding," and play a primary role in the teaching of the word to children.

But *why* are these behavioral dispositions so generally connected with what we have been speaking of as the "mental components" of understanding? Why, for example, is being able to say aloud the right answers so generally connected with the mental components? This is the question that anti-dualists will want to ask. They will have in mind a two-pronged offensive. If the answer is that the connection is necessary, then they will question the notion of a logical connection between something behavioral and something "mental." They will ask us to think again about whether the "mental" items here really are mental; perhaps they are just phantoms, or not at all part of what we mean by "understanding." If the answer instead is that the connection is not necessary, then the anti-dualists will want to ask how we know that it generally obtains. The apparent alternatives for dualists then would be either an untenable dogmatism, in which one generalizes about all minds on the basis of one's own mind, or an implausible skepticism.

Nevertheless, my answer is that the connection is not necessary. We shall construct a class of imaginary cases which bears this out, if the description indeed is not self-contradictory. Then we can deal with the difficulties remaining for the dualist.

Let us imagine that pharmacists develop a drug, Cartesine, which has the following effects. During the period in which the drug has an effect (i.e., until it has worn off, or its antidote, Rylene, has been administered), the subject experiences dissociation between mental components of understanding on one hand, and words and deeds on the other. When presented with a problem, for example, the subject says to himself the words that constitute the solution, along with several sentences of explanation, with some mental accompaniments characteristic of understanding. Meanwhile, the subject voices an incorrect answer, and in general behaves stupidly. Physiological examination discloses that certain crucial nerves are blocked by the drug. When the drug has worn off, or the antidote has been administered, the subject is able to voice the correct solution along with a reasonably articulate explanation of it, and claims that he had said these to himself while under the influence of the drug.

Now, it might be suggested that the effect of the drug could be construed as, not the dissociation that I claim, but rather stupidity followed by a false memory of having seemed to understand something. And, indeed, this interpretation always could be placed upon the phenomena. But if the memories of unspoken sentences were elaborate enough and able to be reported at any time that Rylene was administered, and if the physiological evidence of nerve blockage or comparable phenomena were great enough, we would, I think, consider the "false memory" account to be highly implausible. The account in terms of dissociation would have a simpler and less contorted relation to the facts.

All of this is fantasy, of course, even highly improbable fantasy. But highly improbable fantasy can be used to make a philosophical point. For example, it may be a highly improbable fantasy to imagine the sun's not rising tomorrow; but if it is conceivable at all, this tells us something very important about our knowledge of the future. It tells us that our knowledge of the future does not rest on anything like deductive proof, and that there is a logical separation between, on one hand, statements about the present and past and, on the other, statements about the future. In much the same way, what is philosophically important in the story of Cartesine is not its extreme improbability, but that it is conceivable. If there is no logical contradiction in the Cartesine story, then we can infer the separability, in principle, of mental components of understanding from simultaneous or nearly simultaneous behavioral components.

This requires a closer look: the case of Cartesine is close to cases in which we, ultimately, would deny the occurrence of an adequate set of mental components of understanding. (By an "adequate set," I mean one such that a person possessing it would, in normal circumstances, and in the absence of any behavioral evidence, be justified in attributing understanding to himself.) Take, for example, the case of a man who experiences some mental phenomena that do frequently constitute a part of understanding. He says to himself the solution to a problem, and at the same time has a sense of things falling into place, or the resolution of an intellectual tension. But his solution is wrong, and we deny that he understood anything. Clearly, he lacks an adequate set of mental components of understanding: whatever the sense of things falling into place, and so on, one is not justified in claiming understanding if the solution one voices to oneself is wrong.

This familiar case, however, is different from the Cartesine case, in which there is a great deal to suggest that the subject did possess an adequate set of mental components of understanding, which was not reflected in behavior. All that the familiar case shows is that our own judgments that we have an adequate set of mental components of understanding are not infallible—a point which the dualist can readily grant. To grant this point is not to concede that one is never in a privileged position to know that one understands something. Clearly, we are often in such a privileged position. We often know that we understand something even before we have announced the solution or performed the task. (But this is not to suggest that we normally claim understanding as a result of, or by virtue of, inspecting our states of mind: such an account would be false. It seems more correct to say that we often claim understanding as a result of the presence of some qualities of our states of mind.)

The Cartesine case is open to the following objection from the anti-dualist. The case cannot be presented as an example of understanding, or even of an adequate set of mental components of understanding, divorced from all behavioral dispositions. For what is described does include behavioral dispositions; they are not erased, merely deferred by the action of the drug. One can still make dispositional claims of the form "If Rylene is administered, then the subject . . ."

Of course, the anti-dualist is right about this. The Cartesine case is intended as only the thin edge of the wedge. Let us imagine, now, a universe in which the following cases occur. (1) Some people who have taken Cartesine show signs of nerve blockage, and behave in the manner described, until the drug wears off or Rylene is administered, at which time they show signs of having possessed an adequate set of mental components of understanding, which had not been reflected in their behavior. (2) Some people who have taken Cartesine do not show signs of nerve blockage (and in general have no neurophysiological signs of their condition, or of mental components of understanding), but otherwise fit the pattern of the subjects in case 1. (3) Some people who have taken Cartesine show signs of nerve blockage, and in other ways fit the pattern of case 1, except that neither time nor the administration of Rylene removes the effects of Cartesine. (4) Some people who have taken Cartesine do not show signs of nerve blockage (and in general have no neurophysiological signs of their condition, or of mental components of understanding); otherwise they fit the pattern of case 3. (5) Some people who have not taken Cartesine suddenly show signs of nerve blockage, and behave in other ways like the subjects in case 1; after a short period of time, the nerve blockage disappears, and they show signs of having possessed an adequate set of mental components of understanding, which had not been reflected in their behavior. (6) Some people who have not taken Cartesine suddenly begin to behave like the subjects in case 1; they do not show signs of nerve blockage (and in general have no neurophysiological signs of their condition, or of mental components of understanding). The administration of Rylene brings them out of it. (7) Some people who have not taken Cartesine suddenly begin to act like the subjects in case 6; they have no neurophysiological signs of their condition, or of mental components of understanding. However, neither time nor the administration of Rylene reverses their condition.

These cases compound extreme improbability, and the mind boggles at the vision of a world in which they all occur. But, again, what is philosophically important is not the degree of fantasy involved, but whether the world described is conceivable. We might, comparably, imagine a world in which not only did the sun not rise tomorrow, but in myriad other specified ways the future did not resemble the past. Such an imaginary world might verge on the chaotic, but as long as we can describe it consistently, it can be used to make a philosophical point.

Now, in a world in which only cases of kind 7 occurred, it would be very easy to assume unquestioningly that people who behaved as if they lacked all components of understanding in fact did lack all components of understanding. In a world in which there were abundant cases of the first six kinds, this assumption would be less easy to make. In either world, there would be logical room for doubt—and even more so in a world exhibiting abundant cases of all seven kinds. In this world (the world of many varieties of systematically discombobulated people), there would be considerable evidence that an adequate set of mental components of understanding could be severed from its immediate manifestation, and some evidence that an adequate set of mental components of understanding could be severed from any disposition to manifest it at any time. Thus, in this world, we would not be able to infer with entirely unruffled assurance from the fact that a subject lacked a disposition to behave in a manner consonant with understanding that the subject lacked an adequate set of mental components of understanding.

It may be that there are, or will be, data from which we can infer that the world I have been describing (the world of many varieties of systematically discombobulated people) is not, and cannot be, our world. Those holding a view that we shall consider later—which equates "the mind" with the brain and central nervous system—will certainly want to insist that there are neurophysiological correlates in any case in which a subject says to himself the words that constitute a solution to a problem, along with several sentences of explanation and other appropriate mental accompaniments. Thus such a thinker would rule out, on actual or hoped-for empirical grounds, cases of types 2, 4, 6, and 7. The world which includes these cases would be classed among fairy tales.

The quarrel at this stage of the argument is not with this

philosopher. Let us, for the sake of argument, accept his claim that the world under discussion in fact cannot exist. This, however, is distinct from accepting the claim that there is some logical contradiction in the existence of such a world. If there is no logical contradiction, then the point now at issue is established: namely, that it is logically possible that an adequate set of mental components of understanding could exist without accompanying behavioral dispositions.

But on what grounds could anyone claim that there is a logical contradiction? It might be argued that "understanding" implies certain behavioral dispositions, and that therefore these behavioral dispositions *must* be present in cases of understanding. But note that the cases at issue were not presented as cases of understanding, but merely as cases in which mental components of understanding were present. This, then, sidesteps the objection.

What could we say about cases in which familiar mental components of understanding might be present without the normal behavioral dispositions? It is important, first, to distinguish between two kinds of cases. On one hand, there are cases in which some familiar mental components of understanding (e.g., the sense of clarity, the release of intellectual tension) are present, but other important mental components are absent (e.g., there is no disposition to say to oneself what amounts to a correct solution, and the clarity is more apparent than real). On the other hand, there are cases in which there is an adequate set of mental components of understanding. In the former cases, it is simple to know what to say: the subject, despite the way it may seem to him, lacks understanding. The latter cases are more difficult.

In these latter cases, I suggest that we would not know what to say. These cases would involve a breakdown of the familiar boundaries of language. If we ascribed to the subject an adequate set of mental components of understanding, we thereby are inclined to ascribe understanding; but to the extent that the subject behaved stupidly, we thereby would be inclined not to ascribe understanding. A mirror image of this tension is to be found in the familiar cases of computers which perform sophisticated operations. They exhibit the behavior we associate with understanding, but we assume that they lack the mental components; and we hardly know what to say. If we speak of the computer as "understanding" what it reports on, we do so in an inverted commas, tentative sense. We are comfortable in ascribing understanding (in a normal, not inverted commas, sense) only in cases in which we are prepared to ascribe both some characteristic mental components and corresponding behavioral dispositions. Thus the dualist account under discussion does not imply that understanding can exist in the absence of characteristic behavioral dispositions. No logical contradiction can be attributed to the account on that score.

What other objections can there be? It would seem that there are two major sources of further objections. One is a purported logical principle: that there cannot be factual claims that are in principle unverifiable, or facts that are in principle unknowable. The other is the difficulty, previously mentioned, of how we know about the minds of others.

Let us consider the first source of objections. The account that has been given implies, and, indeed, any dualist account must imply, that it is logically possible that someone who is behaving stupidly and uncomprehendingly nevertheless might possess an adequate set of mental components of understanding. It might seem that the claim that the person possesses these mental components is, in principle, unverifiable; and the fact, if it is one, is unknowable. Some philosophers will appeal, then, to the logical principle that any unverifiable claim is meaningless, and that any hypothesis that includes unknowable facts is meaningless. One way to meet this challenge is with a peremptory counterchallenge. On what basis is the crucial "logical" principle asserted? How do we know that it is true? There is, however, a less headlong way to meet the challenge.

Under the hypothesis (of seven varieties of discombobulation), there never will be a subject of whom it is certain that behavioral dispositions associated with understanding will not manifest themselves. Let us take an extreme case. Suppose that a man fits the pattern of case 7. He has not taken Cartesine, but suddenly begins to behave stupidly and uncomprehendingly; he does not show signs of nerve blockage (and in general has no neurophysiological signs of his condition, or of mental components of understanding); Rylene does not help. We keep the subject alive until his ninetieth birthday, at which point he dies; during all this time the condition does not change. We cannot have entire theoretical certainty, though, that during the subject's ninety-first year of life there might not have been a dramatic reversal, so that the subject would have provided evidence to convince us (or, at least, to give us reason to consider it not highly unlikely) that he had possessed an adequate set of mental components of understanding all along. Similarly, in a case of types 3 or 4, it always will seem possible that, if the subject had lived longer, the condition would have been reversed, and behavioral evidence provided that the subject had possessed mental components of understanding.

Thus behavioral evidence of mental components of understanding is never ruled out. At worst, we lack the evidence; but it is never impossible that, in time, the evidence would have been available. My argument requires that there is a logical possibility that the behavioral evidence of mental components of understanding never will be forthcoming, even if the subject lives forever; but this logical possibility, of course, does not preclude the possibility that the evidence will be, or would have been, forthcoming. Now, few philosophers today would deny the possibility of truths that, strive though we may, we are in fact unable to learn, as long as the truths are not in principle unknowable. But there is nothing inherent in the truths about mental components of understanding that prevents behavioral evidence from being available. Indeed, in real life such evidence frequently is available. Often, of course, it is not: there are cases in which the subject dies suddenly, is secretive, or simply is not asked to provide the evidence, and has no opportunity to do so. What makes the hypothesis under discussion peculiar, then, is not that in the case of certain subjects there is no evidence—this happens often enough in real life. It is rather that, *ex hypothesi*, even though an adequate set of mental components of understanding exists, there is contrary behavioral evidence; and the evidence that would tend to confirm the presence of the mental components of understanding is not provided. But it never is impossible that the confirming evidence will be, or would have been, provided.

Thus the hypothesis under discussion does not involve claims that are in principle unverifiable. It is merely designed to illustrate the logical separability of mental components of understanding from the appropriate behavioral dispositions. It does not involve anything that is on principle unknowable.

Having said this, we have to add that the cases included in the hypothesis are all cases in which ample behavioral evidence might still leave us in some doubt. Even after the aged ex-idiot behaves in a manner to suggest that he had possessed an adequate set of mental components of understanding all along, we might wonder whether he had—especially if there has been no nerve blockage or other neurophysiological evidence of his condition. If "verification" is given a strong interpretation, in terms of evidence that will allow a consensus of reasonable people to be confident of the correct answer, then it is true that the hypothesis includes some cases in which verification is not possible. However, any principle that insists that meaningful claims are verifiable is considerably more plausible if "verification" is taken in the weak sense that merely stipulates that evidence will be available which makes it more reasonable to reach a certain conclusion than it otherwise would be, than if "verification" is taken to require overwhelming and conclusive evidence. It is difficult to do justice to the actual practice of historians and social scientists without recognizing that there often are cases in which the evidence concerning someone's motivations, or the character of an action, is not entirely conclusive; and it appears doctrinaire and implausible to insist that in principle there must be some arrangement of ideal evidence which is conclusive.

What, then, about the problem of our knowledge of other minds? The summary treatment that present space allows will not do justice to the problem. But it should indicate the lines along which a dualist solution could lie. It is important to make clear that a dualist need not lapse into untenable dogmatism or implausible skepticism on this issue.

It is clear that, to the seven kinds of cases discussed earlier, one could add an eighth kind: that of a person who has from birth appeared to be an idiot, with no neurophysiological signs of any components of understanding. There could also be a ninth case: a stone, or some other inanimate object. My argument commits me to saying that there is some logical possibility of mental components of understanding even in these cases.

However, "logical possibility" should not be taken as meaning anything like "real chance." There is the logical possibility that the stone will begin to talk, solve problems for us, declare its love for another stone, and display wounded feelings. That is, there is no logical contradiction in the story of a stone that does all these things. However, no reasonable person would expect stones to act in that way; and, if a stone did suddenly behave in such a manner, it would be an unreasonable person who said, "I'm not surprised."

My position, in short, is that we know that congenital idiots and stones (not to mention computers) do not have mental components of understanding; and we know that most of the people we encounter every day do, in some matters, possess mental components of understanding. How do we know? In order to answer this, we have to recognize the similarity of this problem with certain other problems that have bedeviled philosophers. Take, for example, the problem of the "reality of the past."

J. J. C. Smart has argued that the hypothesis that the universe began to exist ten minutes ago (with everything just as it was ten minutes ago) is "a meaningful one."[3] "Indeed, though there are no possible observations or experiments which could distinguish between this hypothesis and the more usual one, there are considerations, hard though they may be to formulate, of simplicity and plausibility, which should determine us to reject the 'ten minutes ago' hypothesis."[4]

Smart's line here seems entirely correct, not only for the reality of the past, but also for the problem of other minds. We *could* imagine that the world was created ten minutes ago, and that at this point God created us with memories (which *seemed* to tell us of things past), and that God also created the world with fossils in it, old newspapers, historical records, and rocks with carbon characteristics that normally are taken to indicate great age. The hypothesis that the world was created ten minutes ago can be made to fit all the evidence we have, but at the cost of extreme elaborateness and artificiality. (Why would God, or any other being, create false memories, old newspapers, etc.?) In much the same way, we *could* imagine that other people are like robots, that when they express pain they have no feeling, and so on; but this too is to construct an extremely elaborate and artificial view of the world. The assumptions necessary to support anything other than the usual view of other minds are, in their way, as baroque and implausible as those necessary to support the denial of the reality of everything that happened more than ten minutes ago.

This, it must be stressed again, is just a sketch of a solution to the problem of other minds. It is inserted here merely to indicate likely lines of defense. If an objection to a dualist treatment of understanding is that it incurs enormous difficulty *vis-à-vis* the problem of other minds, it is important to see, even in brief, that the probable weight of this objection is not great.

Now, it may be said, I have dealt with some objections to dualism, but not with the most fundamental and central objection. This is that one-half of what the dualist claims exists in the world simply does not exist. I have argued that mental components of understanding are logically separable from the behavioral dispositions with which they are generally conjoined. But in this argument I have assumed that there are qualities of mental states, some of which might be termed "mental components" of understanding. And this is to assume, among other things, that there are qualities of mental states to begin with.

In reply, one must appeal ultimately to introspection. Indeed, dualism cannot be made plausible without the evidence of introspection. Anti-dualists often are challenged in other ways: one familiar challenge, for example, is to ask the anti-dualist whether he would be willing to undergo an operation without an anesthetic. But his reluctance could be interpreted as a behavioral quirk, or as reluctance to incur the correlates of certain supposed mental states; and such arguments, memorable though they are, can have little weight without the supporting evidence of introspection.

Thus, ultimately, I am assuming that we all know that there are certain qualities of mental states which are characteristically associated with understanding. What I think to be the case is this: everyone, or almost everyone, knows that there are certain qualities of mental states which are characteristically associated with understanding. But some ingenious philosophers have shown that understanding cannot be ascribed in the absence of certain behavioral dispositions. Understanding has been envisaged by them, and their audience, as a "this or that." Either it is mental or it is behavioral. But since (as these philosophers have shown) understanding cannot be ascribed in the absence of the appropriate behavioral dispositions, the solution (it appeared) was that understanding was analyzable in terms of behavior. Our argument thus far was (to adopt fashionable parlance) not designed to *prove* statements of familiar facts, but rather to recall people to a sense of them. It was to do this by establishing the coherence and plausibility of a third alternative to the two that had been debated. Understanding can be logically related both to behavioral dispositions and to mental states, without the two being logically related to one another. Once we see this, we can regain a sense of the facts.

If understanding is not purely mental, what is purely mental? The familiar qualities of mental states that are associated with understanding are purely mental; but if we try to characterize these, we encounter many difficulties, difficulties that will be discussed later in this chapter. In the meantime, we shall present a more easily characterized case of a purely mental event.

Talking About an Image

A case of a purely mental event, and the linguistic problems it raises, can be presented as follows. Suppose that someone says, "Think of a number between one and ten." Not everyone will respond in the same way. Someone may have a visual image of the number six floating through clouds. Some may have no image at all, but just a disposition to make appropriate responses to questions like "Is it prime?" Others, including the present writer, will respond typically by invoking the auditory image of a number. It is this case, and this auditory image, that I wish to consider.

My claim is that the occurrence of the auditory image is a purely mental event, that the image is observable only introspectively, and that (subject to qualifications to be explained shortly) such images need not be connected to, or even correlated with, manifestations in behavior.

The qualifications on my position (and one of the chief respects in which it differs from traditional dualism) can be illustrated by reference to a quotation from Wilfred Sellars. The first half presents a view with which I agree; the second half is part of what I am concerned to refute.

> Once again the myth helps us to understand that concepts pertaining to certain inner episodes—in this case *impressions*—can be primarily and essentially *intersubjective*, without being resolvable into overt behavioral symptoms, and that the reporting role of these concepts, their role in introspection, the fact that each of us has a privileged access to his impressions, constitutes a dimension of these concepts which is *built on* and *presupposes* their role in intersubjective discourse.

and

> It also makes clear why the "privacy" of these episodes is not the "absolute privacy" of the traditional puzzles. For, as in the case of thoughts, the fact that overt behavior is evidence for these episodes is built into the very logic of these concepts as the fact that observable behavior of gases is evidence for molecular episodes is built into the very logic of molecule talk.[5]

We can see the truth in the first half of what Sellars says, and the falsity in the second half, if we examine how we can learn to report auditory images of numbers, or to understand such reports. If I have an auditory image of "seven," how can I report this, and what basis could you have for understanding my report?

Perhaps it would be best to approach the case of my auditory image of "seven" by means of another case, which in some respects is similar, but in one or two important respects is different. This is the case of talking (silently) to oneself. It is related to auditory images of the kind under consideration, roughly as process to product.

In his *Philosophical Investigations*, Wittgenstein asks how one might teach someone the meaning of the expression "to say something to oneself."[6] The commonsense view is as follows. "Rather it seems to us as though in this case the instructor *imparted* the meaning to the pupil—without telling him directly; but in the end the pupil is brought to the point of giving himself the correct ostensive definition."[7] This Wittgenstein calls an "illusion."

Wittgenstein is concerned to reject the view that, in the case of talking (silently) to oneself, one can impart meaning to someone without telling the meaning. Indeed, to impart meaning in this way sounds magical, and there is something lacking in the commonsense view as Wittgenstein reports it.

An inner process, it is often said, stands in need of outward criteria. That is, we cannot explain what is going on "inside" us (it is said) except in terms of outer manifestations. But do outward criteria remedy the deficiency here?

Suppose that we teach a small child what it is to talk silently to oneself. We say, "It's what you typically (but not always) have when you later *are inclined to say*, 'I heard myself say "such and such" but no one else could possibly hear it.'" This is perverse. It certainly cannot make sense to the child until the child knows *why* someone would be inclined to say, "I heard myself say 'such and such,' but no one else could possibly hear it."

Some might say here that the outward criteria must be physiological. Look at the larynx or the brain. Wittgenstein has the best comment on this. "But then did we learn the use of the words 'to say such-and-such to oneself' by someone's pointing to a process in the larynx or the brain?"[8] The answer, of course, is "No." Thus, whatever correlations there may be between larynx or brain and talking to oneself will not explain how we learn to tell others about our talking (silently) to ourselves.

How, then, does the child learn what it means to talk to oneself? Let me suggest that there are two possible ways—used either alone or in combination—for the learning to take place. First, we might display talking to oneself as the limit of a series. That is, we might say something loudly, then less loudly, then less loudly still, whisper it, and so on. Alternatively, we might simply tell the child that talking to oneself is *like* talking aloud, except that there is no sound.

Now, this teaching does not require the teaching of outward criteria, if by outward criteria are meant ways that will tell us in the great majority of cases whether other people are talking to themselves. The child may convince us that it has learned the meaning of "talking to oneself," knows when it talks to itself, but genuinely does not know (except in a few cases) when other people are talking to themselves. If we loosen the requirement for outward criteria, of course, so that outward criteria may govern only a minority of cases, then the teaching does require conveying outward criteria. It would be odd to claim, as things now stand, that the child has learned the meaning of "talking to oneself" if the child were not able to conjecture that a man pacing about with lips moving, gesticulating in a conversational manner, was talking to himself.

Are there logical connections between items of behavior on one hand and talking to oneself on the other? It is true that the meaning of "talking to oneself" cannot be taught except by means of behavioral items: the words, gestures, and so on, of the teachers. It is true also that the meaning of "talking to oneself" must be taught in relation to the meaning of something behavioral, that is, talking aloud. It is true, further, that there are characteristic behavioral accompaniments, or manifestations, of talking to oneself. The most notable is the person's report afterwards. But there is no logical necessity that in any given case, or even in the majority of cases, what in fact we take to be behavioral manifestations will manifest themselves. Indeed, we can conceive of a world in which most people whose lips move, and so on, and who give reports afterwards of talking to themselves, in fact have not talked to themselves; and most people who talk to themselves successfully conceal the fact. Such a world would involve, among other things, systematic lying; but it is worth bearing in mind that, while it is logically impossible for most people to lie on most subjects most of the time, it is possible for almost everyone to lie almost always about some specific matter.

There is some temptation to say one of two things about the world in which talking to oneself no longer has what we now take to be its characteristic behavioral manifestations. One possible comment is to insist that, even in this world, there still would be outstanding examples of talking to oneself, and that the outstanding examples would involve, for example, moving one's lips, a report afterward, and so on. After all, to teach a meaning, we need outstanding examples. And, of course, these must have behavioral elements. How else can teaching take place?

It might be replied that, in a world in which correlations between talking to oneself and certain behavioral manifestations no longer exist, what are now outstanding examples would lose their role. This then leaves room for a second possible comment. If this is so, then, it might be said, in the world described it would be simply impossible to teach the meaning of "talking to oneself." This is not to deny that people might talk to themselves; it is merely to deny that, in that world, we could talk about talking to oneself.

These comments are, as I shall argue, several shades more plausible with regard to talking to oneself than to my auditory image of "seven." That is a major difference between the two cases.

The plausibility of the comments with regard to talking to oneself can be seen as follows. The two ways of teaching the child the meaning of "talking to oneself" both involved comparison with talking aloud. Whether talking to oneself was conveyed as the limit of a series or as like talking aloud except for inaudibility, the core of the teaching was that talking to oneself could be understood as importantly similar to talking aloud. It is possible to argue the following. In a world in which talking to oneself loses its present relation to behavioral manifestations, the great majority of cases of talking to oneself will no longer be importantly similar to cases of talking aloud. Therefore, unless a few cases of talking to oneself that remain importantly similar to talking aloud can be treated as outstanding examples, and the great majority of other cases of talking to oneself can be treated as deviant cases, it would be impossible to teach the meaning of "talking to oneself." Even scientific information about the larynx and the brain would not help: in such a world, what would there be to correlate with the scientific reports?

I do not affirm that the foregoing line of thought is correct; but it may well be correct, and certainly has great plausibility. However, a similar argument with respect to the auditory image of "seven" is not nearly so plausible. In order to see this, we should examine how we would ordinarily teach a child the meaning of "auditory image of the number seven."

Once again, it will not do to say to the child, "It's what you typically (but not always) have when you later are inclined to say, 'I had an auditory image of the number seven.'" This would beg the all-important question of why one would be inclined to say such a thing. Neither do we normally appeal to the larynx or the brain in order to teach a child this bit of language.

It seems to me that the only way we can (and do) teach the meaning of "auditory image of the number seven" is by means of analogy. That is, we say that to have this auditory image is *like* hearing "seven" spoken; only it seems in some sense "inner" (this functions as a hint rather than as a precise direction), and in any case the "seven" cannot be heard by anyone other than oneself.

If this seems a profoundly unsatisfactory account, I can only ask the reader to provide a better one; I cannot. It is worth pausing, however, to ask why this account should seem to many philosophers to be profoundly unsatisfactory.

There are three elements that may seem particularly repugnant. First, there is the central role of analogy. To many philosophers, arguments from, or appeals to, analogy will be especially suspect. But, we may inquire, how can the linguistic system of an individual, or of a group, develop if not by analogy? Furthermore, even if we examine routine use of language, rather than what we would consider change within the linguistic system, we encounter something like analogy.

The cases encountered are never precisely the same as those used in teaching; in a changing world we always are talking about something slightly different from before. Yet these ordinary minor linguistic adjustments are never considered guesswork, and we and our friends know that we are using language properly as we apply it to slightly new cases. Thus something like analogy is a routine part of the use of language. It is only when the analogy spans, as it were, too great a gap that worries are generated and we feel unsure of the appropriateness of language. Still, not all significant gaps are problematic. If tomorrow the world's first green monkey is born in a zoo, the keepers will know to call it a monkey.

Secondly, it may be disturbing that the teacher will rely on a hint (that the image will seem somehow "inner" in relation to an ordinary sound) rather than a precise direction. But how *could* one provide a precise direction, we might wonder. Leaving this to the side, we still may ask what is wrong with giving a hint. The likely answer, I think, is that hints are too indefinite. One is not able to be sure whether one has taken the hint properly. Part of the response to this worry is to point out, as Wittgenstein does in *Philosophical Investigations*, that even what are ordinarily accounted precise directions are subject to interpretation.[9] But, as he remarks, "The sign-post is in order—if, under normal circumstances, it fulfills its purpose."[10] A hint is as good as a precise direction, we might say, if it accomplishes its purpose.

But how do we know that it has accomplished its purpose—in one's own case, or in anyone else's? This leads us to a third disturbing element in the account I gave of teaching "auditory image of the number seven." In this account, the teacher points toward a kind of item in inner experience to which the phrase "auditory image of the number seven" refers. But, it might be said, if there is no way of telling whether any pupil has learned to use the phrase "auditory image of the number seven" properly, then there is no way to distinguish between proper and improper usage; if so, there is no such thing as proper usage.

However, we sometimes can tell that someone has used the phrase "auditory image of the number seven" improperly. Suppose that someone says, "I just had an auditory image of 'seven'; it had three syllables," or "I just had an auditory image of 'seven,' and it was all *s*'s and *z*'s." Or it is said, "My auditory image of 'seven' was predominantly red at the center, with a violet aura." Clearly, in these cases language is not being used appropriately.

But can we ascertain in any case that this bit of language *is* being used appropriately; that is, that "auditory image of the number seven" is being used in relation to something to which it truly refers? Well, if a man is a sober, reliable, native speaker of English, and, better yet, both passes a lie detector test and repeats his story under scopolamine, we can say with confidence that the man did have the auditory image of the number seven that he reported, and used language appropriately in reporting that image. What more is wanted? Is it that we should be able to inspect the image that is reported? Or is the demand here really for some *conclusive* verification? If so, our argument in chapter 5 suggests that the demand cannot be met even for the physical world.

Even if it is conceded that, in our present world, the meaning of "auditory image of the number seven" can be taught in the manner I describe, what of a world in which neither a man's statements nor his other behavior ever gives even a moderately reliable indication of whether he has an auditory image of a certain number? (Asked which number between one and ten they were thinking of, people answer randomly, telling the truth one-tenth of the time. Scopolamine and lie detector tests correlate so badly, in all their varied uses, with other evidence that we judge them no longer to provide evidence.) Could the meaning of "auditory image of the number seven" be taught in such a world? We have already seen that, in an analogous situation, there is a strong case for saying that we could not teach the meaning of "talking to oneself."

However, there is an important difference between the two cases. "Talking to oneself" must be taught by means of analogy with "talking aloud"; and, in a world in which there are no behavioral correlates of talking to oneself, this analogy can be argued to fail. (In such a world, what now counts as pretending to talk to oneself might have more in common with talking aloud than would talking to oneself.) "Having an auditory image of the number seven" must be taught by means of analogy with "hearing 'seven.'" In a world in which there are no behavioral correlates of having an auditory image of the number seven, this analogy still will hold.

Thus, I contend, even in the world in which there are no behavioral correlates of the auditory image, we can teach the child the meaning of "auditory image of the number seven." What is essential in this teaching is the analogy, and not some private and uncheckable ceremony. It is true that if the child in fact has an auditory image of "seven," and grasps the analogy between this and the outward sound "seven," this will facilitate the teaching greatly. It might be tempting to say of this case (to borrow Wittgenstein's ironic words) that "the instructor *imparted* the meaning to the pupil—without telling him directly; but in the end the pupil is brought to the point of giving himself the correct ostensive definition." But the irony would be misplaced here. For one thing, the teacher does *tell*, by means of analogy, the meaning of "auditory image of the number seven." And it is not necessary to have the auditory image to understand the meaning of the phrase. Analogies can be grasped by someone who has not experienced both terms of the analogy.

Now I am in a position to explain my agreement, and disagreement, with Sellars' general claims, as applied to this case. We can see that the concepts used in reporting an auditory image of "seven" are "primarily and essentially intersubjective." "Auditory image of seven" is *grounded*, as it were, to the outer and generally audible sound of "seven": were it not, we could not report our auditory images, or understand such reports. It also is true that "auditory image of seven" is not a phrase which only one person can understand. It presupposes a public use within a linguistic community in which everyone can use the same words to report, inquire about, or incite auditory images.

It is true that overt behavior is evidence for the existence of episodes involving auditory images. But is this evidential relation "built into the very logic of these concepts"? Consider again the world in which neither a man's statements nor his other behavior ever gives even a moderately reliable indication of whether he has an auditory image of a certain number. In such a world, what a man said and his other behavior would not count as evidence for a conclusion about the character of his auditory images. Thus the evidential relation between behavior on one hand and auditory images on the other rests, not on what is built into the very logic of concepts, but rather on the assumption that people do not generally deceive us about such things as their auditory images. The crucial assumption, as in the more general problem of other minds, turns out to be factual, rather than some kind of logical truth.

Thus far I have made a case for saying (with qualifications) that the auditory image of "seven" need not be connected to or correlated with manifestations in behavior. The occurrence of the auditory image does not require behavioral accompaniments, or any corresponding behavioral dispositions: in this sense it is purely mental. Also, since there is no behavioral component of the auditory image, it is observable only introspectively. Thus the auditory image of "seven" provides a useful test case in the debate between dualists and anti-dualists. If the account that I have given of it is largely correct, then dualism must be taken seriously.

This image must not be regarded, however, as a typical purely mental event, or even as a typical mental image. Its very definiteness, which enhances its usefulness as an example, renders it atypical and importantly different from, say, visual images of speckled hens. Any balanced account of the mind must stress the indefiniteness of so much of the mental. The polemical implications of this, as we shall see, are important.

Reducing the Mental to the Physiological

The classic example of the indefiniteness of (much of) the mental is that of the image of the speckled hen, possessing an indefinite number of speckles. Other examples are visual images in which it would be impossible to say what color certain objects are, because they have no color. In some dreams certain facets are indistinctly indicated, so that while the dreamer can report what he was doing in the dream, he cannot say whether he was angry or sad. Questions like "What color was it?" or "Were you angry?" then are unanswerable, and not because what is asked about lies on a linguistic borderline.

Even if we put this indefiniteness to the side, much of the mental, along with intentional action, poses peculiar difficulties of description. It is because of this that poets traditionally have been held to have special powers of describing both states of mind and human actions. Where there is only one clearly appropriate mode of description, the report of any experimental subject will do. But it seems to take special skill to describe much of the mental. Similarly, anyone can report sizes of armies, dates, and so on, but a Gibbon has a special role in describing late Roman and Byzantine history.

Some of the philosophical implications of this will be explored in chapters 8 and 9, and in the next chapter we shall explore the concept of precision more fully. But the difficulty in describing much of the mental with any precision is relevant to a present problem. Can the mental be reduced to the physiological? Our difficulties in describing the mental create an obstacle that may justify an answer of "No."

A number of different ways of equating the mental with something physiological have been suggested. We shall consider one—the most prominent, and perhaps the most straightforward. It is found in the work of a number of contemporary Australian philosophers, most notably Professor J. J. C. Smart.

Smart "wishes to resist" the suggestion that to say, for example, "I have a yellowish-orange afterimage," is to report something "irreducibly psychical." It seems to Smart that "science is increasingly giving us a viewpoint whereby organisms are able to be seen as physio-chemical mechanisms." Some people, in describing human beings, insist upon including descriptions of conscious states and events (such as the yellowish-orange afterimage). But, says Smart, "that every-thing should be explicable in terms of physics (together of course with descriptions of the ways in which the parts are put together—roughly, biology is to physics as radio-engineering is to electromagnetics) except for the occurrence of sensations seems to me frankly unbeliev-able."[11] Smart looks forward to a science in which a complete set of laws will be able to be stated without any reference to sensations or to anything that is "mental." Thus, in terms of this science, it will not be necessary to think of the "mental" as existing. Given the viewpoint of scientific realism, one would conclude that the mental does not exist, since it is an unneeded category in the best possible science.

The first thing to note about Smart's view is that it rests, in large part, upon a prediction about the future of the sciences. What is being predicted is that the kinds of explanation that have been arrived at in the physical sciences eventually will be able to be provided for all events, even events that at first sorting seem "mental." When this millennium is reached, and even thoughts and moods can be explained in physical terms, then we will be able to leave the mind, or anything pertaining to the mind, out of our statements of laws without losing anything.

An analogy often used by philosophers of this persuasion is that of the reduction of lightning to electricity. Lightning certainly had seemed to be a special kind of entity in its own right. But research enabled us to "conclude that lightning is nothing more than a motion of electric charges, because we know that a motion of electric charges through the atmosphere, such as occurs when lightning is reported, gives rise to the type of visual stimulation which would lead an observer to report a flash of lightning."[12] Lightning, then, is just electricity. Similarly, when our scientific knowledge has developed appropriately, we shall see that the mind is just something neuro-physiological. The science of the future will be unified, and will have no need for talk of "the mind."

This is a bright picture of the future of science. In its optimism it attracts, understandably, many psychologists as well as philosophers. But it is worth inquiring into some of the details of this attractive package. We might ask for a more detailed account of the kinds of laws that are expected to spread from the physical sciences to other branches of knowledge. And we might ask, especially, about the process by which it will be possible for our explanations of human actions and expressions of feeling to develop to the point at which mental entities can drop out. Like many utopian blueprints, political or intellectual, the Smartian account of the future of the sciences is singularly lacking in crucial details.

Smart's view is a philosophical conclusion appended to a prophecy about the future of the sciences. If the prophecy is correct, there is still room for debate about the philosophical conclusion. How can we identify the mental state of having an image of a speckled hen, we might wonder, with a neurophysiological state? The former involves the occurrence of an entity (the image) which has a number of speckles such that, for any X, X is not equal to the number of speckles; no neurophysiological state, presumably, will involve the occurrence of any entity with this quality—unless, of course, we speak of a neurophysiological state as involving the occurrence of the image of the speckled hen, in which case we have granted the occurrence of a mental entity. But, leaving this to the side, we have every reason to suppose that the fundamental prophecy about the future of the sciences is unfounded. The imprecision of the descriptions we can provide of most psychological states does not allow for development of the kinds of laws that those who think like Smart evidently count upon.

Suppose that we try, in some science of the future, to explain the state of mind that impelled Shakespeare to write his Sonnet 29, which begins:

> When, in disgrace with fortune and men's eyes,
> I all alone beweep my outcast state . . .

(We can assume, for the sake of simplicity, that the state of mind that impelled the poetry was in this case roughly the same state that is expressed in the poem, although we know that poems do not always come into being in this way.) We can try to explain this state of mind in terms of neurophysiological factors, just as we explain lightning flashes in terms of electricity. To make the parallel complete, we would have to arrive at a generalization of the form "Neurophysiological conditions X give rise to the type of experience that would lead someone to report the 'When, in disgrace with fortune and men's eyes . . .' state of mind." If we arrive at this generalization, then, presumably, just as we say that lightning is just electricity, we will be able to say that the "When, in disgrace with fortune and men's eyes . . ." state of mind is just neurophysiological conditions X.

How can we expect, in any future development of the sciences, to arrive at the required kinds of generalizations?

First, we should note that when Shakespeare says "When, in disgrace with fortune and men's eyes . . ." the expression is meaningful, and not just in an emotive way. One can tell that the feelings which are both expressed and described in the first part of the sonnet are much more like those one typically has after publicly saying some very stupid things than like those one typically has after winning a prize. But it would be chivying language to count on a much more precise application of what Shakespeare says. X fails an examination, and this is publicly announced; Y is jilted at the altar. X says that his states of mind are like those described in the first nine lines of Shakespeare's Sonnet 29; Y, asked if the description applies to his feelings, says that he would not put them this way. Are X's states of mind more like Shakespeare's than Y's are? Questioning the two will help us to form a judgment; but, unless the answers are surprising (e.g., if Y was secretly glad), it is very possible that we shall lack any grounds for a confident conclusion. If X decides that "I feel like a dope" characterizes his state of mind better than does "When, in disgrace with fortune and men's eyes . . . ," how does this affect our classification of states of mind? Do we still credit him with the "When, in disgrace with fortune and men's eyes . . ." state of mind?

In the hoped-for future science, we would expect a fully comprehensive set of generalizations connecting neurophysiological states with states of mind. This requires either a one-one or a many-one mapping of neurophysiological states onto states of mind: that is, we must be able to associate a definite state of mind with any given neurophysiological state, although it would be allowable that more than one neurophysiological state would share the same state of mind. But if some people in neurophysiological state X says that their state of mind is that of "When, in disgrace with fortune and men's eyes . . . ," and other people in neurophysiological state X prefer the formulation "I feel like a dope," and yet others in state X prefer a variety of other formulations, and if some people in neurophysiological state Y say "I feel like a dope," what do we say? It certainly would be high-handed to assume that subtly different formulations of states of mind do not correspond to subtly different states of mind. But how, given the unlimited welter of formulations of states of mind, do we arrive at our generalizations? It is very hard to see how we could possibly arrive at the requisite generalizations unless we had a determinate and precise classifications of states of mind, and very hard to see how this classification could be achieved.

It might seem that we can escape the difficulties by correlating states of mind with neurophysiological states, and then arriving at causal laws which explain these neurophysiological states and do not mention states of mind at all. But this project encounters the same difficulties. As one contemporary philosopher has asked:

> For how are the neurophysiological sequences to be established in relation to the relevant mental states? The task is not wholly daunting when we think of very simple sensations. We associate a wince with a certain sort of painful sensation. But our mental life is rarely, if ever, restricted to discrete simple items of that sort.[13]

Nor will it help if we abandon attempts to correlate states of mind with the neurophysiological, and instead attempt to correlate reports of states of mind with the neurophysiological. Given the variety of language available for such reports, and the complexities of shadings within the language, we may well doubt that this could produce precise correlations. The psychologist may insist on a "multiple choice" system of reporting states of mind, limiting in advance the options, in the hope that this will lead to precise correlations. But what, then, of people who complain that none of the options that the psychologist presents does justice to the states of mind that are being described? Do we try to pretend that what defies the psychologist's classifications does not exist, or that it really fits them?

The moral seems to be this. We should hesitate to project a future character for psychology that is closely modeled on that of physics. Speculation about future knowledge of the mind is extremely difficult, especially if we try to put aside preconceptions. As Wittgenstein remarked of a hypothesis like Smart's, "Now ask yourself: what do you *know* about these things?"[14] As Wittgenstein points out, accounts of this kind are *a priori* very convincing to us. But this says more about our need to simplify than about the value of such accounts.

Notes

1. Cf. Friedrich Nietzsche, *Thus Spake Zarathustra*, trans. Walter Kaufmann, in the *Viking Portable Nietzsche*, ed. Kaufmann (New York: Viking Press, 1954), p. 146.

2. Gilbert Ryle, *The Concept of Mind* (New York: Barnes & Noble, 1949), p. 53.

3. J. J. C. Smart, *Philosophy and Scientific Realism* (London: Routledge & Kegan Paul, 1963), p. 10.

4. Ibid.

5. Wilfred Sellars, *Science, Perception, and Reality* (London: Routledge & Kegan Paul, 1963), p. 195, Sellars' italics.

6. Ludwig Wittgenstein, *Philosophical Investigations*, trans. G. E. M. Anscombe (New York: Macmillan, 1953), no. 361, p. 114. (Cf. also no. 344, p. 110.)

7. Ibid., no. 362, p. 114, Wittgenstein's italics.

8. Ibid., no. 376, pp. 116-117.

9. Ibid., no. 28, pp. 13-14; no. 85-87, pp. 39-41.

10. Ibid., no. 87, p. 41.

11. J. J. C. Smart, "Sensations and Brain Processes," in V. Chappell, ed., *The Philosophy of Mind* (Englewood Cliffs, N.J.: Prentice-Hall, 1962), p. 161.

12. U. T. Place, "Is Consciousness a Brain Process?" in Chappell, *The Philosophy of Mind*, p. 106.

13. II. D. Lewis, *The Elusive Mind* (London: George Allen & Unwin, 1969), p. 182.

14. *Philosophical Investigations*, no. 158, p. 63, Wittgenstein's italics.

SUGGESTED FURTHER READING

The classic sources for the debate over dualism are the following.

Descartes, René. *Meditations*. There are many modern editions of acceptable translations.

Ryle, Gilbert. *The Concept of Mind*. New York: Barnes & Noble, 1949.

Recent work on the philosophy of mind is contained in the following.

Shaffer, Jerome. *Philosophy of Mind*. Englewood Cliffs, N.J.: Prentice-Hall, 1968. This presents a clearly written and perceptive overview of the field.

Chappell, Vere, ed. *The Philosophy of Mind*. Englewood Cliffs, N.J.: Prentice-Hall, 1962. A strong and well-organized collection of essays. It includes essays by Smart and Place closely pertinent to the final section of this chapter.

Dennett, Daniel. *Content and Consciousness*. London: Routledge & Kegan Paul, 1969. An important and influential anti-dualist work.

Rundle, Bede. *Perception, Sensation, and Verification*. Oxford: Clarendon Press, 1972. This contains an interesting discussion of what can or cannot be said about the mental characteristics of animals.

Matson, Wallace. *Sentience*. Berkeley: University of California Press, 1976. This contains an interesting comparison (in chap. 4) between human cognition and the cognition that machines are known to be capable of.

Lewis, Hywel. *The Elusive Mind*. London: George Allen & Unwin, 1969. A spirited and often telling defense of dualism.

8 Can Human Activities Be Objectively Described?

It is very tempting to assume that, for any reality, there is a definite truth that corresponds to it. "The truth" may be something that we have not entirely attained. We may approximate it, and then through argument and effort we may come to approximate it even more closely. But even if it is graspable only in theory, or in some idealized future state of wisdom, "the truth" provides the basis for an important claim: that there is a single optimal account or description of any set of events or states of affairs, such that any competing account or description is either inferior or synonymous. We may call this claim the claim of objectivity.

We may speak of "objectivity" generally, or we may speak of the "objectivity" of various areas. Indeed, it makes sense to discuss problems of objectivity piecemeal: there is no reason to assume that all kinds of statements that people make have equal claims to, or hopes to, attain objectivity. Earlier in this century, a number of philosophers denied the objectivity of ethics. There was no reason to believe, they suggested, that there was "the truth"—or, indeed, truths at all—about right, wrong, good, and bad.[1] The implication was that the social sciences, or at least the physical sciences, were in a more fortunate position. But there have been numerous challenges, over a considerable period of time, to the claim that history and the social sciences are objective. It has been pointed out that values inevitably intrude into history and the social sciences; if they are not expressed in the final account that the historian or social scientist provides, they yet will have played a part in his or her selection of the data to report on.

Furthermore, historians and social scientists generally work on the basis of an explicit or implicit theory: natural law, Marxism, liberalism, and so on. These theories shape the results of historical work or work on the social sciences. But, unless we can claim that there is an objectively correct theory, we cannot claim that there is even a theoretical possibility of objectively correct accounts in history and the social sciences.

The objectivity of the physical sciences also has been challenged, mainly on the grounds that theoretical assumptions interact with scientific data in such a way that it becomes implausible to speak of an objective collection of scientific data. Philosophers used to believe in "the neutral given": that what we experienced was itself independent of scientific theory, and could be used as an impartial basis for selection between scientific theories. As we pointed out in chapter 6, it is now widely accepted that this is not the case, and that what we experience has a great deal to do with the concepts with which we are armed, the systems of measurement we accept, and the theoretical assumptions that delineate the possible results of experiment.[2]

The argument of chapter 6 suggests the conclusion (whether or not one is agnostic about the character of physical reality) that *no* knowledge developed within a linguistic framework can reach the ideal of objectivity. Competing scientific theories can be viewed as competing versions of a linguistic framework or (to put it another way) competing but overlapping linguistic frameworks. Competing linguistic frameworks are always possible, and no optimal account will be reached because no one (not the agnostic and certainly not the anti-agnostic) will be able to claim that an account developed within a linguistic framework perfectly corresponds to a reality that is outside of linguistic frameworks. If someone claims to have arrived at a linguistic framework that is itself optimal, consideration of the history of revolutions in science, as well as of the variety of approaches to reality that pass from being unimaginable to being imagined, should induce skepticism. If this line of thought is correct, there will be no perfect science, no perfect history, and so on.

Even if no perfect physics is possible, one might claim that physics is objective in *this* sense: that *if* one takes for granted the linguistic framework involved in a given theoretical approach, *then* there are optimal answers to questions of physics. Given the Celsius scale, and current assumptions regarding measurement, we can say that the temperature of a given body of water is 20 degrees Celsius, and no different answer is as good. What physics tells us about the world may be revised as theories fall and rise. But the revision rarely affects our account of such banal realities as the temperature of water. And even in a case in which a revision of accepted theory was that cataclysmic, we could say that, *given* a theory, we can find an optimal account of the temperature of the water, and that in *this* (intratheoretic) sense there is objective truth about such things as the temperature of water. To put the point in a different way: physics cannot be objective in the sense of entirely capturing some absolute reality that is independent of theory, but physics can be objective *relative to* a given theoretical framework.

Can other areas of knowledge be objective in this latter sense? In this chapter we shall consider the problem of intratheoretic objectivity only as it affects the subjects that describe and explain human behavior, subjects such as history, sociology, anthropology, and social psychology. And we shall consider the problem only as it affects description of human activities: explanation and prediction will not be considered here, although the latter will be taken up in the next chapter. The argument of this chapter is that totally objective description, as defined by the ideal of a single optimal description of any set of human activities, is beyond the reach of these subjects, even if one takes for granted a fixed theoretical framework. It also will be argued, however, that the correct view of these subjects does not lie at the opposite extreme—that the impossibility of total objectivity does not mean that "anything goes," or that these subjects can be viewed as totally subjective.

The Problem of Precision

The argument that the subjects under discussion cannot attain entirely objective description rests on an argument that they cannot attain entire precision of language.

What is meant by "precision"? We can distinguish two parameters of precision. One parameter is that involved in fineness of measurement or classification. If someone asks, "What temperature is it today?" and we answer "40 degrees Fahrenheit," this is only fairly precise, in the sense that we could have given the temperature to the tenth decimal place. In the same way, if we say that the color of a wall is green, this is only fairly precise, since we have not specified the shade of green.

The other parameter is more difficult to characterize. Suppose that someone asks, "What was the condition of black people in the United States in the 1920s?" and we have a choice among answering, "On the whole, they were badly treated," or "They were discriminated against systematically," or "They were oppressed." Someone asks what the effect of civil rights legislation was, and we can reply, "An improvement of conditions," or "Some elimination of discrimination and some increase in opportunities," or "Oppression became more covert and less systematic." The difficulty of choosing the right language in cases like these is very different from the difficulties that on occasion can arise in answering questions of the form of "What temperature is it?", "What color is it?", "On what date did it happen?", or "How many people voted for it?" In the latter kind of case, we have to apply a preestablished system of measurement or classification, and precision within the system is a matter of how finely we measure or classify. In the former kind of case, we scarcely are measuring. We are classifying, in the trivial sense in which any application of general terms represents classification; but there is no chart of classification that we can consult in the way that we can consult a color chart.

What counts as precision when there is no preestablished system of measurement or classification? It is very tempting to say that the concept of precision is totally out of place here, that it makes sense to talk about precision only where measurement is involved, or where there is a preexisting system of classification comparable to that of colors. But this would be a mistake.

Consider the following two accounts of the situation of black Americans in the early twentieth century, and the results of civil rights legislation.

1. In American society in the early twentieth century, the position of black people was generally unfortunate, in terms of housing, educational opportunities, and the jobs that were open to them. There was systematic and open discrimination. One effect of civil rights legislation was that discrimination became less systematic and open; another was that a number of people were brought to realize the unfairness of the previous treatment of black people, with the result that there was some (but not total) improvement in housing and educational opportunities, and many jobs previously closed to black people became open to them on fair terms.

2. In American society in the early twentieth century, the position of black people was generally unfortunate; in lots of ways they had a bad time. People were very mean to them most of the time. One effect of civil rights legislation was that people weren't so mean to them. Also many more black people were allowed to get a good education, and a number of black people got good jobs. So things got better, although they still were not very good.

Now, neither of these is put forward as a definitive, or even a really good, account of the events it describes. But it is pretty clear that No. 1 is superior to No. 2 and that the superiority is the direct result of language choice. It is not flatly wrong to say that in the early twentieth century people were very mean to blacks most of the time, but "systematic and open discrimination" is the better phrase. It places the treatment of black people in the 1920s in a different comparison class. To speak of people as having been "very mean" most of the time is to suggest a series of emotion-charged moments of hostile behavior. "Systematic and open discrimination" suggests something much more clearly continuous, which could be unthinking, and which at some moments might be emotion-charged but at others could be entirely matter-of-fact. To say that the effect of civil rights legislation was that people were not so mean to blacks is to suggest that the count of hostile actions was lowered: this is correct, but less revealing than to suggest that a continuous pattern of behavior was changed. There is something vague about saying "a number of black people got good jobs." This leaves open the possibility that this happened simply by administrative fiat, and it also does not say whether the number of black people who got good jobs was disproportionate or, at the other extreme, less than a fair number. To say "many jobs . . . became open to them on fair terms" is to suggest the latter, and it suggests also that the change was largely a matter of there being more fair competition than there had been previously.

In other words, while No. 1 undoubtedly has its defects, No. 2 illuminates less, and is in some ways slightly misleading. It is an example of what any careful teacher would consider poor student writing. And, I suggest, the teacher might say to his pupil, "You should try to write with somewhat more precision."

One way to put the difference between the two parameters of precision that I have been describing is this: great precision along the first parameter is fine measurement or classification; great precision along the second parameter is constituted by the *mot juste*, the appropriate wording. The historian or social scientist who wishes to be precise, in both ways (or senses), about the changed status of black people in the United States will give the numbers of black people who have reached various educational levels and the numbers holding jobs of various descriptions, and also will be extremely careful in his choice of words.

Now, when we inquire about relative precision in history and the social sciences, our concern is with the second parameter of precision and not the first. We need not worry, that is, why social scientists discussing the status of minority groups do not invariably record the exact numbers of members of minorities who hold managerial positions. That such details are not invariably reported rests in part on the contingent matter of the unavailability of some exact figures, but more generally on the fact that (as Wittgenstein remarked) what is not precise for some purposes (e.g., a census) is precise enough for others (e.g., most work in sociology). We normally do not want extreme precision of the first kind in accounts of the social sciences or in historical writings. However, in many cases we could get it if we wanted it.

What we are concerned with, then, is choice of language. My contention is that, in this parameter, there cannot be optimally precise writing in the social sciences and history, and that this is one of the factors that leave room always for new, competitive accounts.

Consider the concept of the *mot juste*, the "right word." It may be tempting to suppose that for any scene, or series of events, there is a single set of words that collectively occupy the role of the *mot juste*. But the inexhaustibility of literary and historical production should cause doubts on this score. And these doubts should be magnified into disbelief if we consider what is required to qualify as a *mot juste*.

There are two factors that appear relevant. One is that any use of a general word, phrase, or description involves comparisons. It suggests a relationship to a class of cases that customarily would be described by the word, phrase, or description. If the cases to which the locution customarily applies are very different from the case at hand, then we might say that to use the locution in this case is misleading.

On the other hand, we might not. Consider the following. "Pretend," "make believe," "feign," "act as if" are near synonymous expressions, with subtle differences of meaning.[3] These near synonyms evoke somewhat different comparisons, and are "at home in" somewhat different kinds of cases. "Make believe that," for example, is at home in cases of innocent diversion, such as the telling of fairy tales or children making believe that there is a man in the moon. "Feigning" is a more serious business, as when one feigns illness to escape work.

Thus it is appropriate to say "He made believe that the rings in the meadow had been left by fairies," and not normally appropriate to say "He feigned that the rings in the meadow had been left by fairies." Conversely, "He feigned madness in order to escape imprisonment" is more appropriate (more precise, we might say) than "He made believe that he was mad in order to escape imprisonment."

Along these lines, it is appropriate, in a treatment of Russian history, to say "Stalin feigned suspicion of the Old Bolsheviks in order to facilitate his purges." But is it altogether inappropriate to say "Stalin made believe that he suspected the Old Bolsheviks in order to facilitate his purges"? The implicit comparison with the world of fairy tales might be apt in this case—it might be an apt irony. Often a word that is normally inappropriate can introduce enlightening or revelatory comparisons to the description that includes it. A good deal of what is called wit has this character.

The second factor is this. The choice of a locution frequently is a choice of how much to say, or to suggest. Someone who thinks that Stalin genuinely was suspicious might speak of him in the late 1930s as "paranoid": this is to suggest, for good or ill, a whole psychoanalytic background that is not so clearly suggested by speaking of Stalin as "deeply suspicious." To speak of the traditional treatment of blacks in America as involving "systematic and open discrimination" is to call attention to institutional and legal factors that are not so clearly called into play if we speak of "great meanness." Perhaps the two extremes of the presence of this factor in social scientific and historical writing could be designated as "illuminating" and "flat." But someone who believes that Stalin was indeed paranoid will be prepared to argue that "paranoid" is the precise word for Stalin, and that any rival word will be imprecise.

Now, there clearly are bad forms of writing in history and the social sciences: one thinks of unilluminating descriptions and misleading comparisons. There are clearly good ways of writing in history and the social sciences. But is there, for any set of human activities, an absolutely best way of writing a description of it?

It looks as if the answer is "No." We may speak of the *mot juste*, but as contests among wits disclose, there typically is more than one *mot juste*. There is not one best choice of words for a description of human activities any more than there is one best painting possible of a landscape, or one best poem that can express a set of emotions. Let us analyze the grounds for this answer.

First, it has to be said that some sets of comparisons evoked by a social scientist's or historian's choice of language will be better than others. Superiority may involve suggestive value in enabling us to understand better why things happened as they did, the usefulness of placing in a broad context what had appeared unique, the illumination involved when the reader recognizes some connection between what is familiar and the unfamiliar activities the social scientist or historian describes, and perhaps many other factors as well. But to maintain that only one set of comparisons is appropriate, and fully definitive, is to misunderstand what comparisons are and what their function is. They are guides to the perception and understanding of the reader. Any comparison that becomes established will have fulfilled its function, and in fulfilling its function will sink to the level of a cliché. The merest wit or novelty of comparison on the part of the next social scientist or historian that deals with the subject matter will be superior.

In much the same way, the choice of words that illumines or suggests relevant material for some readers will be illuminating or suggestive for no one if it becomes well established. To call Stalin paranoid might be extremely effective description for an audience only slightly acquainted with psychoanalytic theory, and only slightly prepared to view statesmen in psychoanalytic terms; nowadays one wants more in a description of Stalin. Thus one can praise a social scientist's or historian's choice of language as precise, or condemn it as imprecise. But these are relative terms. There is no ideal of precision that plays a part here.

One qualification has to be placed on the foregoing. Not all elements in the writing of history and the social sciences pose the linguistic problems described. If we ask, "What is the condition of black people in America today?" we have a choice to make among descriptions, and we confront the shifting problem of finding apt descriptions. If we ask, "What is the number of black college students in America today?" there are, refreshingly, no difficulties of this kind. Problems of linguistic choice do not loom large when we answer questions of the form of "How many?" or "On what date?" or "How much money?" Economics, which to a large extent answers questions of the last kind, is thereby largely exempt from the difficulties of language that beset, say, sociology and history; and it would appear that the conclusions of this chapter do not firmly apply to economics. (If economics is not entirely objective, this is for other reasons than the one explored here.) That part of political science that deals with voting behavior also might be argued to be exempt; although, insofar as it explores the reasons why people vote as they do, it too will give prominent place to descriptions beset by the difficulties under discussion.

Why cannot all of the social sciences, and also history, consist entirely of sentences like "The number of black college students in the United States is . . . ," or "39,000,000 people voted for political candidate X," or "48.7 percent of those questioned said that they opposed abortion"? (Some might put the question another way. Why are distressingly literary elements so pervasive in the writing of history and most of the social sciences, preventing them from assuming their rightful places as sciences?)

Let us take the question first as it relates to history. Part of the answer is that some accounts that fit under the general rubric of history—accounts that would be called "chronicles"—come at least close to supplying what is asked for. (We should bear in mind, of course, that we are dealing with just one dimension of the problem of objectivity, and that we are dealing merely with objectivity *given* a theoretical framework. I do not claim that chronicles are "objective"; and especially do not deny the thesis that interpretive and theoretical elements are inextricably woven into the mesh of the chronicle. But the one worry about objectivity on which we are concentrating appears far less acute in relation to chronicle than in relation to the ordinary historical study.) Chronicles can consist of dates, sizes of armies, reports of who won what battle, lengths of the reign of kings or presidents, election results, and so on. One could have a chronicle-history of the United States which would consist of national election results: who got how many votes, when a person took office, length of term, and so on.

If old chronicles fit within history, it is partly an honorary classification, because of their antiquity, and because they do provide source materials for the historian. New chronicles, represented by almanacs and digests of the year's events, are not customarily classified as history. And we can see that there are important differences between typical historical writing and what a chronicle supplies. The difference is only in part a matter of what one might call the flatness of writing of the chronicle. It is also that history tells us about things that are beyond the scope of chronicle. Chronicle can tell us that Richard Nixon was elected president, and how many votes he received; history tells us what appeal he had, what the national mood was at the time, and how this national mood was related to events of the previous two decades. An account that told us simply the results of national elections would be unacceptable as a United States history, and even a much fuller summation of what could readily be put into numbers (an almanac of almanacs) also would be unacceptable.

A similar point can be made about such fields as sociology and social psychology. A sociological account of the condition of black people in America might consist entirely of statistical tables: for example, reporting the number of black Americans in various occupations, the number at various educational levels, and so on. But this would be inadequate. It would leave out, or at best hint at, what it was like to be black in America at a certain time. It also would omit an analysis of the facts behind the statistical tables—the attitudes and practices that made the tables what they were.

A social scientist may attempt to have it both ways, by relying very heavily on questionnaires. The questionnaires serve the purpose of getting at the facts, about attitudes and practices, behind the statistical tables. But their results can themselves be formulated in statistical tables. Thus the questionnaires may seem to make possible the ideal of entirely precise social science which is not limited in its subject matter, which tells us everything that we want to know.

The difficulty is that questionnaires, just like ordinary descriptions, must involve linguistic categories, both in the formulation of the questions and in what is allowed as a possible answer. The questionnaire imposes categories that suggest certain comparisons and not others, and that lead to answers that cumulatively are illuminating or flat. Except on the most simple matters, a subtly different set of questions will always produce a subtly different set of answers. Thus social scientists cannot, by relying on questionnaires, escape the problem of precision under discussion.

Good social science, and good history, cannot be written on significant topics without there being a limited precision of language. Or so it seems at present. But why is it so? And must it always be so?

Limitations of Language and Types of Reality

It helps, in answering these questions, to contrast history and the social sciences with physics. Descriptions in physics focus on measurable qualities. Consequently, the physicist does not have to struggle as the historian does with the problems of choice of language. This contrast could be argued to be a matter of degree rather than kind, on the basis of the role of something like metaphor in the construction of physical theory. But, in any case, it is plausible to say that on the level at which theory is applied rather than formulated, in descriptions of states of physical objects, the physicist does not have to struggle with the problems of choice of language facing the historian or social scientist. And we might say that, at least in the second parameter, descriptions found in physics are precise in a way in which the historian's or social scientist's descriptions generally are not. The major job here of the physicist is to quantify, to find the right number; an important part of the job of the social scientist or historian is quite different, involving finding the right words.

"How lucky for the physicist!" one might murmur. But is it luck? Could social scientists and historians, if they work at it, make their descriptions quantifiable in the way that descriptions in physics are quantifiable? And if they could, why haven't they?

One possible solution is that the social sciences and history cannot be as precise (in the respect under consideration) as physics, because what the social scientist or historian characteristically tries to describe is more complex than what is described in statements like "The temperature of the water is 20 degrees Celsius" or "The weight of that object is 397.36 grams." This solution has an obvious plausibility, but it is in fact inadequate.

It is true that complexity introduces difficulties into physics: there are notorious difficulties in prediction as the number of bodies whose behavior is to be predicted is multiplied. But we are considering description, not prediction. Furthermore, we are considering a particular difficulty in description, one involving choice of words. The difficulties in description in physics stipulated by Heisenberg's Uncertainty Principle are well known, but they are different from what we are considering.

Suppose that we have a number of more or less warm, more or less bulky objects, and we want to describe them. It does seem that the number of objects to be described can be multiplied indefinitely without bringing about difficulties in finding ways to describe their temperature and mass. Further, we can multiply indefinitely the number of physically measurable qualities of the objects that we want to describe without producing cases in which finding the right set of words will be a problem.

Is the source of the difficulty in description in the social sciences and history that what the social scientist or historian characteristically tries to describe is more complex than what the physicists describe? If so, then the word "complex" cannot have its normal meaning. For, if we make what is described by the physicist more complex, in the ordinary sense, by multiplying the number of objects and qualities to be described, we still do not introduce the kind of difficulties with which social scientists and historians labor.

The answer that the crucial difference is complexity, interpreted in the ordinary way, appears wrong. However, it may be that the correct answer is not far from this. The word "complex" might be intended to point toward the claim that what the social scientist or historian characteristically describes is in some sense "beyond" what one can describe in terms of measurements. A less misleading way of putting this claim is to speak of what the social scientist or historian describes as "richer" than what can be described in terms of measurements, rather than as "more complex." To understand this claim, we have to distinguish indisputable fact from supposition or extrapolation.

What is indisputable fact is this. The development of the physical sciences was made possible in part by systems of measurement. These made it possible to provide "objective" (in one sense) accounts of the objects to be described or explained. (The physicist professionally does not describe the immeasurable qualities of the objects he studies: he describes the weight of the painted canvas, but not its aesthetic properties) Systems of measurement are also available, to some extent, in the biological sciences, economics, and physiological psychology. They are available only in a very limited way in history and the social sciences (e.g., for dating, giving sizes of populations or electorates, or providing occupational distributions of various groups).

To this fact one can conjoin the following suppositions. The development of systems of measurement, in a much more thorough and satisfying way in some subjects than in others, cannot be viewed as an accident. It is not that the physicists got lucky. Nor is it the case that the genius of Western culture produced developments in that direction, and that in some other civilization the sociologists and historians might have systems of measurement as elaborate and satisfying as those the physicists enjoy in ours. Nor is it the case that, eventually, the balance will be righted, and that history, social psychology, and sociology will develop systems of measurement comparable to those in physics. Many social scientists, it is true, look forward to such a day, with a fervor comparable to that of messianic expectation. But we may extrapolate the differences under discussion, and say that what is now the case will continue to be at least roughly the case. These suppositions seem to me immensely plausible. It is not clear how they can be proved correct or incorrect. But they can be argued for, as follows.

If systems of measurement were to come to play the same role in history and the social sciences as in physics, one of two things would have come to be the case. Either the unmeasurable human activities which are described in the social sciences and history would have been "reduced" to what we now already can measure (e.g., perhaps neurophysiological activity), or in some independent way systems of measurement would have been developed for all or virtually all of what the social sciences and history describe.

One argument that human activities cannot be reduced to what we now already can measure parallels the argument, given in the last chapter, that states of mind cannot be reduced to neurophysiological states. In order to correlate two kinds of realities, or two kinds of data, we have to be able to classify precisely the items in both sets. We cannot correlate what is imprecise with what is precise, or reduce what is imprecise to what is precise. Therefore, since we cannot on the whole precisely describe human activities, we cannot reduce them to what we are now able to describe precisely.

A second argument is this. The subjects, such as history or sociology, in which systems of measurement play the most rudimentary role, are all subjects concerned with human purposive behavior. We might distinguish between these and other subjects on the basis of the character of what they describe. Behavior has meaning, in terms of the purposes or choices of agents, and as such is different from mere movement. D. W. Hamlyn has argued that descriptions of behavior must be regarded as "interpretative."[4] "No fixed criteria," he insists, "can be laid down which will enable us to decide what series of movements shall constitute 'posting a letter.'"[5] This suggests that descriptions of behavior (which are the heart of history and the social sciences), even though they of course are descriptions of something that involves movement, are not translatable into descriptions of movement. This again suggests the irreducibility of what the historian wants to say.

Some readers may feel that this argument misses the point. Behavior *is* movement. In a given case, to make an angry gesture *is* to move one's right arm one foot higher and eight inches forward, and so on. If everything about the body can be described precisely, in terms of the position and motion of bits of matter, why cannot behavior be described precisely? Admittedly, the descriptions would be uncomfortably complex and elaborate, and perhaps too complex and elaborate for us at present to be able to spell out; but in theory the precise descriptions would be attainable.

There is some truth to this objection. If any bodily change can in theory be described precisely, then in theory also any behavior can be described precisely, at least insofar as the behavior is bodily movement. But this is *not* to say that what the historian or social scientist has to say about behavior can be said precisely. It is much less enlightening to hear that a man moved his arm forward eight inches, and so on, than to hear that he made an angry gesture. The latter description, which transcends mere physics and belongs to the realm of the historian and the social scientist, introduces the element of classification and comparison. It is this vital added element that seemingly cannot be conveyed by specifications of movement. And, insofar as it implicitly includes meanings that demand this added element, a human action is not just movement.

If what is described in history and the social sciences cannot be reduced to what is described in the more precise disciplines, then why do not historians and social scientists develop independently their own methods of measurement, with perhaps an associated special terminology, in order to make their subjects more precise? Part of the answer is that they have tried: the efforts have been especially intense in some of the social sciences. The major result, however, has not been greater precision, but a kind of mock precision involved in the use of jargon.

The main argument, in short, that history and the social sciences cannot develop independently extensive systems of measurement for the most significant elements of their subject matter is that attempts have been made, and have been unsuccessful. This is not conclusive. But then no conclusive argument is possible in cases of this sort. How can one show that a proposed linguistic system is inadequate until one has seen it? A record of lack of success, while not conclusive, may provide the best evidence that we can have.

If the foregoing line of thought is correct, then the answer as to why greater precision is not forthcoming in history and the social sciences rests in brute fact. Some qualities (e.g., the temperature of an object, or the date of an event) lend themselves to measurement; others do not. Thus the answer to the question "Why cannot historians and social scientists be more precise?" may be "They just cannot be; that is all." If questioning continues, we can point out that historians and social scientists talk about human motivations and projects, as well as dates and population sizes. And the former topics do not admit of precise description (of the kind we are considering). Now, this could be alleged not to be an answer at all. If so, then the reply is that there is some point at which explanations must stop. A reasonable account will point out where this is.

If the precision of history and the social sciences is limited, then so is their objectivity, even if we assume a theoretical framework within which work is done. There is always room for alternative accounts, because no account (even one existing only in theory) ever can claim to consist of just the right words, involving just the right comparisons. If the heart of description in history and the social sciences consists of points of view, rather than measurement, then there is always room for new points of view.

This conclusion must not be misinterpreted. First, it does not mean that a subject, such as physics, that does have extensive systems of measurement is entirely objective. We have indicated that a number of worries and problems are bound up in discussions of "objectivity," and some of these worries and problems do occur in relation to physics. Physics at best has what we called "intratheoretic" objectivity.

Secondly, to say that history and the social sciences are not entirely objective is not to say that they are entirely the opposite of objective, or that in them anything goes.

Any practitioner in history or the social sciences knows that there are working standards of objectivity, which can rule out an account because of bias, preposterous causal claims, simple inaccuracy, or extreme imprecision of language. These standards in fact have a peculiar role in relation to the practice of historians and social scientists. They operate primarily as exclusionary. That is, standards of objectivity in practice operate primarily to demonstrate that certain accounts are unacceptable—"beyond the pale"—rather than positively to demonstrate that an account is *the* correct account of a set of human activities. The standards may determine that an account is acceptable, but only in relation to specified competitors.

Thus we can acknowledge that history and the social sciences are not entirely objective, in the sense of being able to produce optimal accounts only in the cases of human activities of the simplest sorts (and then only if a given theoretical framework is assumed). Yet they recognize that there are standards of objectivity that pervade these disciplines. The correct answer to the question "Can human activities be objectively described?" is "To some degree, but not entirely."

Notes

1. See J. Kupperman, *Ethical Knowledge* (London: George Allen & Unwin, 1970).

2. In the extensive literature on this, the classic work is T. S. Kuhn, *The Structure of Scientific Revolutions* (Chicago: University of Chicago Press, 1962).

3. The demonstration of this is owed to an unpublished lecture of J. L. Austin's.

4. D. W. Hamlyn, "Behaviour," in V. Chappell, ed., *The Philosophy of Mind* (Englewood Cliffs, N.J.: Prentice-Hall, 1962), p. 62.

5. Ibid., p. 63.

SUGGESTED FURTHER READING

The objectivity of history has been discussed prominently in the following recent works.

Danto, Arthur. *Analytical Philosophy of History.* Cambridge: Cambridge University Press, 1965.

Dray, William. *Philosophy of History.* Englewood Cliffs, N.J.: Prentice-Hall, 1964. Chap. 3 contains an especially clear and good discussion.

Gallie, W. B. *Philosophy and the Historical Understanding.* London: Chatto & Windus, 1964.

Mandelbaum, Maurice. *The Problem of Historical Knowledge.* New York: Harper Torchbooks, 1967. An extended attack on historical relativism.

Walsh, William. *Introduction to Philosophy of History.* London: Hutchinson, 1951. Chap. 5 contains an interesting and provocative discussion of the role of perspectives in history.

The following general books in philosophy of the social sciences are recommended.

Ryan, Alan. *The Philosophy of the Social Sciences.* London: Macmillan, 1970.

Winch, Peter. *The Idea of a Social Science.* London: Routledge & Kegan Paul, 1958.

9 Free Will

Free will is usually contrasted with determinism. It is assumed that if we are determined, we do not have free will, and vice versa. In what follows we can determine the legitimacy of this contrast. Then we can ask whether in fact we are determined, and whether we are free.

To say that we are determined is to say that, given the antecedent conditions of our actions, we can act in no way other than that in which we do act. Determinism, then, is the view that all human actions are determined by antecedent conditions, so that they could not be other than what they are. It is important, as we later shall explain, that the thesis of determinism maintains more than just that all of our actions are caused. It maintains that all of our actions are caused in such a way that, given antecedent conditions, they have to be what they are.

The standard contrast between free will and determinism rests on a line of reasoning something like the following. We *seem* to have free will: that is, we are frequently aware of making choices in cases in which more than one option appears to be genuinely open. However, there have been cases in which people have been willing to say that someone felt free, but in fact was not free. These are cases in which what seemed a free choice turned out to be utterly predictable.

In the 1950s, before it was generally recognized that drug addiction could be overcome by will power, exercised in appropriate living conditions, commentators often said that drug addicts were not free with respect to the drug habit, however they felt. The drug addict might feel himself to be in the process of making a choice whether to take the next dose of the drug, might feel both alternatives genuinely to be open, might say things like "Perhaps I won't"; but, according to these commentators, the fact that the addict's taking the next dose was entirely predictable meant that the "free will" in this case was an illusion. If we can know in advance what the addict will do, then the addict in fact is not exercising free will.

This kind of comment was made about an unusual and extreme case, that of drug addiction. Further, it is worth bearing in mind that there was some practical point to the comment. To say that someone is not exercising free will is to some extent to absolve that person of responsibility. It is also to rule out appeals to the person's good sense, or subtle forms of pressure; it places the person instead in the category of things to be managed. "So-and-so cannot help himself, so we must take care of him," it says.

Nevertheless, a conceptual point is involved: conduct that seems free is not free if it is entirely predictable. And what is a point only about extreme cases can be converted into a point about every case. Suppose that in five hundred years psychology advances to the point at which all human actions are entirely predictable by psychologists armed with the appropriate data and sophisticated computers. From this vantage point, it would appear that the only difference between the choice of the drug addict who genuinely cannot help himself and the choices we all make daily will be that in the former kind of case the outcome is easy to predict, and the factors that make the man act as he does are obvious. That prediction of what we choose is more difficult, and the determining factors less obvious, will not make our choices any more free. If psychology makes this kind of advance, in other words, the difference between us and the easily predictable drug addict will turn out to be just a matter of degree.

Thus the case for saying that determinism conflicts with free will runs as follows. In individual and unusual cases, nowadays, if we can recognize that someone's choice is determined, we deny that the choice is free. If this is generalized, if we come to be in the position to recognize everyone's choices as determined, we would deny that anyone's choices are free.

Does Determinism Conflict with the Ascription of Free Will?

The foregoing argument is not conclusive. Many philosophers would affirm both determinism—that all of our choices are determined—and free will. The opposite of freedom, they would say, is not predictability, but constraint. A man is not free if his hands are tied, or if there is a gun to his head; but if what he does is the result of his own unconstrained choice, then he has free will whether or not his choice is in fact entirely predictable.

One of the motivations for holding a view of this sort is to be found in the connection, already remarked upon, between characterizing a choice as free and ascribing responsibility to the person who makes the choice. In the 1950s when we denied that the drug addict had a free choice of whether to take drugs, we were also denying his responsibility. This may seem only just; but if psychologists eventually show that all of our choices are determined, do we then deny responsibility to everyone? This might seem unreasonable. In a future society in which every choice is known to be determined, we still might feel free to blame people, attempt to persuade them, appeal to their reason, and so on—all actions which presuppose that people are responsible for their behavior. Further, there would still be a point to blaming people, attempting to persuade them, appealing to their reason, and so on: even though it would be the case that we would be determined to do these things, and that these activities would be determined to have certain results, it also would be the case that the activities of blaming, persuading, and so on, would have a genuine causal impact on what people chose. They would have an impact, and thus there would be a point to them, and in that respect they would make sense.

An argument against regarding free will and determinism as opposites, in short, is the following. If everyone is determined, it still makes sense to treat people as responsible. If they are responsible, then they are free. We deny responsibility, and freedom, only in the cases in which there is constraint, as when a man has a gun to his head. In our common mode of judgment, someone can be spoken of as making free choices even if the choices are in fact determined.

Here we have an example of the kind of conflict about words that occurs frequently in philosophy. We have a strong tendency to equate freedom with lack of determinism, and thus to conclude that if we are determined we are not free. We also have a strong tendency to equate freedom with responsibility, and thus to conclude that if we are not free we are not responsible, and if we are responsible we are free. If we are given what look like strong theoretical reasons for asserting that we are determined, and at the same time have strong practical reasons for continuing to regard ourselves as (in most contexts) responsible, then it looks as if we have strong reasons both for regarding ourselves as not free and for regarding ourselves as free. This is like a neurotic conflict: its roots are deep, and it is difficult to get rid of.

One plausible move is to attempt to save the situation by insisting that there are multiple senses of "free" and "freedom." In one sense "free" means "undetermined"; and in this sense, and this sense alone, if we are determined, we are not free. In another sense "free" means "unconstrained"; and in this sense, even if we are determined, we may be free, and hence responsible.

Now, there is a great deal to be said for this way of putting matters. No doubt we do use words like "free" and "freedom" in multiple ways. What we mean by political freedom, for example, is quite different from what is in question when we discuss determinism. Even if we are determined, we may have political freedom. Also, when we say of a man that he is "free to leave the room," we mean something quite different from a denial of determinism.

Nevertheless, a case can be made for saying that, if we are determined, we also are constrained, at least in cases in which we might be alleged to be "responsible." Thus, if "free" is taken to mean "unconstrained," in this sense also, if we are determined, we are not free in cases in which we might be alleged to be responsible.

Consider again the case of the drug addict, as addicts were viewed in the 1950s. Once we come to believe that psychological and physiological factors are such that the addict's taking the next dose is entirely predictable, we also come to view these factors as constraining the addict. Once we assent, that is, to the proposition "Given factors X, subject Y has to do Z," we will say not only that factors X determine Y to do Z but also that they constrain Y to do Z.

Suppose that five hundred years from now psychologists score the complete success that we had imagined, and we are able to predict with entire certainty that subject Y will order pie with his next lunch. This prediction is based on computer data, comprising facts W about Y's heredity, environment, body metabolism, nervousness, greed, and so on. Then will we not say that factors W constrain Y to order the pie? They make him do it in the same sense as that in which factors X constrained the drug addict: because of them, it was inevitable that the subject acted as he did.

There is a complication here that is worth pointing out. We might be a shade more hesitant in speaking about "constraint" in some cases than in others. The word "constraint" is at home in cases in which the subject might well have had some wish, or should have had some wish, to do the opposite of what he or she did. Thus we are comfortable in speaking of constraint in the case of the drug addict because we think that the addict either might well have had some wish not to take the drug, or should have had such a wish. In the case of the pie eater of the future, we similarly would feel most comfortable in speaking about constraint if the subject was overweight, or had some other good reason not to eat the pie. If the subject was thin, and eating the pie was entirely harmless, it might seem a trifle strange to speak of constraint. But in this kind of case we will not speak of "responsibility" either. We speak of responsibility only in cases in which the subject might well have had some wish, or should have had some wish, to act differently.

The fact remains, under our hypothesis, that even the thin pie eater had to eat the pie, given the antecedent conditions, and that these conditions made him eat the pie. We have to say this much, even if we do not wish to use the word "constraint" in the case of the thin pie eater. In any case in which we might wish to ascribe responsibility, and to claim that Y can be held responsible for Z, we would also use the word "constraint." The reason the overweight pie eater did not pass up the pie (even though he should have), or why his momentary wish to pass up the pie was ineffective, was that factors W constrained him to eat the pie.

All of this follows if we are determined. Probably the most reasonable thing to say is this: there are *some* senses in which we can be said to be free even if we are determined. We can be politically free, and we can be free in the (related) sense of being not coerced. (To say that we are not coerced is to say that external factors do not have a primary role in determining what we do.) If psychology advances over the next five hundred years in the manner imagined, we would have to adjust our ways of speaking; there would be more than one option in our doing this. We could decide, for practical reasons, to speak of people as "responsible" in certain situations if they were free in the sense of being uncoerced. Thus the overweight pie eater and the drug addict, not to mention the criminal, would be spoken of as "free" in the sense of "uncoerced," and thereby responsible. Alternatively, we could sever the general connection between speaking of people as "free" in some sense and speaking of them as responsible, and could decide instead to speak of people as responsible if and only if pressure from us might change their conduct. In this case, we would hold the ordinary criminal to be responsible, but perhaps would not hold the drug addict to be responsible; a decision on the overweight pie eater might depend on empirical investigation. However we decided to speak about "responsibility," and whatever senses of the word "free" we resorted to, there would remain a primary sense of the word "free" in which, if we are determined, we are not free. It is clear that, historically, this is the sense of "free" that philosophers generally had in mind when they spoke of "free will." Therefore, we can say that determinism does conflict with the claim that we have free will.

But are we determined? The major reason given in recent years for maintaining that we are has been an optimistic view of the future of psychology, and of the social sciences in general, of the sort outlined above. This has obvious links with the optimistic views attacked in chapters 7 and 8. We can examine now whether there are grounds for being skeptical of the optimistic view of the future ability of social scientists to predict with certainty any human action.

Is Determinism True?

Consider this puzzle. "There can and should be causal sciences of human society: why do they (except to a limited extent in economics) still not exist?"[1] The question can be extended beyond the sciences of human society so as to include psychology as a putative science of the human personal sphere. In what follows I shall provide a partial solution to the puzzle, which will also serve as a basis for a negative view of the prospects of the development of psychology and other social sciences to provide a basis for determinism. This will amount to a case against determinism.

The anti-determinist argument is, in outline, the following. The kinds of scientific laws that determinism requires are possible only if we can describe precisely the entities and events governed by these laws. Since, as was argued in the last two chapters, it is by and large not possible in the social sciences to have extensive precise description of what we most want to understand and predict, the kinds of scientific laws that determinism requires are by and large not possible in the social sciences. Therefore determinism fails: it fails because, as a matter of fact, the subject matter of the social sciences lacks the characteristics that would make the application of a deterministic account possible.

An analogy might be found in the reasoning that has convinced physicists that they cannot predict with certainty the behavior of individual elementary particles. They cannot make such predictions because, in the first place, it is impossible to describe precisely both the position and energy of the particle at a given time. One commentator speaks of the "older view" that "electrons are in precisely defined states but that we (because of our crude techniques of investigation) cannot know what these states are; *we* cannot define them precisely although they *are* precisely defined." This older view seeks, he says, "what no physical theory can hope for—a knowledge of nature that transcends what our best hypotheses and experiments suggest."[2]

Because "in quantum mechanics there exists no concept of 'the exact state of the microparticle,'" all laws within quantum mechanics are "irreducibly probabilistic. . . . Therefore, it becomes a reasonable metaphysical possibility that nature is fundamentally indeterministic."[3] It should be pointed out that we can give some *rough* description of both the position and energy of a particle at a given time: for example, we can describe the energy and say, "It is somewhere in this building." What is declared impossible by current physical theory is a precise description of both position and energy. And from limitations on our ability to describe, there follow limitations on our ability to predict.

I should stress that this sketch of the case for indeterminism in quantum physics is presented as, at best, analogous to the case against determinism in the social sciences. It is not being presented as the foundation of a case against determinism in the social sciences. And it certainly is not being presented as the foundation of a case for saying that human beings are free.

Someone might suggest the following. We are made up of elementary particles. If the behavior of elementary particles cannot be predicted with certainty, then our behavior cannot be predicted with certainty. However, it does not follow, from the fact that the behavior of individual elementary particles cannot be predicted with certainty, that the behavior of very large conglomerations of elementary particles cannot be predicted. Indeterminism on the level of individual elementary particles does not entail indeterminism on the level of human-sized objects. There is, for one thing, the possibility that the activities of the particles whose individual behavior cannot be predicted with certainty do not yield independent variables, so that even though we cannot be certain whether one particle among a very large number will go to the left or the right, we can be certain that between 49 and 51 percent of the total will go to the right. Even if the activities of individual particles do provide independent variables, so that there is a minute possibility that a human being will do something very strange and unexpected on the basis of a large number of elementary particles in the human being's brain unexpectedly all behaving in the same way, this would not create a case for a very full-blooded indeterminism as applied to the activities of human beings. Someone who wants to deny the thesis of determinism, as applied to human behavior, is unlikely to be satisfied by the statement that, while human behavior is predictable with virtually complete certainty, there is always a one-in-a-zillion chance (but no more) that the prediction will turn out to be false. It certainly seems possible to arrive at a stronger denial than this of the determinist view of human behavior.

There is a further complication, which we need not explore at this point. Even if we could show that human actions were functions of the activities of elementary particles, and were undetermined for this reason, it can be objected that this indeterminism does not constitute freedom. To act randomly is hardly the same thing as being free. Because of this, some writers have gone so far as to argue that freedom, far from being incompatible with determinism, actually requires it.[4] This is a second reason for holding that the thesis that human beings have free will is not derivable from indeterminism in quantum physics. It also raises a point that we shall have to deal with later; after we provide our own argument for holding that determinism regarding human behavior is false, we shall have to argue that we are free in a sense which does not imply that we act randomly.

The case against determinism is not that we are made up of elementary particles, whose states cannot be described precisely; it is that our states, like the states of elementary particles, cannot be described precisely, and that the imprecision goes much deeper, and has much more significance, than the imprecision of possible descriptions of elementary particles in our brains. Even on a macroscopic level, we elude precise description. At least, some facets of us elude precise description. On the macroscopic level our bodies can be described precisely, at least in many respects (we can be precise about height and weight, but not about posture and facial expression). If the neodualist account argued in chapter 7 is correct, we have minds; and a great deal of what is mental cannot be described precisely.

Suppose that we consider the state of Julius Caesar, deciding whether to cross the Rubicon. A great deal about Julius Caesar could be described precisely: his blood pressure, his gene structure, how many troops he thinks he has, and so on. Other things cannot be described precisely: the way he looks when he is facing toward Rome, his mood, his attitude toward Pompey. How could we, on the basis of a description of Caesar's state, and other antecedent factors, predict with entire certainty what his decision would be?

There are only two ways in which this might be possible. One is that it could turn out that the only relevant causal factors are those that we can describe precisely, such as Caesar's blood pressure, gene structure, neuron firings in the brain, and so on. We then might be able to produce laws connecting these factors to what Caesar does. In this event, we might speak of such factors as Caesar's mood as irrelevant to science, meaning that the mood is real enough, but that it does not play any role in the causal chain of events.

To take this line is to claim that what human beings do is a function of physiology, and related physical and chemical facts about the situations they are in, only. Now, this is possibly correct; but what must be said is that there is no reason whatsoever, at this stage in the development of human knowledge, to think that it is correct. To the contrary, our moods and feelings seem to affect what we do. That is, it often seems that we act in a certain way because, in large part, we are in a certain mood or feel a certain way.

It was argued in chapter 7 that no strict correlation can be produced between mental items (with some, on the whole unimportant, exceptions) and physiological items. If moods and feelings do affect what we do, and if we cannot replace them by physiological items in accounts of why we do what we do, then it is false that we can regard what human beings do as a function of physiological, physical, and chemical facts only.

The second possibility is that we somehow produce deterministic causal laws which enable us to say that, given Caesar's genes, moods, and so on, along with various other facts about the situation, he was certain to cross the Rubicon. To arrive at such causal laws is the dream of many psychologists. Many philosophers, also, have faith that such laws ultimately will be found.

But how can they be? If Caesar's mood and feelings are genuine causal factors, then it must make a difference whether we describe Caesar's mood and feelings before his decision as X and Y, rather than W and Z, or A and B. We must know, further, that mood X has in general a certain causal impact, which mood W or mood A would not have. In order to know this, we must be able to arrive at causal laws of the form "Mood X, in conjunction with other factors D, E, and F, produces action Q." But how can such laws be arrived at?

One of two conditions would have to be met. Either it would have to turn out that we can know that certain moods, and only certain moods, count as mood X. This requires an objective and precise use of the label "X." Or, if we cannot attain this precision, we would have to know that any mood that might with some plausibility be labeled "X" produces, when in conjunction with factors D, E, and F, action Q. The first condition cannot generally be met, as was argued in chapter 7. What of the second condition?

The answer is that in some cases the second condition can be met, but in a way which leaves further difficulties. Suppose we say this: in conditions which include the offer of a better paying job elsewhere, if a man is in a mood that could be termed anger (i.e., that is anger or something like anger), he will quit his job. Here we have a causal law of the kind we need. But what of the kind of mood that, with the same associated factors, will lead to his not quitting his job? Perhaps we can say that if his mood is one of enthusiastic loyalty, then, in the conditions specified, he will not quit his job. But what if his mood is one that could be described as amused and affectionate irritation with his boss, and could also be described as one of slight unease, or one of uncomfortable involvement, or simply as one of irritation? How do we predict what will result from this difficult to describe intermediate kind of mood?

The point is this. It may be possible (although even this is debatable) to arrive at some causal laws of the sort desired: causal laws describing combinations of moods and conditions in which it is guaranteed that a person will quit a job, move house, or behave in various other ways. But even if we could arrive at absolutely reliable predictions in certain extreme or easy kinds of cases, that does not mean that we could arrive at absolutely reliable predictions in every case. If anyone in a mood that could be described as X, in conditions D, E, and F, will do Q, then what of the person in a mood that could not normally be described as X, but is not totally unlike what would normally be described as X? Even if we can predict with certainty in some cases that a man will do Q, we will not be able to predict with certainty in every case whether or not a man will do Q, unless we can draw precisely the boundary between the kind of mood that in those conditions leads to Q, and the kind of mood that in those conditions does not.

Thus our previous analysis of the precision of language that can describe such things as moods implies that the first condition for causal laws of behavior cannot be met, and that, even if the second condition is met, it still will be impossible for us to arrive at a comprehensive set of causal laws of behavior that will allow us to predict all human actions with certainty.

The upshot of the argument is this. If moods and feelings genuinely are uneliminable causal factors of human action, and if moods and feelings cannot be described precisely, then determinism is false.

Freedom and Causation

Does the falsity of determinism imply that we are free? Here we must confront a difficulty mentioned earlier. To deny determinism might be taken as an assertion that we act randomly. But random action can hardly be considered free action. Indeed, our conception of free action is such that we normally do not consider an action of ours free unless it is in some sense really *our* action. But an action is not really our action unless it is caused by, among other things, something in us. If determinism is false, then, it might be hard to see how we could be free.

In order to see through this difficulty, it is important to become clear about a relevant distinction. This is the distinction between saying that factors X cause Y, and saying that factors X determine Y to happen.

The distinction is neatly illustrated by a claim sometimes made about psychoanalytic explanation. According to some schools of psychoanalysis, all of our actions are determined by psychic antecedents; this is said even of seemingly random actions or slips of the tongue. If a man is asked to pick a number between one and ten, the psychoanalyst, after suitable examination, will be able to explain why he chose the number he did. But, it has been said, if the patient had picked a different number, or if he goes on to choose a second time, the psychoanalyst will be able to find a cause for the choice of that number also. Thus there are assignable causes for more than one alternative. If X causes Y, but W was available to cause Z (Z being different from Y), it becomes far from clear that X *determines* Y to happen. To find the cause of an action need not be to find something which determined that action to be performed. Thus a philosopher can reject determinism but yet agree that there is no action without a cause. Indeed, as Jean-Paul Sartre has remarked, "To speak of an act without a cause is to speak of an act which would lack the intentional structure of every act . . ."[5]

Sartre's view is that the cause of one of our actions is constituted as a cause by the value we place on it. It becomes a cause because we regard it as such, and act accordingly. Thus fatigue causes one man to rest, because he takes his fatigue seriously and acts accordingly; another man might press on without resting. An unfortunate childhood might cause one man to steal, because he regards certain incidents of childhood as disturbing in a way that justifies theft; another man with much the same background might shrug off these incidents, and not steal.

Sartre also claims that we are aware of a spontaneity in our own activities, and of an openness that allows for more than one choice in any situation. This awareness is "phenomenological": it is awareness of the structure of our experience. Phenomenological evidence is not scientific evidence: it does not involve scientific apparatus, or observation of the world around us, since it is obtained by what might broadly be termed an introspective (and also an analytical) process. But this seems not to be a conclusive reason for disregarding phenomenological evidence. If we have an independent reason (the one given at some length above) for concluding that determinism is false, and if the question then arises as to how we can be said to be free if there are no determining causes of our actions, there seems no compelling reason not to rely on Sartre's phenomenological evidence to solve our difficulties.

Thus we can say this: every human action Y has a cause, or set of causes, X. We have argued, on the basis of the fact that such things as moods and feelings appear to be uneliminable causes of human action, and that they cannot be described precisely, that determinism as a general theory is false. To say that X caused Y is not to say that, if X occurred, Y had to occur. That Y occurs, and that X is constituted as the cause of Y, both come to be true as a result of human choice. We can experience ourselves as making choices, and there is no reason to disregard this experience.

Our choices, at least for the most part, are not determined; but for all that, the actions that result are not random occurrences. The actions are caused, and in a great many cases we can predict that they will probably be performed. In some cases (e.g., perhaps those of certain drug addicts, or extremely angry people), but not in all cases, we may be able to predict an action with certainty. In the normal kind of case, in which we cannot predict an action with certainty, it still will be true that the action can have its reasons, as well as its cause, and the agent can experience the action as having originated from a causal complex that includes his or her decision. This is far different from the random behavior of elementary particles.

None of this amounts to proof that we are free and not determined. However, it does, I think, amount to a very strong argument— one that places the burden of proof on the shoulders of the determinist. The determinist needs more than a utopian view of the future progress of the social sciences. The determinist needs solid evidence that the hoped-for progress can actually take place. The issue is one of facts: facts about us, and also about the future of the social sciences. On the basis of present evidence, and the conclusions about language that have been argued for, it appears to be a fact that people have free will.

Notes

1. J. L. Mackie, "The Inductive Process," *Times Literary Supplement*, March 7, 1975, p. 257.

2. N. R. Hanson, "Quantum Mechanics, Philosophical Implications of," in *Encyclopedia of Philosophy*, ed. P. Edwards (New York: Macmillan, 1967), Vol. 7, p. 44, Hanson's italics.

3. Ibid., p. 46.

4. See for example R. E. Hobart, "Free Will as Involving Determinism and Inconceivable without It," in *Free Will and Determinism*, ed. B. Berofsky (New York: Harper & Row, 1966).

5. J. P. Sartre, *Being and Nothingness*, trans. Hazel Barnes (New York: Philosophical Library, 1956), pp. 436-437.

SUGGESTED FURTHER READING

The debate between proponents of determinism and of free will has received much attention from contemporary philosophers. The following are good collections of essays on this subject.

Berofsky, Bernard, ed. *Free Will and Determinism.* New York: Harper & Row, 1966.

Dworkin, Gerald, ed. *Determinism, Freedom, and Moral Responsibility.* Englewood Cliffs, N.J.: Prentice-Hall, 1970.

Honderich, Ted, ed. *Essays on Freedom of Action.* Boston: Routledge & Kegan Paul, 1973.

Lehrer, Keith, ed. *Freedom and Determinism.* New York: Random House, 1966.

Morgenbesser, Sidney, and James Walsh, eds. *Free Will.* Englewood Cliffs, N.J.: Prentice-Hall, 1962.

The following contain extended statements on the issue.

Holbach, Baron d'. *The System of Nature*, trans. H. Robinson. New York: Burt Franklin, 1970. Chaps. 11 and 12 contain a defense of determinism.

Berofsky, Bernard. *Determinism*. Princeton: Princeton University Press, 1971. A defense of determinism.

Sartre, Jean-Paul. *Being and Nothingness*, trans. Hazel Barnes. New York: Philosophical Library, 1956. Sartre claims that a careful analysis of the difference between human and inanimate reality shows that we must be free. The beginner should not be deterred by the difficulty of Sartre's introduction. The book becomes steadily more accessible.

10 The Existence of God

The history of philosophical discussions of the existence of God has to be understood in relation to the historical character of philosophy in general. Philosophy has frequently been regarded as the ultimate bastion of rationalism—the area of knowledge (besides mathematics) in which reason, with little or no outside assistance, could solve major problems. Thus a very common traditional approach to the existence of God has been in terms of proof. Philosophical discussion of God has tended to center on the issues of whether and how the existence of God could be proven.

The proofs of the existence of God that have been offered, criticized, and debated by philosophers can be divided broadly into two categories: those in which reason requires no outside assistance (e.g., the proof proceeds simply from a definition of what we mean by "God"), and those in which there is minimal outside assistance (the proof proceeds from factual evidence, but the factual evidence is familiar and readily available to all without special effort). The model for proofs of the first type is mathematical; for those of the second type it is armchair science, of the sort that was more common before the ascent of the experimental method during the Renaissance.

Proofs of God's Existence

The prototype of the first kind of proof was propounded by St. Anselm, an eleventh-century theologian. St. Anselm, in his *Proslogium*, defines God as "something than which nothing greater can be conceived." That is, the meaning of the term "God" is that it refers to the most perfect being imaginable. This "something than which nothing greater can be conceived" exists as an object of thought; that is, we can have this idea. Even if our conception of God is different from, and of something more finite than, the traditional Judeo-Christian conception, we can manage to have the idea of "something than which nothing greater can be conceived." Thus, though St. Anselm's definition articulates a particular conception of God, a Judeo-Christian one, this does not provide an objection to the proof. As long as we have the idea he refers to, we cannot object to the start of the proof. What is crucial is whether the existence of the being than which nothing greater can be conceived can be proved; whether it is, finally, referred to as God, or by some other name such as Zizzzl, is immaterial.

Anselm argues that the being than which nothing greater can be conceived must exist in extramental reality, as well as in thought, because otherwise we would be able to conceive of a greater being (a being just like it except that we conceive of it as existing in extramental reality). In other words, if Anselm's God does not exist, then (he argues) we would be able to conceive a being greater than the being than which nothing greater can be conceived. This is a contradiction, an absurdity. In mathematical proofs, a familiar way of proving that something is the case is to prove that its denial leads to an absurdity. In the same way, if denying the existence of God leads to an absurdity, then God must exist.

Two things must be noticed immediately about St. Anselm's proof. The first is that, as was suggested earlier, the model clearly is proofs in mathematics. This is not to say that Anselm's proof is in some sense mathematical, or that God is being viewed as in some sense mathematical. It is simply that the pattern of the proof and what is expected of it correspond to what someone who had taken, say, a course in Euclidean geometry would thereby find familiar. Mathematics traditionally is the area in which, most visibly, reason reigns supreme, and the work of experience is limited to preparing the scene before the curtain goes up. Reason alone tells us that the Pythagorean theorem (which concludes that the square of the longest side of a right triangle equals the sum of the squares of the other two sides) is valid, and it would be mad to attempt to establish the theorem by taking measurements of sample triangles around the world. In the same way, St. Anselm is claiming that reason alone can tell us that God—the being than which nothing greater can be conceived—exists. In some remarks St. Anselm qualifies this somewhat: the reason required to realize that God must exist itself requires faith. Perhaps it is that we shall be blind and stupid on this issue unless we have the proper background of faith. But with this qualification, in St. Anselm's view the existence of God can be determined by reason alone, just as the conclusion of Pythagoras's theorem requires reason alone.

The second point is that St. Anselm's proof incorporates a crucial assumption: that a being which was otherwise perfect but existed only in thought would somehow be less great, or less perfect, than a being which was like it but existed in extramental reality as well as in thought. This assumption is at the heart of the proof. The crucial argument, after all, is that if God did not exist (i.e., did not exist in extramental reality), this imagined God would be less great than something which was like God but which we conceive to exist in extramental reality, and therefore a God which did not exist would not be the greatest being conceivable—thus contradicting the original definition, and showing that to assume that God does not exist leads to a contradiction.

The comparison of an unreal God with a real God, however, is mind-boggling. How could we decide which is greater? And what sense can the comparison make?

St. Anselm's crucial assumption would appear to make sense only if we think of God, if God does not exist, as having a kind of being even while lacking (extramental) reality. If we reason this way, it becomes tempting to think of the hypothetical God who does not exist as being inferior to, or less great than, a comparable being that does exist.

But this in turn requires the following view. God and other beings must be thought of as having various qualities, which we may call predicates. A man, for example, may have the predicates of being twenty years old, six feet tall, good at mathematics, named Smith, and so on. God has the predicates of being all-knowing, benevolent, just, merciful, and so on. Predicates that it is good to have may be spoken of as perfections. Thus Smith's perfections include being good at mathematics. God's include being all-knowing, benevolent, just, merciful, and so on. In addition, to have extramental reality is, at least for a basically good being, a perfection. Thus Smith is more perfect if he exists than if he does not. Once we accept this view, it may seem intuitively clear that what is defined as the being than which nothing greater can be conceived must exist (extramentally), since not to have extramental reality would be to lack a further perfection, or aspect of greatness, which that being imaginably might have had.

But should this view be accepted? It was challenged vigorously by Kant, and subsequently by many others. The argument is that the function of the word "exists" is not to add to the description of what we are talking about, but rather to posit that something in reality corresponds to our words. When we say that Smith exists, we are not reporting one more interesting, or not so interesting, feature of what Smith is like. Rather we are saying something quite different: that there is a Smith, not just in the pages of a book but in the real world. In the same way, we may praise God by speaking of God as omniscient, omnipotent, and so on; but we are not praising God by saying that God exists; rather we are claiming that the being we have been talking about is "out there."

If this challenge is correct, then existence is not a predicate. And if existence is not a predicate, it is not a good predicate. Hence it cannot be argued that a God possessing extramental reality would be greater, or more perfect, than one lacking extramental reality: the two lists of good qualities, or aspects of greatness, could be the same.

It should be stressed that even if the foregoing challenge leads one to reject St. Anselm's type of argument, this does not imply that God does not exist. There are still two other alternatives. One is that God exists, but that God's existence cannot be proven. The other is that God's existence can be proven, but not in the manner of St. Anselm's attempt. This latter alternative has been embraced by a number of thinkers, notably St. Thomas Aquinas.

St. Thomas is the most prominent exponent of a type of argument for the existence of God known as the "cosmological argument." Cosmological arguments, or proofs, are unlike St. Anselm's in that they do draw from experience. However, what they draw from experience is highly general, and available, facts about the world. Reason does not do all of the work, as it did for St. Anselm, but it does almost all of the work.

In the *Summa Theologica* St. Thomas set forth five "ways" to reach rational conviction of the existence of God. The first three of these proofs generally are termed cosmological. The first argues from the general fact that there is motion in the world; the second from the general fact that there are causes and effects in the world, and the assumption that every event has a cause; and the third from the fact that there are contingent realities in the world (things that exist but imaginably might not have existed).

The First Way of St. Thomas may be summarized as follows. What is in motion must have been set in motion by something else, and that something else must have been set in motion by something else, and so on. We can continue backwards, discovering the moving source of motion of the moving source of motion of the moving source of motion, and so on, of the motion that we see. But there cannot be an infinite variety of steps backward. Therefore there must have been a first mover, a being whose nature is so special that it can be an unmoved mover. This unmoved mover is God. God can be spoken of as a first cause, although, strictly speaking, since he is outside of time, he is outside of the series of events he causes.

We may note briefly that there are at least two questionable assumptions in play here. One is that motion must always have a source. Perhaps this is true of all the motion that we see now, but must it have been true of all motion always, including the motion at the beginning of the world? Some might contend that the first motion in the world would have been so special an event—so different from what we normally see—that it could count as an exception to this generalization. The other questionable assumption is that which rules out the infinite variety of steps backward. Why cannot there be an infinite regress of this kind? It is not *prima facie* evident that the notion of a world without a beginning is self-contradictory. Certainly one would want to see this assumption proved.

Much the same comments can be made about St. Thomas's Second Way, in which he argues that every event must have a cause, so that we can inquire as to the cause of the cause of the cause, and so on, of the events we see. But there cannot be an infinite regress. Therefore there must be a special first cause, which does not itself need a cause. This *causa sui* is God.

Again we might wonder how far we rationally are entitled to generalize. There are philosophical difficulties involved in determining what we mean by saying that every event has a cause: what is a cause? But even if we put these to the side, and agree also that every event that we perceive has a cause, can we assume that every event in the history of the world has had a cause? Can we assume this of the special events at the beginning of the world? And we can wonder again how St. Thomas can be rationally certain that there cannot be an infinite regress. What may have seemed intuitively obvious to St. Thomas may not be intuitively obvious to others, and one would like to see proof.

The Third Way proceeds as follows. The things that we experience are contingent: they are capable of not existing; they come into being and pass away. But if everything were of this character, then there would have been a time when nothing at all existed. But had there been such a time, then nothing would have come into existence, and there would be nothing even now. Therefore there must be something the existence of which is necessary, that is, which in its nature has to exist, and which does not come into being or pass away. So there is at least one necessary being. The necessity of necessary beings cannot, in every case, be caused by some other being; hence there must be one necessary being that is the source of its own necessity. This is God.

It is not clear, however, that a world in which all beings were contingent would be a world in which there once was nothing. Why could there not have been an infinite succession of contingent realities, or a collection of contingent realities that flickered in and out of existence? And, even if there once was nothing, why would that imply that nothing now would exist? Why, that is, need we assume that from nothing comes only nothing?

The doubts that one may entertain of the Third Way are related to those relevant to the first two Ways. For example, St. Thomas can rule out the possibility that there has been an infinite set of contingent realities only by denying that there could be an infinite regress (of contingent realities). To doubt the correctness of St. Thomas's denial of the latter is to doubt the correctness of his denial of the former. The assumption that a contingent reality could not have come out of nothing has intuitive links with the general assumption that every event (including, presumably, any primal existence of a contingent reality) must have a cause. If this general assumption is doubted, it becomes less clear that one should assume that only nothing can come from nothing.

The Fourth and Fifth Ways, although they are not cosmological, share with the first three the same degrees of reliance on experience and on intuitively appealing assumptions. The Fourth Way argues that we find in the world degrees of various kinds of perfection, and that these gradations imply a maximum. Just as fire is the maximum of heat, and thereby (in some sense) its cause, so also God is the maximum and cause of the perfections we see in the world. Those acquainted with the mathematics of limits may be especially qualified to question the assumption that any perfection must have a maximum. The Fifth Way argues that there is design in the world, and thus there must have been an intelligent designer. To many this may seem an especially appealing argument (about which we shall say more later). But it is not *a priori* certain that useful patterns cannot be the result of accident, rather than of intelligent design.

A fair comment on St. Thomas's proofs might be this: they are ingenious and plausible, and it is possible to maintain that they are valid. However, a very strong case can be made for saying that none of them is valid, on the grounds that in every case key assumptions themselves require proof. A plausible argument that appeals to what seems intuitively right is not thereby a proof: there are stricter standards for what counts as proof, even if we are talking about "proof" in the natural sciences or concerning everyday realities.

If we are justified in rejecting the proofs of both St. Anselm and St. Thomas, then there is room for the following two comments. First, it should be stressed again that their defeat—if it is a defeat—is not a defeat for the forces of religion, but rather for the forces of rationalism in religion. If, in fact, there is no valid proof of the existence of God, that does not in any way preclude God's existence; it merely precludes the attempt to extend the territory of reason to such matters as the existence of God. This is the conclusion that has been drawn by some extremely devout opponents of unbridled reason in religion. Secondly, it is possible to argue that the failure of proofs is not a defeat for the forces of rationalism in religion, but merely a check. It can be argued that to say that the existence of God cannot be proved is not to say that reason is totally useless in relation to the existence of God.

In order to understand the latter position, we have to distinguish among three ways in which rational considerations can be relevant to a conclusion. First, in some cases it is possible to prove a conclusion in a narrow sense of "proof." That is, in these cases it is possible to begin from correct premises and to construct an inference such that, if the premises are correct, the conclusion must be correct. This is the procedure of mathematics and of deductive logic, and the procedure that St. Anselm hoped to bring into relation to the existence of God.

Secondly, there is a broader sense of "proof," which comes into play in cases in which considerations are adduced which are such that any reasonable person could be confident of the correctness of a conclusion on the basis of these considerations, even though it is not logically impossible that the premises of the argument are correct and the conclusion false. For example, you can "prove" to a man that it is raining by having him look outside and then put his head outside the window (so that he can feel the raindrops falling). This is not proof in the first sense, and it remains logically possible that the man's statement of the evidence ("It looked like rain, and drops of water fell on my head") could be true and yet the conclusion false. But in normal circumstances this logical possibility is not something one dwells upon, and the man to whom you have proved that it is raining in the manner described can reasonably be confident of it. We do speak of this presentation of very strong evidence as "proof." The general run of proofs in the natural sciences or concerning everyday realities are of this character.

Thirdly, there are cases in which it is impossible to prove something even in the broader sense—the evidence or arguments are not strong enough to entitle a reasonable person to be entirely confident of the conclusion—but yet there are arguments or pieces of evidence which provide a rational basis for a conclusion. There may, for example, be evidence which would entitle a reasonable person to believe that it was raining on a certain day five hundred years ago. That is, the evidence would make it more reasonable to believe that it was raining then it would have been if the evidence did not exist, and one could cite the evidence as one's basis for so believing; but the evidence was so fragmentary that there was room for reasonable doubt on the matter (and, indeed, the evidence might be so fragmentary, or mixed in character, that the case might be one in which, as we say, reasonable people can disagree).

Even if it is agreed that rational considerations are not relevant to the existence of God in either of the first two ways, this does not rule out the third kind of relevance. Even if we cannot prove (in either the narrow or broad sense) the existence of God, we might decide that there is evidence, or are considerations, to make it more reasonable to conclude that God exists than that God does not. Clearly the third division here covers a great deal of territory. We might conclude that the evidence rationally justifies a high degree of confidence in the existence of God, or, at the opposite extreme, that it lends only slight support. The territory left to faith is also variable, as is the territory actually occupied by faith. One person might conclude that the rational evidence lends only slight support to the conclusion that God exists, but nevertheless have enormous confidence that God exists, because of faith. Another, reviewing the evidence and his or her own spiritual state, might conclude that there is only slight rational support and very little faith besides, or considerable rational support and entire faith.

Religious Evidence

Two kinds of evidence that have been adduced with considerable plausibility as relevant to the existence of God are (1) the order in the world, and (2) the goodness, or lack of goodness, of events in the world. Ever since St. Augustine spoke of "God's daily miracles," it has struck many people that the regularity to be found in such matters as sunrises and sunsets, and the structures found in such things as snowflakes and human cells, provided signs of God's work. Something like this is the basis of St. Thomas's Fifth Way; and, even if the Fifth Way does not amount to proof, it can be claimed to be an argument of some strength.

The regularity of the world has seemed even more striking since David Hume showed in the eighteenth century that one could not prove (at least in the first sense of "prove") that the sun would rise tomorrow. Recent biological discoveries have also made it seem something of a miracle that the structures required for animal life came together in the primeval ooze. It is very tempting to argue that there are too many unexplained cosmic coincidences unless one posits a God who is responsible for the regularity of things, and for life.

On the other hand, at least since the Book of Job was conceived, people have been struck by the suffering and misfortune in a world supposedly ruled over by a good God. If God exists, and is perfectly good, how does one account for earthquakes, fires, wars, cancer, plagues, and so on? This is known as the "problem of evil," and it is a problem for any religion, such as Judaism, Christianity, or Islam, that posits the omnipotence of an all-good God. It is not a problem for religions, such as the Zoroastrianism of ancient Persia, which deny the omnipotence of a good God.

Traditionally, believers have explained much of the evil and suffering in the world in terms of free will. The argument runs something like this. True virtue is enormously valuable. But true virtue requires free will: there is no real merit in a compelled or automatic right choice. Thus God created humanity with free will. Furthermore, free will is meaningless, and in fact not really free, if people always make the right choices. For there to be free will, and hence true virtue, there must be a situation in which people freely make the wrong choices: there must be sin and vice. Sin and vice exist for there to be the greater good of true virtue.

This reasoning is designed to reconcile the hypothesis of divine providence with the fact of human wickedness. It can be used to explain why there are wars, murders, muggings, and so on. Further, it can be used to explain why wicked people sometimes seem, throughout their entire lives, to be enormously successful and contented, and why virtuous people are sometimes extremely unsuccessful and miserable to the day that they die. If virtue always visibly triumphed and vice always visibly failed, the argument runs, there would be little difficulty, and hence not much merit, in being virtuous; ordinary prudence would suffice. Only in a world in which wickedness often visibly triumphs and virtue often brings misery, can virtue represent a serious challenge. Only in such a world, indeed, can virtue have real meaning and real value.

This general line of argument has more force in explaining wars, murders, and muggings than it does in explaining earthquakes, cancer, and plagues. The former can be assigned to man's free will, but hardly the latter.

Still, it can be argued that earthquakes, cancer, and plagues form part of the challenge that makes it difficult, and therefore especially meritorious, to be virtuous. In the Book of Job, Job's virtue is represented as especially meritorious in that he rose above the deaths of his children, painful boils that covered his body, and so on: these too had a role to play in making possible the heights of Job's probity. We may want to complain, as Job complained; but, it has been argued, if we could appreciate the over-all design of the universe, we would see the function of all of these things.

Since we human beings cannot perceive the over-all design of the universe, this answer is irrefutable. We may be left with doubts, though. Even if natural evils, as well as human wickedness, are required by God as challenges to human virtue, need there be as much evil as there is? Would not life be amply challenging to the virtuous even if, say, cancer did not exist? Perhaps human wickedness is required if there is human free will, and perhaps there must be *some* calamities of nonhuman origin to add to the challenge, but need there be as many natural evils as there are? It is often said that the evils in the world are like shadows in a well-constructed picture, which serve to set off the bright spots and enhance one's appreciation of the whole. But need there be so many shadows? The God powerful enough to bring good out of evil is powerful enough to bring good out of good.

It is characteristic of appeals to the order in the world, or to the goodness or evil in the world, as St. Augustine pointed out, that the kind of weight they appear to have is intimately related to the prior state of faith one brings to them. God's "daily miracles" are disesteemed by many, but to those with faith they may seem to constitute proof of God's existence. Conversely, the evidence against the existence of God that evil and suffering provide may seem insignificant to those who have faith, and very strong to those already inclined to doubt the existence of God. Thus it is especially difficult to arrive at a dispassionate or an "objective" evaluation of these arguments.

However, let me suggest, very tentatively, that the order in the universe provides at least *some* rational support to the hypothesis that there is an omnipotent, perfectly good God, and that the evil and suffering in the world provide at least *some* rational support to the contradictory hypothesis. To say thus that the rational evidence is divided is not, of course, to say that any reasonable person must be hesitant in his or her opinion on the matter. It is abundantly clear that reasonable people may differ in their estimates of the weights of evidence, and that reasonable people may have considerable faith, of a positive or negative sort, which fills in the gaps left by reason.

To speak of the hypothesis that there is an omnipotent, perfectly good God is also to call attention to a question that we thus far have ignored. When a philosopher attempts to prove or disprove the existence of God, it always is reasonable to ask what kind of God he is talking about; and, if he claims to prove the existence of God, it is reasonable to ask what he can claim to have proved about God. The God St. Anselm and St. Thomas Aquinas had in mind in constructing their proofs was, obviously, the Christian God. But the God whose existence they claim rationally to have established is characterized in such general terms that there is nothing that need be unacceptable to Moslems or Jews. A Moslem or a Jew could accept the existence of St. Anselm's being than which nothing greater can be conceived, or St. Thomas's unmoved mover. St. Anselm and St. Thomas believed in the Trinity; but, clearly, even in their accounts, the trinitarian nature of God is left to the domain of faith and not brought within the sphere of rational proof.

If the order in the universe is adduced as evidence for the existence of God, it is not clear what this God must be like, apart, of course, from being orderly. This is a point that David Hume made in his *Dialogues concerning Natural Religion*. If it is argued that the design of the world requires there to have been a designer, it is not clear what logic compels us to think that the world should have had only a single designer, rather than, say, a team of designers. It is not clear also that a very good world requires there to have been a very good designer. A number of fantastic possibilities can be raised as to how the world conceivably was designed; even if they are not serious possibilities, the fact that we cannot rule them out logically helps to show the limitations of reason here.

Conversely, the existence of evil and suffering in the world can count rationally against the hypothesis of God's existence only if we stick to a certain highly traditional view of God's goodness. The Book of Job argues, in effect, that God's justice is different in character from anything that we are capable of imagining: Job's friends who think that God's justice is like the very best human justice have to pay a penalty, since they have insulted God by bringing him down to a human level. If we hypothesize a God whose conception of goodness is not necessarily ours, it becomes far from clear what rational weight the existence of evil and suffering in the world has.

There are certain conceptions of God that make debate on God's existence still more unclear. If someone says "God is love," what are we to count as evidence for or against the hypothesis that God exists? If someone says that God is the order in the universe, there are similar difficulties.

Traditionally, people who believe in God have been willing to identify God with love, or with the order in the universe, only metaphorically: they have meant more than *that* when they asserted that God existed. But what did they mean? From the point of view of some philosophers, it is not entirely obvious.

It has been suggested, for example, that religious claims are "pseudo-statements."[1] Even though they seem to be factual claims that can be true or false, their character is quite different. They have meaning only in terms of a system of attitudes—of potential responses to the world—of the believer. It has been suggested also that statements about God take their meaning from the moral commitments that are built into them.[2]

These suggestions have value because they remind us that statements about God are frequently not *just* statements about God, that they frequently have other dimensions. A certain theological position (e.g., a Christian one) may be so intimately connected with a certain moral stance that to profess the former, unless there are special disclaimers, can be generally understood as profession of the latter. Thus someone who says that he is a Christian, and then advocates torturing innocent people, can be accused of insincerity.

But is this all that there is to theological claims? Even if we grant that very frequently, at least in normal contexts, statements of theological position will have implications for one's life, including moral implications, is this all? Most people who believe in God would say that there is more to it than that, that besides the moral commitments and the characteristic religious attitudes, there is the fact—at least they affirm it to be a fact—that a God exists, as it were, out there. When they say that God exists, they mean, among other things, that God exists.

Why not take the claim "God exists" to mean that God exists? If this is what religious people generally think they mean, why can they not mean what they think they mean? There seem to be only two possible reasons. One is the remoteness from experience of what believers claim to be talking about. The other, not totally separate, is the apparent insolubility, at least by reason or in terms of evidence, of the issue raised by the believer.

The most radical assault on the claim that the existence of God is a serious problem is derivable from the insistence of some philosophers that the meaning of a factual claim is its verification, coupled with the assertion that there is nothing in our experience which will serve to verify either the claim that God exists or that God does not exist. The atheist will say that all the facts pointed to by the theist can be accommodated equally well by an atheist hypothesis, and the theist will say the same about the facts appealed to by the atheist. If one confronts this, it may be tempting to say that whatever meaning "God exists" has is not factual.

John Hick has attempted to meet this assault on its own ground in the following manner. Even if present experiences can be explained on both the theist and atheist hypotheses, this may not be true for experiences after death. The Christian hypothesis, Hick says, is that we will be given a new "spiritual body."[3] The new spiritual body will not itself demonstrate God's existence: we would be assured of God's existence if we experience the fulfillment of God's purpose for ourselves, or experience communion with God as Christ.[4] In other words, verification after death. There is an interesting asymmetry in what is proposed here. If you hold Hick's religious views, you will find verification after death if you are right, but presumably you would never discover that you were wrong; the atheist, conversely, could never have the satisfaction of finding that he was right, but might (in unspecified ways) find out that he was wrong.

If our question is "Does God exist?" the picture must, however, be more complicated than this. One of the possibilities, after all, is that God exists but that the full Christian doctrine Hick espouses is not correct, in which case it could be that we will find out that God exists in a different way from that Hick hypothesizes, or that, despite the fact that God exists, we will be denied any verifying experience after death. We also must not be too quick to assume that, if God does not exist, there thereby cannot be any experience after death.

Further, even if we die and have the experience that Hick describes, the import of these experiences would be open to question. It may seem farfetched to talk of a last joke of a cosmic deceiver, but it may be less farfetched to hypothesize a final dream which takes on an intense air of reality. Dreams—ordinary dreams—are said to last only a few seconds, even when the dream events seem to occupy much longer periods of time. Why could not the final second or two of life involve a dream of peculiar significance, which seemed to encompass a very long time, perhaps even an eternity? This might be, in certain esoteric views, the real meaning of heaven and hell: one gets the final dream one deserves.

What this suggests is that after-death experience, if there is any, need not be entirely decisive with respect to the existence of God. It is arguable that even the kind of after-death experience that Hick hypothesizes would not prove that God exists, although it certainly would give strong support to that conclusion.

It seems highly implausible, however, to insist that proof, or entirely decisive, foolproof verification, is required for a claim to have factual meaning. Most of the factual claims that are ordinarily debated, especially those in history, do not admit of this. Hick has successfully provided an example of conceivable evidence that would have genuine weight in relation to the question of the existence of God. In doing this, he has decisively undermined the position of those who have denied factual meaning to claims of the existence of God.

We might generalize with regard to the issue of meaning here by means of the following principle. The principle is neither comprehensive nor restrictive, and merely outlines one kind of factually meaningful claim.

> A claim is factually meaningful if we can conceive of an experience (1) in relation to which someone who makes the claim, and who takes the experience at face value, would say "This is what I was talking about," and (2) which could reasonably be considered to provide support to the claim, so that it would be more reasonable to make the claim on a basis that included that experience than on a basis that was equivalent except that it did not include that experience.

This principle seems at least as plausible as any obvious alternative. It implies that the claim "God exists" is factually meaningful.

Is the claim true, however? It seems perfectly consistent to say that there is no *rational* basis for being certain of what the correct answer to this is, but that yet there is a correct answer. The major difficulty is in knowing what the correct answer is.

It is worth mentioning, at this final point in the discussion, that a number of able philosophers in this century have discussed the existence of God as a problem of what "language game" we decide to play, or of what labels we decide in accordance with our perspective to apply to what we experience.[5] Why would they do such a thing? Part of the answer is that there is *some* truth in what they say. (It is hard to find philosophy that is totally devoid of truth.) The case for affirming the existence of God does depend, in part, on what one means by "God" and how the language is to be used in general. Similarly, one's view of the evidence for and against the existence of God does depend obviously on perspective, which will be mirrored in the language that one finds appropriate in describing the world. On the other hand, this chapter has argued that it is absurd to regard the issue as entirely one of language or of perspective.

The main reason, I suggest, why these philosophers have tried to treat the problem of the existence of God as primarily linguistic is that it is (by tradition) a philosophical problem, and they were wedded to the view that philosophical problems are primarily linguistic. This book has developed an opposite view: that a number of important philosophical problems are not primarily linguistic, and instead are problems about reality. The problem of the existence of God is probably the hardest for the linguistic (or philosophy-as-logic) approach to accommodate. This is one reason for putting it last in this book: the hardest fighting occurred earlier. But the reader might reflect that, even if the arguments of the previous chapters were ill-founded and the conclusions about the character of the issues wrong, still there is at least one philosophical problem which is a problem about reality.

Notes

1. See the discussion of "pseudo-statement" in I. A. Richards, *Science and Poetry* (London: Kegan Paul, Trench, Trubner & Co., 1935).

2. R. B. Braithwaite, "An Empiricist's View of the Nature of Religious Belief," in *The Existence of God*, ed. J. Hick (New York: Macmillan, 1964).

3. John Hick, "Theology and Verification," in *The Existence of God*, pp. 260–261.

4. Ibid., pp. 269–271.

5. See for example the essays by Malcolm and Wisdom in *The Existence of God*.

SUGGESTED FURTHER READING

A good source book of arguments—pro, con, and other—concerning the existence of God is the following.

Hick, John, ed. *The Existence of God*. New York: Macmillan, 1964.

The following contain classic statements of rational arguments for the existence of God.

St. Anselm. *Proslogium.* In *Basic Writings.* La Salle, Ill.: Open Court, 1962.

St. Thomas Aquinas. *Summa Theologica.* Selections in *Basic Writings.* New York: Random House, 1945.

Descartes, René. *Meditations.* Many modern editions of acceptable translations.

The following develop skeptical or negative views.

Hume, David. *Dialogues concerning Natural Religion.* Many modern editions. There is much debate still over just where Hume does stand, but it is clear that he rejects the claim to rationality of standard proofs of the existence of God.

Feuerbach, Ludwig. *The Essence of Christianity.* New York: Frederick Ungar, 1957. This is a sharply written attack on all conventional religion.

A highly sophisticated argument for regarding all important religious matters, including the existence of God, as matters of faith is to be found in the following.

Kierkegaard, Sören. *Concluding Unscientific Postscript*, trans. David F. Swenson and Walter Lowrie. Princeton: Princeton University Press, 1960.

Index